Complete Home Decorating

CAUTION

Complete Home Decorating

A step-by-step guide to achieving the best results for your home

Phil Gorton

This is a Parragon Publishing Book
This edition published in 2005

Parragon Publishing
Queen Street House
4 Queen Street
Bath BA1 1HE
United Kingdom

ISBN: 1-40545-911-5

Printed in Indonesia

Produced by The Bridgewater Book Company Ltd, Lewes, East Sussex, United Kingdom

Photographer Steve Gorton
Decorators Philip Rogers, Michael Harradin and Phil Gorton
Illustrator Coral Mula
Plan Illustrator James Neal

Contents

Introduction	6
How to use this book	8
Planning	10
Color	20
Painting	32
Paper finishes	66
Wood, brick, and tile finishes	92
Floors	154
Woodwork	184
Furniture facelifts	202
Stylish space savers	212
Accent accessories	224
Appendices	236
Glossary	248
Index	252
Acknowledgments	256

Introduction

As the world enters a new millennium, people's lives have never been more stressful, their workstyles more fractious and time-specific, or their lifestyles more fragmented. Relaxation at the end of a difficult day is consequently more of a basic requirement than ever before, and to be able to wind down in comfort and style in esthetically pleasing decorative surroundings is not so much a bonus as a necessity.

Relaxing in familiar surroundings usually involves personal input to the area in question. Favorite colors and textures, controllable lighting, displays, pictures, and mementoes all act as a "welcome home." Whether "home" is owned, mortgaged, or rented, or whether it is a house, cottage, or apartment, the decorative personal touch is essential if home is to be where the heart is.

Employing third parties to do decorating work is expensive, time-consuming, carries no real guarantees, and still requires a lot of personal input. Channel the energies of personal attention into the task itself, always being aware of its possible complexity, whether it is merely deciding on color schemes for walls or whether it involves a complete makeover, so popular on television. Home improvement programs, in order to retain viewer interest, edit down technical job sequences from hours to seconds, leading the unwary into the erroneous belief that a decorating job can be done in the time it takes on TV. The most important function of this book is to bring a sense of reality to the initial discussions and scheduling, allowing decorating decisions to reflect a proper timescale, and to take into account the available skill levels.

Throughout these pages a proper professional approach is encouraged, from the drawing up of a detailed plan to the application of top quality materials and power tools in a safe and responsible manner. The tools required are discussed at the start of each chapter. Step-by-step sequences show each job in progression and can be easily followed and understood.

Whether these pages help with a simple painted frame or a complex zonal plan, hopefully, after the project is completed, you will experience much greater satisfaction in having done a quality job in the home, rather than paying to have one done.

How to use this book

Any job must start at the beginning, and so must you in your assessment of it. "Designer's notes" cover not only the esthetics, but also the practicalities of a scheme. When the idea becomes a working plan, the pages on tools, equipment, materials, and hardware will illustrate what you need in order to follow the step-by-step sequences in each project.

Designer's notes

When making notes, the designer always considers the features that are inherent in the original design of the room, and their current status and condition. Whether these features are emphasized or visually disguised by the new color scheme will be a decision for the room's occupants, influenced by some basic color rules.

Designer's questions

Color for emphasis

"Designer's notes" pages in each major section of the book offer tips on how professionals approach each aspect of home improvement.

In each major section of the book the tools and equipment necessary for carrying out the projects in that section are listed. Where appropriate, tools are separated into basic and advanced categories.

Tools and equipment

As with all tools of the trade, investing in cheap, badly made decorating equipment is a recipe for failure. There is nothing quite as expensive as trying to save money. An inferior tool can ruin a job or a finish by underperforming at a crucial stage, so invest wisely. Here is a selection to start off your essential toolkit for painting.

Tools and equipment

Sugar soap and sandpaper

Brushes, pads, and rollers

Rollers and brushes

Top tips on the use and maintenance of tools are included in the tools and equipment pages.

A handy visual reference is provided so that you can familiarize yourself with the tools mentioned in the book.

Tools and equipment for specific projects are described and illustrated throughout the book.

Practical, color illustrations offer step-by-step guides to carrying out improvements in your home.

Top tips can be found throughout the book. These nuggets of information will help you to hone your home improvement skills.

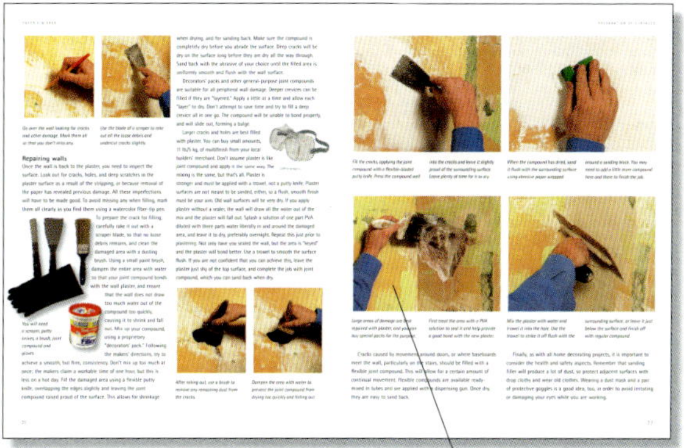

Easy-to-follow steps are illustrated with color photographs throughout, so you can see what you need to do at each stage of the home improvement project.

PLANNING

In today's competitive, consumer-orientated marketplace, modern businesses must have carefully considered strategies and working schedules to ensure their survival and growth. You are probably aware of this requirement in your own daily working life and the same is no less true of planning home improvements. Most households already have some kind of general strategy for running the home smoothly, varying from a basic task "duty roster" on a kitchen notice board to a complex time-specific system that includes family members and budgets, all logged onto a home computer. Forward planning is an essential part of running a home and is equally vital when it comes to making improvements, whether major or minor.

90
91
92
93
94
95
96
97
98

Practical considerations

No matter how small the job appears to be, forward planning is needed when you are considering refurbishing or decorating your home. Inspiration gained from a magazine or television "makeover" needs to be turned into a plan of action if home improvement is to be successful. Here are some tips on what to think about before you start.

Clear brief

Imagine you have an independent builder taking on the job. What he would expect from his client is a clear brief, detailing all that is required from the finished work, which materials are going to be used, and which color scheme is required. Just because you intend to tackle the project yourself, don't skimp on the details when devising the plan of action. And beware: "making it up as you go along" is liable to end in unsatisfactory results.

When planning a refurbishment, seek inspiration from a variety of sources, including magazines.

Measure the room, draw a plan, and collect color cards, paint testers, and material swatches.

Questions to consider

Whether you live alone or with others, it is worth considering the following questions:

- Is the planned change suitable for the particular room that you have in mind?
- Is it necessary?
- Is it practical?
- Will everyone in the house benefit?
- How long will it take?
- How much upheaval will there be?
- Can you live with it in the long term?

Budget

If the household members like the ideas and are happy to live with the works in progress, then you need to consider:

- How much will it cost?
- Is it affordable?

The job budget involves adding up prices taken from builders' and decorators' lists. You might need to include the cost of any new tools required (whether bought or rented), delivery charges for materials, and/or rubbish clearance.

Skills and time

Presuming a reasonable skill level with a basic tool kit (the skills and tools required for each job are discussed throughout this book), try to devise a logical order of work, bearing in mind the following factors:

- The amount of work needed each day will depend on the size of the project, but don't take on too much in one go. Popular decorating programs on television may give the impression that a room can be completely transformed in a mere 25 minutes, including a commercial break, but this is far from being the truth.
- Be realistic in assessing how long you think each part of the project will take.
- Cutting corners on any part of a job may lead to difficulties later on and may ultimately add to the time the job takes.

Implications of refurbishment

The eventual resale value of your property is not the only thing to bear in mind when assessing standards of workmanship. Removing period features from a room for "modernization" generally does not meet with approval today, so consider all the implications before you start. Sympathetic decorating and subtle changes can sometimes be more beneficial than wholesale refurbishment.

In years to come, you may tire of the changes you have made and seek to reinstate an earlier look, but if you have disposed of vital features, you may encounter considerable difficulty in replacing them. Give yourself time to come to terms with your plans; put them away for a while, then come back to them. Don't be afraid to change your mind or tone down some of the more ambitious aspects of the project.

Before

After

Assessing room functions

If your work is not confined to one room and a complete makeover of the house is needed, then your plans must be more elaborate. Maybe you've just moved in or your family circumstances have changed dramatically. Whatever the reason, the first step is to assess the basic areas—living, working, and sleeping—plus the role of the kitchen and bathroom.

Living areas

The living-room must cater for all members of the household, who will use it for different reasons. Its main function is to provide a seating arrangement for family and friends where privacy is not possible. Several activities may take place in this room simultaneously—for example, reading, listening to music or watching television, family discussions, and hobby pursuits, such as playing computer games. Decide whether an open-plan style is in keeping with this lack of privacy, or whether a breakdown of the living-room into two separate functional areas is possible. In a period house, the downstairs living areas would usually have been arranged as a day room, near the cooking area for convenience, with easily cleaned flooring, and a separate evening area, with more luxurious fixtures and fittings, suitable for entertaining.

Working areas

What constitutes work, and what doesn't, may present an ever-changing issue in the contemporary household. Computers are used for schoolwork, business, and family leisure activities. Digital interactive cables have transformed the television into a potential shopping mall and banking service. As certain areas become multifunctional, a study or home office may be a welcome retreat. This is a real necessity if you work from home full time; otherwise, professional commitments can easily spill over into everyday family life.

Sleeping areas

The younger members of a household often consider their

Living areas often benefit from being divided into separate areas for different functions.

This bedroom in the loft area of the house lends itself to several purposes at once: a sleeping area, with storage in the foreground, a sewing area, and, at the back of the room, a shower area.

edroom space to be out of bounds to anyone not specifically nvited. These areas are already catering for several activities, and nust be furnished accordingly. The bedroom used solely for its ntended purpose is usually the parents' room, traditionally the argest. Consider the benefits of young children sharing this room nstead. It will double as a nursery or play area, possibly freeing up a room elsewhere in the house. A good night's rest, however, relies on peace and quiet, so the location of bedrooms away from sources of noise is very important.

he kitchen

Generally the working hub of the home, the kitchen is frequently n use for food preparation, cooking, dishwashing and general leaning. Home to many major labor-saving devices, such as the vashing machine, dishwasher and food processor, it may need to ccommodate several family members at the same time and to louble as a breakfast or snack room. Easy access to other eating reas, such as a dining-room, may be needed, so that cooked food eaches the table quickly. A large serving hatch between the itchen and dining-room may be the ideal solution, providing a ractical and visual link.

The bathroom

In a large household, a second bathroom is a modern necessity, and builders' merchants stock all types of space-saving units with this in mind. If your main bathroom is fitted out traditionally (i.e., with a bathtub), a shower room would be a good idea, along with a second lavatory, possibly incorporated in a downstairs cloakroom. If space precludes all these options, another possibility would be to divide the lavatory off from the rest of the bathroom.

Interconnecting spaces

In an ideal world the home you inhabit would grow and change with you and your family. This is possible if the house layout is flexible. Corridors that have a decorative scheme encouraging adjacent areas to interact, rather than divorcing one from another, are a good start. The décor in any area becomes more interesting if flexible design lets the occupants see through to another, different space.

Linking rooms does not necessarily have to mean sacrificing privacy, either. Decorative screens can be used to isolate parts of the open space temporarily as and when you wish. If you have the room to create open spaces in this way, however, try to avoid overcompensating by adding too much furniture.

Minimalism will not be an option for a family unit, of course, but too much clutter will rapidly reduce or destroy any feeling of spaciousness that you endeavor to create.

Opposite ideas often work well together. For example, a small apartment will appear larger if it is visually sparse. By contrast, a large loft apartment benefits from an aggressive color scheme that is used to reduce the overwhelming impact of the space.

A balcony area surrounded by greenery creates a relaxed environment in which to work.

Accommodating the new

Period housing has many features that can live happily alongside modern innovations in this technological age, and it is worth assessing how modernization will work in your home without removing original features. In addition, you will need to consider how the requirements of the household members will be met by your refurbishment choices.

Original features and new technology

Technology can work in any surroundings, and stylish period features don't have to make way for contemporary interiors to accommodate innovations. Original fireplaces, baseboards, cornices, and decorative moldings can all be updated by adventurous color scheming, irrespective of their Georgian, Regency, Victorian, or Edwardian origin.

Water and electricity supplies in older properties must meet modern standards and regulations, but they can be largely hidden away, and the growing reproduction marketplace supplies period-style radiators and switch surrounds. Brand-name paint manufacturers offer a range of period colors, and architectural salvage yards are full of period pieces for the bargain-hunter.

Opposites can work very well together. A digital sound system can look and sound superb in an elaborate Victorian Sunday room. If you are considering a large-scale refurbishment program, keep your mind and your options open to the possibilities for accommodating new technology in a traditional setting.

Unique family needs

Along with considering room function, period styles, and linked color schemes, you also need to assess requirements that are unique to your family. Every person who lives in the property should be allowed an input because any form of alteration or decoration is a family affair.

Needs alter as the years pass. Children who once shared a room will want to move apart, eventually to leave home altogether. Elderly relatives may join the household. Flexibility is crucial. It may be difficult and time-consuming to adapt a house to fit the occupants, but equally it may be difficult to change the habits of a lifetime to suit the layout of a property.

Here are some points you might need to consider:

- Is there adequate provision in the entrance hall or lobby for wet outdoor clothes, boots, and/or sporting equipment?
- Can this area be cleaned easily?
- Is there space in this area to put down shopping items temporarily, while a cab is being paid off or a vehicle is being unloaded?

A hall area ideally needs to be reasonably spacious, to have a floor surface that is easily cleaned and plenty of room for hanging up coats and storing umbrellas, boots, and shoes.

- Can late-night arrivals get to their rooms directly without disturbing the rest of the household?
- Do all the sleeping areas have easy access to both the bathroom and the lavatory?
- Can a meal cooked in the kitchen be served in the dining area easily and quickly?
- Does the kitchen have a back door, to allow deliveries to arrive and garbage to be removed easily? Is this access protected from the weather?
- Can you view the rest of the property, and any garden where the children may be playing, from the kitchen?
- Is there enough space for all household members in the communal living area, with room for guests?
- Does everyone have access to the television in this area?
- Is there enough storage space and hobby space?
- Can a bedroom double up as a study area or home office during the daytime?
- If a workshop with power tools, such as a garage area, is open to everyone in the house, is it safe?
- Are all potentially dangerous tools locked away?
- Are the bathroom facilities sufficient for the number of people in the house? Is there a separate lavatory?
- If you have a pet, is it catered for in all weathers?

Nobody knows more about your family circumstances than you do, so adapt the questionnaire to your own situation. Put your requirements in writing. They will provide invaluable guidance when you come to make final decisions.

Period fireplaces have an innate charm, and an old fireplace surround can often be adapted to take modern fittings and painted in either traditional or modern colors. In the summer, grates can be filled with pine cones and massed with greenery, so that they do not look redundant at this time of year.

Old radiators still have a certain appeal, and can often be bought at architectural salvage yards and brought back to life. Alternatively, you can purchase a reproduction radiator and enjoy all the benefits of modern technology with the esthetic values of another era.

Major or minor changes?

If your decision involves changing the function of a particular area, consider how major those changes will be. A bedroom to be used as a study, for example, will require largely cosmetic changes, such as new shelving, a worktop for a computer, and décor to be approved by the new inhabitant. However, enlarging a kitchen by, say, connecting it directly to a utility room may involve leveling one of the floors for retiling, removing doors, and matching paneled interiors. Any major kitchen or bathroom work will involve water facilities and the services of a plumber, so consult a reliable local tradesperson before final redesign decisions are made. Electrics are another consideration. Are there enough outlets, and are they in the right place? Is the lighting good enough, especially if the house is old? Unless you have experience in this field, seek the advice of a professional. Major disruptive work needs to be completed before any cosmetic details can be started.

A small space can be successfully multifunctional, as a bedroom, washing area, and work unit, if it is well planned and the various components form an integral whole that is pleasing to the eye.

Making plans

Whether your plan is complex or simple at this stage, whether you intend to divide up a room space or merely paint a floor, you will find a detailed plan on paper makes life a lot easier. It doesn't have to be a work of art, but it does need to be accurate. If you have a computer with suitable software, you can draw up your plans and alter them using a grid system. You might even be able to put together a three-dimensional drawing.

Left: The essential tools required for measuring a room are graph paper, some colored pencils, a notepad and pen, a clear plastic rule, a pair of scissors, a retractable steel measure, and a calculator.

Below: Mark on the plan the room's basic dimensions, noting in particular any unusual shapes that distort the room's appearance, and all the doors, windows, and other features such as closets.

Measuring up a room

To measure up a room, use a retractable steel measure of at least 16½ ft/5 m total length, with a lever to lock the tape at any given distance. Adding distances together from shorter tape measures, or using cloth tapes that are prone to sag, leads to inaccurate figures.

Measure the basic dimensions first—wall height and length. Measure the room from corner to corner to confirm that it is square, or at least square enough for your purposes. Add on any bay window and alcove areas, where necessary, and note down the sizes of the chimney breast, all built-in cabinets, window areas, and doors, marking on your plan which way the doors open.

You will find it easier to write down initial measurements on a rough sketch. You can also add radiator positions and pipe runs, electric outlets and light fittings to this first drawing, even if they are not relevant to the final scheme.

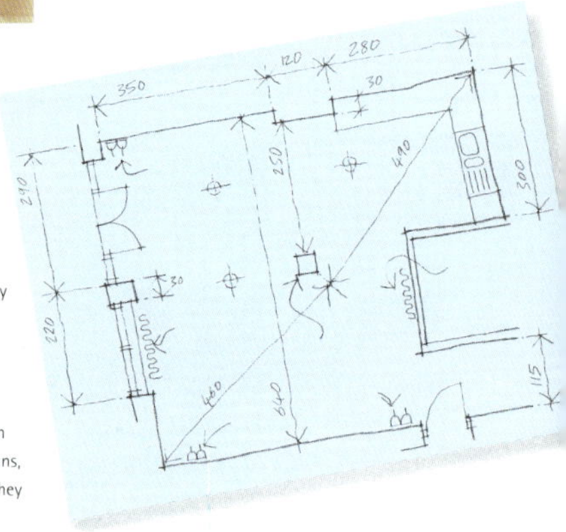

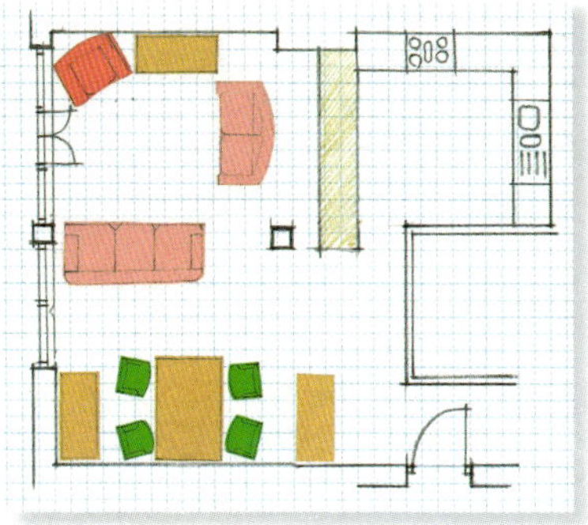

Transferring to graph paper

Using a pencil, not a pen (it's much easier to correct mistakes if you use a pencil as you can erase them when you go wrong), transfer your plan from rough sketch to graph paper and scale the area to size using the squares. Include only the items that you consider relevant from your comprehensive measurements. Simplify the plan as much as possible to reduce the risk of errors due to incorporating too much clutter.

If your room is furnished, or if you know what items of furniture will eventually be included, then represent these objects with small pieces of card cut to scale. You will be able to rearrange items of furniture at will, to establish their best position and to make maximum use of the available space.

Draw in shelving systems or new cabinets to go in alcoves, change access doors, and so on, until the plan is complete and you are quite happy with it.

A plan comes to life when the items of furniture are colored in and you can see how they relate to one another and how they fill the space. Try moving them around to ascertain the ideal configuration.

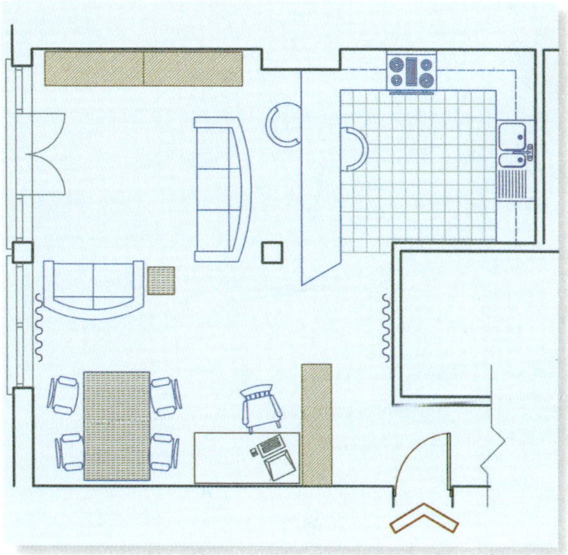

Because of the positions of doors, windows, and chimney breasts there are only so many combinations that will work in any given space. With trial and error you should finally arrive at the perfect solution.

COLOR

Choosing the correct color scheme for your home is vital to your sense of comfort and well-being. Individual tastes in color are, of course, highly subjective, but there are also several important objective factors involved in the selection of color schemes. In this chapter we look at the color wheel, which will help in choosing contrasting and complementary color schemes, and also discuss the importance of natural light, the psychological effects of particular colors, and the visual tricks that can be achieved through careful color scheming. Successful use of color has the potential to transform rooms in an exciting and gratifying way, and in many instances involves no great expense to you, so it is well worth taking your time considering all the choices available.

Designer's notes

When making notes, the designer always considers the features that are inherent in the original design of the room, and their current status and condition. Whether these features are emphasized or visually disguised by the new color scheme will be a decision for the room's occupants, influenced by some basic color rules.

Designer's questions

Before you make plans for redecorating, imagine that you are an independent interior designer looking at your home for the first time and ask yourself the following questions:

- What is the aspect of the room (i.e., which direction does it face)?
- How much natural light comes into the room?
- Is there an original feature in the room? If so, is it to be retained?
- Will the room need joinery additions, such as built-in storage and shelving in an alcove, which will alter its basic shape?
- Can paint schemes be applied to existing features such as doors and windows?
- Will these items have to be replaced (for example, to restore a period feel)?
- Can the desired effect be achieved simply by cosmetic changes or is major work necessary?

Stripping paint away to reveal whatever lies beneath is just one part of the decorating process and can have intriguing results.

Using a similar light color on the walls and furnishings opens up the space and creates a feeling of airiness. This scheme is cheerful and uplifting and enhances whatever light there is in a room.

A room decorated in the three primary colors of red, yellow, and blue, like this bedroom, is bold and invigorating, although some might find it too vibrant to sleep in.

Bear in mind, however, that stripping a wall may involve you in a considerable amount of making good before it is suitable to be left exposed. The original mortar may be in poor condition and need repointing. Don't assume that every wall will be suitable for such treatment; in some cases, the underlying brickwork will have been laid carelessly and will never be attractive to look at. Be prepared to carry out some exploratory stripping of the plasterwork to discover what lies behind.

Other surfaces such as floors can also be stripped. Here, the beauty of the grain of wooden boards can be brought out by careful sanding and varnishing. But again, repairs may be necessary. Always be prepared to amend your plans if it turns out that you can't achieve your desire.

You can make a feature like a fireplace into a focal point by surrounding it with intense color.

Paint can be used to good effect to enhance original features, such as this attractive wooden door.

Color for emphasis

You may feel that an old, ugly tiled fireplace is at odds with your twenty-first century ideal and want to remove it. On the other hand, you may have an older property suffering from 1970s "modernization" that needs the fireplace reinstated. Either possibility will involve a great deal of mess, in the form of soot, so obviously works of this nature have to be tackled first.

If you are in a position to undertake purely cosmetic changes, then you need to examine the features in the room even more closely. Working with what you have is always a good principle in home redecoration. This lets you emphasize the best features of a room using color. An old built-in closet, for instance, when it has been relieved of its multiple layers of paint, may reveal fine, sympathetically crafted woodwork. Using subtle dyes to enhance the grain can make a real feature of the joiner's art.
A pale color on the surrounding walls will emphasize the beauty of the wood and will not compete with it.

Decorating is usually seen as an additive process, which involves bringing paint, paper, or some type of paneling/joinery to a room or replacing the existing scheme. However, it can also be a subtractive process, for example, stripping paint off joinery. So, when you consider your intended wall scheme, you might think about removing wallpaper entirely in order to paint a wall a flat color, or even hacking off the plaster to reveal the traditional brickwork that lies underneath.

The color wheel

The color wheel is a vital tool in the visualizing and selection of color schemes. It shows how all the colors of the spectrum act in relation to each other, and helps you to decide on contrasting or complementary schemes. The more advanced wheel shows how tints and shades of complementary colors can work together.

How color works

When a white light source, typically the sun, consisting of different wavelengths passes through a prism, it splits to reveal the visible spectrum. It is often portrayed as a rainbow effect. The visible part of the spectrum runs from violet through to red. Ultraviolet and infrared, either side of the visible spectrum, cannot be seen by the naked eye (e.g., we cannot see radio waves or X rays). When the walls of a room receive this white light source, they absorb all the wavelengths except those of their own color, which they reflect. The human eye responds to these reflected wavelengths and identifies them as color. So, a wall absorbing all wavelengths except blue, which it reflects into the room, appears to the human eye as a blue wall.

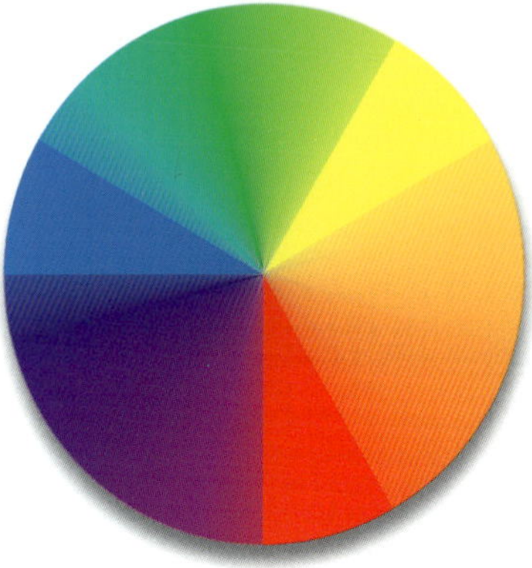

The wheel

The color wheel is a circle based on the color spectrum. The primary colors, red, yellow, and blue, are opposite the secondary colors, green, violet, and orange. Selecting colors that are opposite each other on the wheel, such as red and green, results in optimum color contrast because you are using complementary colors. Selecting colors next to each other on the wheel—say blue and green—results in a more harmonious scheme because they blend into each other in the spectrum. Blending adjacent colors together creates a third set. The wheel is divided up into twelve segments that can be used to plan all your color combinations.

Complementary colors

Complementary colors provide optimum contrast if used together in a room. They can make uneasy companions, however, if used in their purest form. All colors can be lightened by adding white to make tints or darkened by adding black to make shades of those colors. A more complex color wheel shows not only the colors at their most intense, but also the tints and shades in a gradation. This is useful because it shows how the color contrast is increased further if one of the colors is a tint or a shade.

A good example of this is provided by the use of red and green together in a room. Large expanses of these colors in their purest form cause problems for the eye, because they have a similar tonal value, meaning that they reflect similar amounts of light. If you imagine these two colors side by side in black and white for a moment, then they would appear as almost identical shades of gray—neither color would advance or recede. Consequently the eye and the brain become confused. All colors from opposite sides of the wheel have a similar effect if they are of the same tonal value. However, using a tint or a shade of one of them can solve this problem. If you look at the second color wheel, you will notice how dark green will effectively partner red or a tint of red. Conversely, dark red combines well with a tint of green.

Complementary colors in the color spectrum include red and green, orange and blue, and yellow and violet.

Being complementary colors, red and green work better in tint and shade combinations than in pure forms. But just looking at nature should be enough to convince us how well they can harmonize: think of pink wild flowers amid a meadow or of red berries against green foliage.

Using a darker shade with a lighter tint of its complementary color avoids the visual problems caused when similar tonal values reflect similar amounts of light. Left: Red and green in pure form confuse the eye (neither advances or recedes). Right: the pale green recedes, letting the darker red appear dominant.

Light, color and mood

Light and color both play an important role in the way we feel—you have only to think of how much easier it is to get up on bright sunny days than it is when the skies are gray and overcast. So it is important to take into account both the direction that your room faces and the amount of light it receives when deciding what colors to use there.

Natural light

The amount of light reflected by a color, and thus the intensity of that color, depends on the light level that the color receives from the sun. As available light recedes at the end of the day, colors will appear less and less bright, until finally they have no color at all. With this in mind, consider carefully the amount of natural light that enters the room during the day, and what effect it will have. All the walls in the room will work in unison, reflecting the available light received. Lighter colored walls will reflect more light than dark ones, and will project it farther. For example, a bright blue reflected into an otherwise white room will engender a cold blue tint, whereas a bright red will project a warm rose-like tint. When selecting colors, bear in mind that walls reflecting the same color back and forth will intensify that color considerably—otherwise, you may end up with a much more powerful scheme than you envisaged.

The availability of natural light depends on the season. An important point to consider when choosing a color scheme is the light level the room receives throughout the year. The more northerly the property location, the more extreme the difference between summer and winter, so a color scheme reflecting warm summer days also needs to work during long winters under artificial light.

Aspect

Consider the aspect of all the rooms in your intended scheme. Light enters through windows or glass doors, so which direction do they face?

Northern aspect

A room facing north is usually cold, benefiting from direct sunlight only during the height of summer. A warm color scheme will be essential in this room. Red, yellow, and orange will brighten the winter days and reflect what little light there is. Cold blues and greens should be avoided.

Yellow walls will enliven a hallway that faces north and can be rather dark for much of the day.

outhern aspect

room facing south is warm and sunny, with lots of natural light. ou will not need to add to the light levels, so use darker colors, articularly green. When these are combined with lighter tints of rown, blue, and green, a summery feel can be created even during e winter months.

astern aspect

e powerful early light of sunrise becomes less potent as midday pproaches, with no sunlight shining into the room in the fternoon and evening. A mix of color works well here. Both cool ues and warm oranges together will offset the midday change in ghting conditions.

particularly in a child's bedroom, where colors that stimulate the mind will not be conducive to sleep.

There is a place in the home for earth tones such as brown and beige, and for neutral grays, especially in a work area such as a home office. Here concentration is needed and bright colors will be distracting.

A basement or garage workshop containing potentially dangerous equipment is another area where attention should be on the task in hand and not on the decor.

Likes and dislikes of color effects are ultimately subjective. People who share the room space will have individual tastes and preferences, so canvas the thoughts of all the occupants before making a decision on a color scheme.

In east-facing rooms, such as a nursery that receives light in the early morning, a blue scheme looks good and is also restful on the eye, lulling the child to sleep.

Work areas need to promote concentration, so neutral tones are often chosen in preference to vibrant primary colors.

estern aspect

is room will receive afternoon and evening sun, a sunset if nditions are favorable, and dull light in the morning. Bright olors such as reds and yellows will overemphasize the warmth of e afternoon, a more neutral scheme involving greens and grays ill work better.

olor and mood

e psychological effect of certain colors in certain situations ould also play a part in your color scheme selection. Bright olors such as reds excite and invigorate. Cool blues and greens are uch more relaxing. Make allowances for this in certain rooms,

Choosing color schemes

There are various examples of colors and finishes to help you select the right combinations in your color schemes, from color paint cards to sample pots of paint. There are also certain visual tricks that it is worth being aware of, as they can help you make the most of your available space and maximize its potential.

Color cards and sample pots

One of your first steps in selecting colors for your home decorating will be to consult a brand manufacturer's color chart or card – but

this may not be the best way to choose paint. The colored rectangles on the card, while being as accurate as possible, may not be exact. They are very small and are positioned on a white background, which gives a slightly false impression of brightness. Remember, too, that the light reflected and absorbed by a tiny square or rectangle of color will differ immeasurably from that reflected or absorbed by an entire wall of that color. Yellows, for example, will seem much more powerful, because they reflect more light. Blues will appear darker because they absorb more light.

In response, paint-makers have introduced small sample pots of their colors. These provide an ideal way to experiment with your chosen scheme on the wall itself. Small pots of paint, swatches of curtain or furniture fabrics, carpet samples, wood off-cuts, and wallcovering samples can all be used together to give a first impression of what the finished room will look like.

Visual trick color schemes

Combining wall colors of different reflective qualities will let you play visual tricks with the size and proportions of the rooms and their interconnecting areas. Paint one wall red, for example, in an otherwise white room and that wall will appear to advance towar you, shortening the room. Conversely, painting one wall in a cool blue in an otherwise darker room will result in that wall receding visually and appearing to lengthen the room. If the ceiling is too high, paint it in a darker color. You can lower it farther still by painting the top part of the wall (above the picture rail, if there is one) the same color as the ceiling. The opposite effect is achieved by painting a ceiling white to heighten it.

Walls can be made to appear higher if you paint the baseboard the same color as the walls. When all the walls and the ceiling are the same light color, as in monochromatic schemes, the natural angles of the room are much less noticeable. This gives a feeling of increased space, almost as if the room were open plan.

If your rooms are linked by narrow corridors, as in many older properties, light colors will appear to increase the width. A darker color at the end of a corridor will make it seem shorter. The most dramatic change in small or narrow linking areas occurs when the floorcovering is dark and the ceiling is painted in an advancing color, which compresses the space vertically. To expand the horizontals, paint the walls white or use a receding color. Using the same technique in all interlinking areas has a unifying effect throughout the property.

After choosing a color from the card, buy a sample pot. This lets you evaluate a sizeable color area on the wall you plan to decorate.

Red is the dominant color in both these locations.

Left: The end wall advances, making a long corridor appear shorter.

Right: The tint and shade of red act together, appearing to the eye to change the shape of the room.

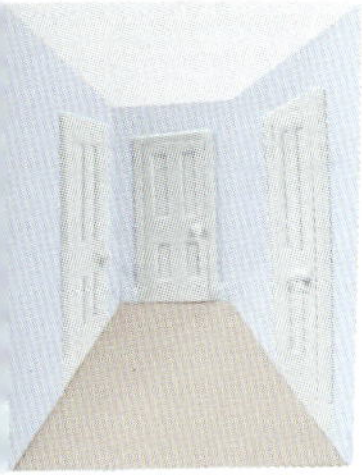

Receding colors are used visually to create a more spacious feeling.

Left: Subtle pale combinations make a corridor appear larger without appearing to alter any of the dimensions.

Right: However, a receding tint of blue on the far wall appears to lengthen an otherwise darker room.

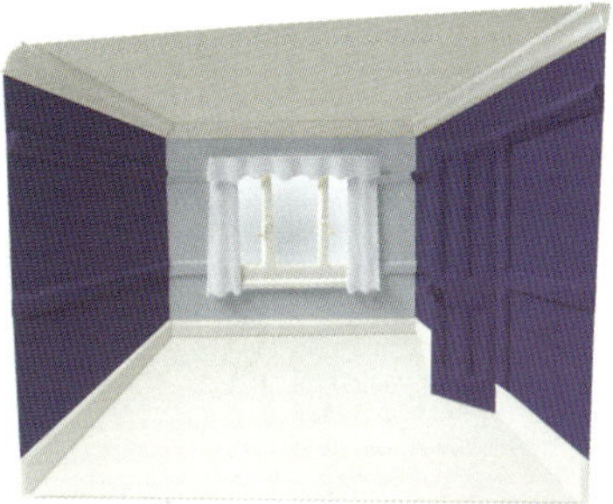

Vertically compressing space by using color:

Left: In a neutrally colored corridor, dominant red and orange appear to lift the floor and lower the ceiling, thereby expanding the horizontals.

Right: A ceiling is lowered visually by use of an advancing color.

Monochromatic schemes

If you are considering a monochromatic scheme, that is, one color only, then the color you choose must form a strong relationship with the fabrics and soft furnishings, the woodwork, and the flooring. Neutral grays, soft beiges, off-whites, and creams are frequent choices because they offset and therefore enhance patterned fabrics, and look good with natural wood finishes.

The term "monochromatic" is a misnomer, because patterns on floorcoverings and soft furnishings, wood varnishes and general household pieces have their own color content.

An easy introduction to such a scheme is to visualize the room and its contents in black and white for a moment. A rough sketch of the room with everything white will let you position colored fabric and carpet swatches, and color in areas clad in wood, such as the fireplace. Adding a touch of harmonious color to the previously white scheme is then straightforward.

Right: A beige and cream color scheme works well in many rooms, complementing natural wood and giving an uncluttered look.

Below: Color scheming—sketch your room and its contents in black and white, then make color substitutions from the chart.

Schemes using contrasting colors, shades, and tints are just as easy to approach in this way. A white room with one black wall, or a white-walled room with black baseboards, cornices, and picture rails, shows the most extreme contrast achievable. Then, simply substitute your colors. Black may become dark green or mid-blue, and white can be softened into cream or pale yellow. The contrast is retained, but your choice of colors will define how dramatic that contrast is.

Schemes using a combination of colors side by side on the wheel would be represented in a black and white sketch by mid-gray. Color contrast is not an issue because these are harmonious colors. There is no dividing line between the gray areas, so any two adjacent colors such as red and orange or blue and green can be substituted.

Swatch watch

When working on a room, designers will make up a swatch or sample board, consisting of colors, materials, fabrics, wallpapers, and wood off-cuts stuck down onto a card to assist the decision-making process. All colors envisaged in the scheme are side by side on the board, and can be held in front of any of the walls for a suitability match. It is easy to put one together by collecting samples from stores. Use the material or paint you are considering, however. Never substitute a cut-out from a magazine because this involves a different printing process and will not be accurate.

When your board is complete, use it to compare differing available light levels, and note down the changes in color in bright sunshine, in dull, overcast, or shadowy conditions, and under artificial light. The artificial light should ideally be the lighting system that is going to be used in the room. If it is going to be different, then find the closest match you can.

To assist in planning your room scheme, make up a swatch board of sample colors and materials.

The great divide

A house is divided into many areas, and you may or may not have a preference for a color linking system, that is to say linking all rooms on one floor by using the same door frame and baseboard color. You may wish to keep these natural divisions and, indeed, emphasize them by using different color schemes. However, one-room dwellings, spaces for both living and working or popular city loft-style apartments are not compartmentalized. Therefore the same contrasting scheme or linking system is advisable throughout. Variations will work, such as substituting a cream finish for white on one wall with the same frame or trim color, but they must not compromise the integrity of the overall scheme. Attempting too many color divisions in an area designated as one space works against the original design concept and is doomed to failure. At best it looks fragmented, at worst it offends the eye.

This loft apartment has a pleasing cohesive look and is visually united by its wooden flooring and units, and by the consistent use of black as an accent color: on the sofa cushions, piano, and dining chairs.

PAINTING

Of the hundreds of weekend tasks that home improvement enthusiasts take on in their homes, the most common is the simple paint job. A vast selection of paints and finishes is now available for all surfaces, and recent additions to paint-makers' ranges have increased the options considerably. This chapter guides you through the selection of paint, offers advice on paint schemes, and shows you how to tackle your first paint job.

Designer's notes

To anyone approaching a makeover for the first time, the vast array of paints must be confusing. The latest paint technology has led to boasts that a professional finish can be attained by a novice. However, it is important to assess modern paints in terms of what they will do, and relate them to older-style paints that may have been used in the house.

Paint types

The paint in your can will be either water- or solvent-based. Both types are made up of pigment, which provides the color, and a binder that holds the pigment particles together. This combination in water is generally called *latex*. In a spirit-based solvent it is known as oil-based *enamel* or *low luster*. Decorators have traditionally used water-based latex paints for interior walls and oil-based finishes for woodwork, such as doors and surrounds, because they are harder-wearing. Today's technology lets the manufacturer offer the choice of water-based enamel or satin paints for woodwork, reducing the drying time considerably.

Traditional descriptions are altering, too. Silk vinyl latex paints are often labeled "washable" or "wipeable." Mat latex is referred to as "nonreflective," which is also nonwipeable. Water-based enamel will often be "nondrip, no undercoat needed" or "one coat only." Often oil-based enamel is offered as "liquid enamel," or, implying use by professional decorators, as 'trade' enamel. As with other "trade" labels, don't be misled by the "trade" label into thinking it is superior.

Traditionally, water-based paints have been applied to interior walls, while oil-based enamel paint has been used on woodwork, but conventions are changing as new materials and finishes are now becoming available.

You may want to offset certain features, such as a fireplace surround, by painting them in one finish against a wall of another finish.

As you contemplate your choice of finish, consider only the durability of water-based versus oil-based paints. Oil-based paints are tougher, longer-lasting, and easier to clean. Water-based paints are easier to use, environmentally friendly, and the job is done in a quarter of the time. You will, however, need to repaint much sooner if you use water-based paints.

Choosing appropriate paints

On walls and ceilings, which are particularly large areas to paint, don't consider oil-based finishes unless you intend to apply a special effect such as ragging, in which case low luster is ideal. Large areas of oil-based paint are unpleasant to apply, environmentally unfriendly, and time-consuming to change. Latex paints are designed for the job, but make sure your wall surfaces are suitable first.

Once you have a color scheme in mind, examine the room. What is the current state of finish? If it is a painted scheme on plaster, liner paper, or wallcovering that can be painted, and you are merely altering the colors, your task is straightforward because paint is the major decorating factor. Perhaps the current finish incorporates wood paneling, tiles, or even a powerful wallpaper pattern that is to be retained on some of the walls. Your paint scheme must take into account what the room inherits from its previous life, and combine with existing materials to achieve a matching or contrasting effect.

Old and new together

Retaining parts of someone else's room scheme may seem unappealing at first, but don't dismiss it out of hand. If the room has a particular feature that dominates it, then it may provide a better visual result if you work with it, not against it. If you like a particular characteristic, it makes no sense to remove or disguise it, and it can become the axis for the new scheme.

In any combined scheme, remember that decorating can be done wall by wall, slowly building up a new look. It doesn't necessarily have to be drastically altered all at the same time. In the same way that you must consider what effect the floorcovering, carpet, or wood floor will have on painted walls, you have to view the walls themselves in relation to each other.

TYPES OF PAINT

Primers/Undercoats	Finishes/Top coats
Stain-blocking primer	Vinyl mat latex
Wood primer	Vinyl silk latex
Aluminum wood primer	Enamel latex
Alkali-resisting primer	Enamel
Penetrating stabilizing primer	Low luster
Red oxide primer	Low luster emulsion
Acrylic primer/Undercoat	Smooth masonry paint
Oil/Resin undercoat	Floor/Tile paint
	Ceiling paint
	Textured paint
	Radiator enamel

For detailed notes on paint types, see pages 246–247.

Adding to a scheme at any time has never been easier. Original paintings, prints, or tapestries can be hung, small areas can be painted as a special effect, or rugs can be used on the floor. This slightly alters the overall appearance, and the way that the walls interact with it, particularly if the scheme is monochromatic and the main color theme is continued in the pictures.

Above: Geometric paintings provide an eye-catching focal point in this neutral scheme.

Below: Kitchen walls need to be washable and will probably be subject to much wear and tear.

As a final thought, you should consider carefully the condition of the walls when you are making your decisions. If you find wood paneling or very heavyweight wallcoverings in the room, it is a good idea to stop and ask yourself why they are there. What are they covering up?

Many enthusiastic decorators have ripped off tongue-and-groove paneling only to find that the wall underneath needs to be taken back to the brick, damp-proofed, sealed, and replastered.

Practicalities

It is important to take into account the function of the room area when choosing paint for a particular scheme. Entrance hallways, for example, may have hooks for wet hats and coats and a place where people remove muddy boots and leave umbrellas. Don't consider a paint scheme that is not washable. Any wood here will need a tough finish, such as oil-based enamel, or, if varnished, an exterior sailboat varnish, to cope with everyday knocks. A wood cladding on the lower, more vulnerable, half of the wall may work to your advantage here.

The walls of the bathroom and kitchen should be washable, but the bathroom is a room that needs to be a warm and friendly place, so you will want to offset the sometimes cold or austere feel of tiles and glass.

Rooms used by all the members of the house need to be both decorative and functional. These are the truly multi-purpose areas, where the philosophy of "change a little at a time" can be both practical and democratic.

Children's rooms and play areas need paints that are washable and tough. Two topcoats are a good idea, so that surface scratches do not reveal a different color underneath. Avoid mat emulsion paints in children's rooms, as these will become shiny where

A deep sea-green is a restful color for a bathroom, offset here by the white units and upper walls.

The paint you select to decorate your bathroom should be washable, warm, and friendly.

inevitable smudges and fingerprints have to be cleaned off. Go for paints with a silk or semisheen finish.

Bedrooms have to be more robust these days because often they double as teenage living space. However, bedrooms are more personal areas, and schemes can be the choice of the individual. The paint job can be bold and imaginative, whereas communal areas sometimes call for compromise. A scheme in the main living area, for example, of bold, pure, vivid colors, may have seemed spectacular when you were doing it, but even after a short while may become rather irritating to the eye.

Instead of the traditional white, paintwork can be given a darker or contrasting color to the paint chosen for use on the walls.

Basic skills: guide to paint

There is more to painting than simply choosing your ideal color. Sound preparation of the surface to be painted is a must; otherwise, you risk having to redo it in the not-too-distant future and ending up with a patchy appearance. You also need to know how best to store your paint and use the tools that are vital to the process.

Wooden furniture must be properly prepared before it is painted. It must be sanded or washed down first, and will then require a coat of primer, undercoat, and finally a topcoat in your chosen color.

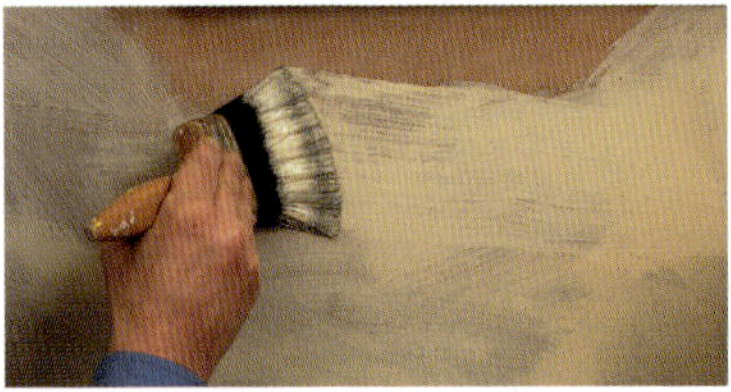

If you don't want your paint to soak straight into the wall, you will need to use either a sealer or a primer before you apply any latex paint. This will stop the paint from being absorbed by the wall.

Before using the "Paint: Types and Uses" table on pages 246–247 as a guide to paint finishes, consider your surface and what type of preparation, sealing, and priming it may require. Latex paint on bare walls needs a sealer to prevent the paint from disappearing into the wall altogether. On old walls you should use a stabilizing primer or a diluted mix of PVA (polyvinyl acetate). New plaster needs a plaster primer; a stabilizer will do, but you must make sure that the new plaster is properly dry or you will be sealing in damp.

Before applying paint to either wood panels or wooden paneling, coat the knots in the woodgrain to stop them from seeping resin, which will show through the paint finish. Use stain-blocking primer for this, followed by a primer, an undercoat, and lastly a topcoat. Traditionally, primer was an oil-based paint, but acrylic primer and combined primer/undercoat have now gained in popularity due to their ease and speed of use, and also because they are environmentally friendly. The latest technology offers enamel or satin finishes in a "nondrip" form that requires no undercoat, just a primer.

Paint pots

However good your paint job, accidental chips and scratches can occur, and a supply of retouching paint is always a good idea. A small amount of paint left in a can is best decanted into a suitable glass jar, with a lid, for storage. The more paint there is in the jar, the less air there is, and less

Brushes, rollers, and paint: the essential components.

chance of a skin forming on the top. Avoid getting paint around the rim of the jar or inside its lid; otherwise, opening it some time later will be tricky. And don't forget to label the jar.

A large volume of paint can remain in the original can. Many tradespeople then store this upside down. If you do so, make sure that the lid is hammered down securely or it may leak out. You may prefer simply to invert the can for a few minutes in order to let the contents run around the lid seal, and then to store it the correct way up.

Color paint charts are useful, but sample pots will be more accurate.

Tongue-and-groove paneling might be hiding a wealth of problems in the walls behind, and it may be better to leave it in place and repaint it, rather than remove it and have to sort out the underlying problem.

Tools and equipment

As with all tools of the trade, investing in cheap, badly made decorating equipment is a recipe for failure. There is nothing quite as expensive as trying to save money. An inferior tool can ruin a job or a finish by underperforming at a crucial stage, so invest wisely. Here is a selection to start off your essential toolkit for painting.

A palette knife, a filling knife and a scraper.

Tools and equipment

For walls and ceilings you will need a set of tools to take off the existing finish, and another set to put on the new scheme. Before you begin, always remember to protect the floor and furniture by covering them with large drop cloths.

Sugar soap and sandpaper

If you are repainting a papered wall, you only need to make sure that it is clean; household liquid soap applied with a soft cloth will remove grease. Make sure the wall is dry before you start painting. Repainting a masonry or plaster wall with latex paint is easier if the wall surface is "keyed" to receive the paint, so lightly abrade the surface with medium, followed by fine sandpaper. Before painting over a enamel, satin, or mat oil-based surface, with either oil- or water-based paint, use flexible silicone carbide paper to remove the surface "sheen." Soak medium and fine-grade sandpaper in a bucket of hot water with sugar soap, an all-purpose cleaner. Abrade the surface as before, using lots of water. Rinse the surface and dry it.

Painter's tape has numerous uses.

Brushes, pads, and rollers

Good-quality paint brushes will apply paint evenly, and will not shed bristles all over the wall. Four sizes—½ in./12 mm, 1 in./25 mm, 1½ in./38 mm and 2 in./50mm—should suffice for any

Rollers and brushes

Mini-roller, spare sleeve, and tray

Textured roller

Four sizes of paint brush, long-handled fitch, retouching brush, and bridge-handled stippling brush

Flogger (dragging brush)

Paint tray and paint pad

Roller handle, extension, foam and pile rollers

Graining roller

A heat gun with various attachments is useful for softening the paint on wooden surfaces so that it can be scraped off.

standard painting job. Larger sizes up to 6 in./150 mm are available, but they may make your hand and arm ache. For larger areas use a paint pad or roller. Always decant the paint into a kettle or bucket. Never paint straight from the can. The pad and roller will have their own loading containers, and as an option solid emulsion has its own tray.

The roller may be foam or fiber. Fiber rollers are available with different pile lengths. The more uneven the surface, the longer the pile you will need. For large areas use rollers, and to reach small awkward places use radiator rollers.

Other equipment

You can reach high ceilings by using an extension pole; however, high corners will have to be done with a brush. It is very important to make sure you are standing on a stable stepladder. An integral top platform is useful for placing your brush and paint kettle. Painter's tape and paint masks can be used to protect adjacent areas of color. If you do overrun, use a soft, damp cloth.

Butane gas torch

> **TOP TIP**
>
> As your brush dries, protect the bristles in plastic wrap and use an elastic band around the end to keep the tips square with the handle. Storing a dry brush in this way will ensure that it always keeps its shape. Avoid leaving brushes soaking in a jar of brush cleaner too long, because the bristles will splay out.

Maintenance

As soon as the job is done, clean the brushes, rollers, and containers. Oil-based paints can be removed with mineral spirits, turpentine substitute, or a brand-name brush cleaner and restorer. Water-based paint can be washed off in hot water and soap. After brushing out excess paint on old newspaper, work the cleaning solution well into the brush, as far up as the handle. Remove partly dried paint with an old comb. Rinse the brush and partly dry it with a soft cloth.

Never leave your brushes to soak overnight, because they will end up with a "permanent wave" that will make accurate cutting-in of colors impossible. To remove excess paint from rollers and pads, simply wash them out in their respective trays. Squeeze the roller and then hang it up to dry; it contains metal parts, and rust will contaminate your next paint load if you do not dry the roller thoroughly.

Preparation materials

General preparation

The finished job is only as good as your preparation. Walls and ceilings need very careful assessment before you reach for the roller and pry open the paint can. They may need to have cracks repaired, and will need to be washed down (and possibly "keyed") before you can apply emulsion or oil-based paint.

The qualities of paint

A thick coat of paint cannot be used to disguise a bad wall. Paint contains a binder, and the binder's job is to ensure that the colored particles (pigment) dry together on the wall as a continuous protective film, on top of, but not hiding, any bumps, cracks, or imperfections. Even thickening agents used in nondrip paints will not cause jelly-like applications to dry out any other way than flat on the wall. It is usually accepted that darker, glossier, more reflective colors show up imperfections more than pale, subtle tones, but this is not a recommended selection criterion. All flat areas of color will emphasize wall damage, and the only proper course of action is to eradicate the problem during preparation.

Repairing damaged walls

Don't be unduly worried, however, if your walls are not in pristine condition. Cracks and crevices in plaster are commonplace. New plaster frequently develops hairline cracks as it dries out, often where large areas meet at an angle, such as a wall and ceiling. A slight settling of the building on its foundations, or a small amount of subsidence, will result in fairly obvious cracks appearing in the plasterwork on the walls and ceilings. Check all around the room thoroughly if this is the case. You may find other evidence of settling, where baseboards meet the walls, and around door frame moldings.

All these cracks can be easily made good, using a decorator's pack of all-purpose joint compound, which comes as white powder to be mixed with water. Cracks caused by movement that is likely to recur, where the stair baseboard joins the wall in the stairwell, for instance, should be repaired with a flexible joint compound. These joint compounds are available premixed in cartridges, are usually applied by means of a simple-to-use cartridge gun, and have a tip that can be cut to fill a specific width.

Holding the cartridge gun at an angle to the wall, squeeze the compound into the crack, then smooth with your finger or a putty knife. When dry, the compound can be sanded down flush with the wall.

Use a triangular scraper to rake out any loose material and dirt in the crack, and to undercut it slightly to give the joint compound a good grip. Then press the compound into the crack using a putty knife.

If the walls have an oil-based paint finish, low luster or flat oil, then in addition to washing them down, you will need to provide a "key" for the new paint finish to adhere to. Lightly abrade the surface using sandpaper wrapped around a sanding block.

Use medium paper for enamel and fine paper for low luster. Alternatively, you can combine both operations by keying the surface while it is wet, using flexible silicone carbide paper. Soak the paper in a bucket of soap and hot water for at least five minutes, while prewashing the wall using a sponge. Using plenty of water, lightly abrade the wall surface to remove the sheen. Finally, wash down the wall with clean water.

Overpainting

Overpainting wall areas with latex paint, whether in the same color or not, is a common task in the home. Provided your walls are sound, you only need to ensure that they are clean and free from contamination by dust, dirt, and grease. Usually, household liquid soap, hot water, and a sponge will do the job. However, if a wall or ceiling has an unsightly stain caused by a leaking roof or upstairs appliance, you must seal it or it will quickly show through the new paint finish. The easiest way is to paint over the stain with oil-based enamel or low luster in an appropriate color, leave it to dry, and then apply the latex. Alternatively, stain sealers are available in spraycan form.

Sand an oil-based surface lightly with sandpaper to provide a "key" for the paint to adhere to.

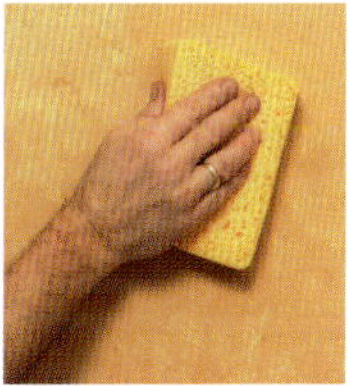

Then wash the wall down using hot water, liquid soap, and a soft sponge to remove any excess dirt.

Preparing paint

Always read the manufacturer's directions, and familiarize yourself with the information on the side of the can. Make sure the top of the paint can is clean before you open it; otherwise, any dirt there may fall into the paint. Insert a screwdriver blade horizontally under the lip of the can and turn it slowly until it is vertical, repeating farther around the rim to pry off the lid. This minimizes damage to the lip, and makes resealing easier. If the can is half-empty, carefully remove any top skin and stir the paint. Any remaining tiny pieces of skin or debris must then be removed by straining the paint. You can do this by decanting it into a paint kettle or bucket through a piece of stretched pantyhose.

Remove the lid of the can using a screwdriver. Old paint may need to be strained into a kettle or bucket.

Abrasives

The generic term "sanding down," referring to surface abrading as a vitally important part of decorating preparation, is still in common use, even though "sandpaper" as such has not been commercially produced for many years. The modern equivalent and all other suitable abrasives are available at your local home center and are outlined here.

Never cut sandpaper with blade or scissors. Fold a sheet into quarters and tear it along the edge of the table.

Preparing the ground

Quality preparation is the key to a quality result, and a smooth surface is essential for a paint or varnish finish. This means rubbing down with the correct abrasive, because using the right materials speeds up the laborious task and gives the best result. Some surfaces must be rubbed down dry (bare woods, surfaces containing water-based joint compounds), some wet (enamel paint that is being recoated), and some, such as floorboards, are suitable for both applications. Common sense and personal preference should also play a part in your decision. Wet abrading of water-soluble materials, including joint compounds, often leads to little more than a pastelike mess; while dry rubbing of dirty, greasy surfaces will clog the abrasive in no time, be both ineffective and expensive because the paper cannot be reused.

Wet or dry?

Traditionally, rubbing down was a dry process, starting with coarser grades and finishing with finer ones, the finest grade of all often being referred to as "flour" paper. However, manufacturers eventually introduced a waterproof paper so that a lubricant could be used with the abrasive.

Initially this waterproof paper was not a popular choice, because of its cost, so it was used only in coach finishing and other high-quality work, and general decorating workers continued to dry rub. Today, silicon carbide used with a lubricant is recognized as a real alternative to dry papers. It is faster and more efficient because of its cutting action, lasts longer, doesn't clog easily, and can be rinsed clean in a bucket. This offsets its higher cost (it is considerably dearer than sandpaper).

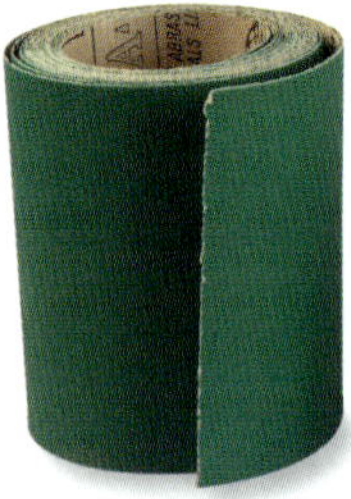

Green aluminum oxide is generally suitable for heavy-duty and machine use.

Left: Cloth sanding belts are available for all belt sanding machines, domestic and heavy-duty machines alike. The abrasive is aluminum oxide; the belt is full resin cloth, flush joined at a 45 degree angle to give maximum life.

Right: Yellow aluminum oxide sheets (here torn from a standard roll) are suitable for hand and block use. You can clearly see the difference in grit sizes.

Abrasive sheets

Conventional sandpaper: coarse, medium, and fine grades in standard sized sheets.

Waterproof, latex-backed synthetic silicon carbide.

Today's cutting edge

The home decorator is able to make the same choices in buying and using as the working professional:

Conventional sandpaper

This is used dry, available in sheets 11 x 9 in. (280 x 230 mm), graded 3 (coarse) to 00 (very fine) or simply labeled coarse, medium, and fine, depending on the manufacturer, suitable for hand or machine use. Cheap but clogs very easily and selection of inappropriate grades can result in scratching of the work surface.

A roll of steel wool. Always wear gloves when you handle this product and, as with other abrasives, wear a dust mask.

Aluminum oxide

This is used dry, available in sheets, 11 x 9 in. (280 x 230 mm), or in rolls 4½ in. (115 mm) wide and sold by the roll or in yard (meter) lengths cut from a roll, or in precut sizes ready-made for machine sanders. Graded in grit sizes, 40 grit (coarse) to 240 (very fine). Electro-bonded, with a grit size giving a more controlled cut, it is frequently used instead of sandpaper in the same type of application because of its longer life.

Silicon carbide

This can be used dry or lubricated; if regularly rinsed in the wet application, it is long-lasting. Available in sheets 11 x 9 in. (280 x 230 mm), graded 100 (coarse) to 1200 (very fine), but frequently found in home centers as a "decorator's pack" containing a couple of sheets of coarse, medium, and fine flexible papers. Tough, flexible, and long-lasting when lubricated, it should be a first choice for painted surfaces.

Steel wool

This can be used either dry or lubricated, available as boxed rolls about 2¾ in. (70 mm) wide, or as pads. Graded from 5 (coarse) to 0000 (very fine), often packed as a kit containing coarse, medium, and fine pads. It can be used as a cleaner or degreaser on flooring to scour wood following the use of water-washable paint remover, or to apply waxes to prepared surfaces. Always wear gloves when using this material.

Rubbing blocks

Use an abrasive with a sanding block to maintain an edge on the corners of the work. Always sand in the direction of the grain, particularly if you intend to apply a varnished finish, because cross-grain scratching will show up badly.

How to paint

It might appear that painting is a perfectly straightforward procedure, but there are numerous tips—on the selection of your brush, roller, pad, or aerosol—that can make the task much easier. If you know how to apply the paint properly and what sort of stroke to use, the result will be much more pleasing.

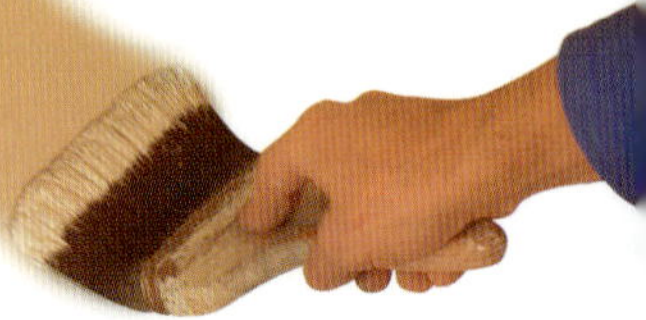

Using a brush

Always select a brush of a suitable size for the job and make sure that it is clean. Ensure that the bristles are in good condition by working the brush up and down on a dry surface. This will make any dust and defective or loose bristles fall out.

For very small wall areas, for blending in, and for finished detail work on roller-painted walls, use a small brush, 1½ in./38 mm or 2 in./50 mm size. Hold it between your thumb and fingers on the metal casing, or ferrule, which encases the bristles.

Larger brushes, although quicker initially, will soon become tiring and difficult to control, and are no substitute for a roller. However, if you decide the large 6 in./150 mm brush is for you, then you will find it easier if you hold it by the handle.

If latex surfaces, the easiest to paint, do not dry out uniformly flat, simply apply a second coat. Oil-based finishes must not dry out at the edges before the entire surface is finished, or the brush strokes will be obvious, so blend in the wet edges continuously as you move from side to side across the surface. Frequent changing of the direction of the brush stroke will result in a more even distribution of paint.

Using a roller

A paint roller is the most time-efficient way of applying a water-based finish to a large area. The only drawback is that you cannot butt up to other color surfaces or into corners, and you will need a small brush to complete the job. Oil-based paints are equally easy to apply, but they will retain some of the texture of the roller in the finish, whereas latex paints all dry flat. If an absolutely dead flat finish is needed in an oil base, use a brush.

- Select a suitable roller sleeve for your wall, remembering that the smoother the surface, the shorter the pile required.
- Pour the paint of your choice into the reservoir of the paint tray, level with the ribbed rolling area.

For maximum control of a small or medium-sized brush, hold it by the ferrule, or metal casing, dip it into the paint to one-third of the bristle depth, and use long, sweeping strokes to apply the paint.

›ll out excess paint on the ›bed area of the paint tray ›fore applying a roller to a ›ll.

Immerse the roller sleeve in the reservoir, then roll it out gently on the ribbed area to ensure an even distribution of paint. Apply the roller to the wall using even pressure throughout, in vertical overlapping strokes. Finish off by changing to horizontal strokes, which will ensure an even coverage. Don't try to cover too big an area each time you load the roller. You may find it helpful if you visualize your wall broken down into imaginary squares and then fill one at a time.

paint spatters onto adjacent surfaces as you roll out the paint, s not because the roller is overloaded, it's because you are iving it too fast. This is always a temptation, particularly when ing an extension pole to paint a ceiling. So, slow down and member that paint splashes from above you can land on your ad. Always wear eye protection.

Using paint pads

Paint pads come in a variety of sizes and the larger ones can be used with an extension pole to reach ceilings. Edging pads are available to cut into corners and angles. Pads come with their own paint tray and special loading roller. Simply pour in your paint, and load the pad by running it back and forth across the ribbed cylindrical loader. Paint in vertical overlapping strokes to achieve a smooth even coat. While paint pads are simplicity itself, bear in mind that they carry less paint per loading than a brush or a roller, so an extra coat is likely to be required.

A roller on an extension pole is ideal for painting ceilings, although you will need to use a brush to fill in corners.

Paint pads are useful for getting a smooth, even surface, without any brush marks, but cannot be used for oil-based paint.

Sprayguns and aerosols are best kept for concentrated detail where the area to be painted is masked off with tape.

Aerosols and sprayguns

Universally available in solvent or water-based form, aerosols are very useful for spraying small areas as special-effect patterns on a plain painted wall, such as colored stripes or squares. They are expensive, however, and require accurate and detailed masking. They are not suitable for spray painting an entire room. For this you would need to rent an electric airless spraygun with a changeable paint reservoir from a local rental center or builders' merchant. These guns have a viscosity measuring cup to ensure that the paint for the reservoir has been thinned down correctly. Useful accessories include a flexible extension tip, for spraying a ceiling, and more powerful models have a fine adjustment control for flexibility of spray volume. It may look simple in the hands of an expert, but unless you are experienced in the use of guns, you are advised to choose another application method.

TOP TIP

Using your second finger as a pressure guide on either the handle or ferrule of a brush can quickly result in a blister, particularly if you have soft hands. An astutely positioned adhesive bandage, or even a length of painter's tape wound around the finger, will protect against rubbing. Try to keep the brush handle and ferrule free of sticky, semi-dry paint or varnish at all times, because this exacerbates the problem.

Special effects: textured paint

Textured finishes were once kept almost exclusively for ceilings but are now becoming increasingly popular on walls—or perhaps just one feature wall in a room—to create a particular look. They also have the advantages of helping to cover uneven surfaces, being simple to apply and being adaptable to your own designs.

Textured paint

Recently built properties frequently have textured paints on ceilings. These appear as fairly uniform overlapping swirls, or single twists in a geometric pattern, usually with very basic light fittings and plain walls with no surround. The advantage here is that water-based paint with added thickeners is used, so the finish is flexible and can disguise cracks and movement in the original surface. The addition of a joint compound will give the paint a smooth finish, which is easily manipulated by a texturing comb. Blending in sand will result in a much rougher appearance. You can decide which finish is right for you. One factor to consider when using textured finishes, however, is their ability to attract and trap dirt and dust. They are therefore best avoided in the kitchen, bathroom, or workshop.

Application

Apply the textured paint with a roller or brush, taking a manageable area at a time – about 3½ sq. ft. (1 sq m) should be ideal. Apply the paint as evenly as you can over the surface area. Make sure that the depth of finish will obliterate any defects that are apparent. Then simply apply the texturing decoration of your choice, using the comb supplied, a sponge, scrapers, or a piece of plastic that has been cut to size. You can also buy patterned roller sleeves in order to create special effects, such as repeating geometric patterns.

Although intended primarily for ceilings, these easy-to-use finishes have become increasingly popular elsewhere—for example on feature walls giving an impression of Spanish or Mexican

A Mediterranean look can be created using textured finishes on the walls.

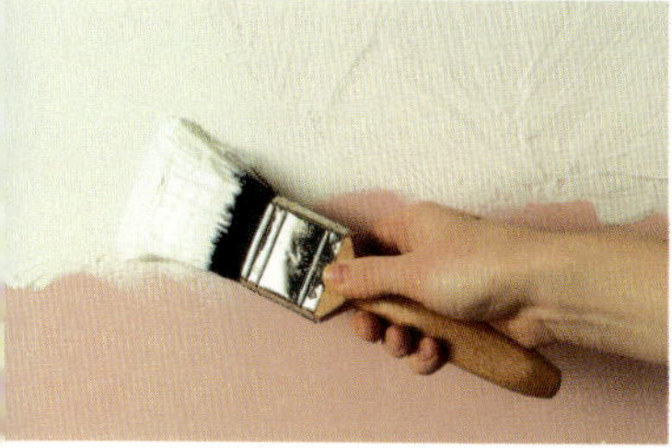

You can apply textured paint with a roller or paint brush. Work on a manageable area at a time, making sure that you spread an even thickness. That way, the results won't be patchy.

A sponge dabbed onto the textured base will create a simple pattern. This is the look often chosen to reflect a rustic style and, when combined with basic furnishings, can be very effective.

styling. It's well worth experimenting on a square of spare hardboard first to see what the effect looks like.

Most of these latex paints are white, but you can add any water-based color of your choice for a Mediterranean-style scheme. Simply treat the textured paint as sealed plaster. The principle of overpainting in various colors can be explored further by using a special texturing base and color waxes, which are available in kit form.

Spread the base onto the feature wall with a trowel or something similar, and then create a relief pattern of your own design. This can be as complex as you like, because the base is reworkable for up to an hour. When you are satisfied with the base texture, brush on one or two coats of your chosen color wax. This will be absorbed into the textured base at different rates, and will dry out to an irregular toned finish, giving the impression of sun-kissed walls.

Apply the textured base to your surface, spreading it out well over a small area.

Brush on the water-based color or wax of your choice when the textured surface is dry.

Textured finishes can be very effective in minimalist surroundings. Like all specialist decorative techniques, they need space in which to work their magic, so the less clutter, the better. Try offsetting a texture against bare unvarnished floorboards, or make a relief feature of one wall and leave the others plain.

Use a comb or piece of plastic cut to size to create a pattern. This might be geometric, swirling spirals, or simply an abstract design. You can rework the textured base for up to one hour.

Special effects: glazes

Glazes are semi-transparent paints that let the underlying base color show through. They have become increasingly popular because they can be used to create a whole range of different effects and are relatively easy to use. With a little practice, you will be able to emulate the look that a professional painter can achieve.

Decorative finishes for walls, from simple rag-rolling to more complex crackle glazing, can be undertaken successfully on correctly prepared wall surfaces. It is always a good idea to experiment on a spare piece of board first. It's a lot easier to throw out a scrap piece of board if you don't like the color or the effect, than to do an entire wall or room again.

The walls in this living-room have been painted porcelain blue with a white glaze swirled in.

Preparation

Whether your intended finish is based on oil or water, a correctly prepared surface is essential. Since several popular effects are common to both oil and water bases, you do have a choice. However, oils are easier to work with because they dry more slowly and are much more resilient. Water bases dry quickly, which is helpful only if you are attempting a multilayered build-up of colors. To achieve the same longevity as oils, a water-based surface needs several coats of varnish.

Rectify any wall defects, cracks, crevices, and holes, as you would for a straight latex roller job. For an oil-based finish on bare plaster, prime the surface with all-purpose oil-based primer-sealer. For water-based finishes you can use water-based primers or PVA thinned with water. Sand the surface of previously painted plaster walls to provide the necessary "key," using a medium-grit abrasive paper. Now apply the underlying coats

Apply your base coat to the wall in the usual manner, using long sweeping strokes.

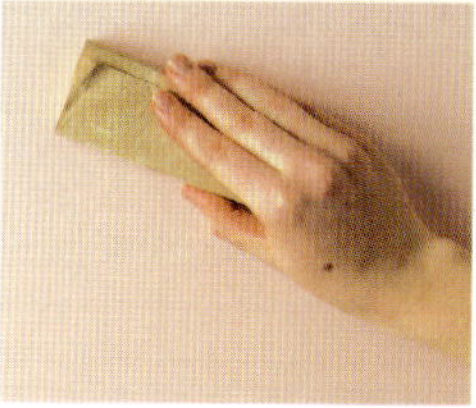

Abrade the surface of the wall between coats with fine grade sandpaper.

Blend a little color with turpentine and mix it into the glaze, avoiding lumps of color.

that will partly show through your glaze. One or two coats of oil-based low luster will suffice for oil finishes; one or two coats of water-based undercoat or latex for water-based finishes. If you decide to add a second coat, lightly abrade the surface of the first using a fine grade of abrasive paper, to remove any irregularities.

Choosing and making glazes

Most finishes require oil-based glazes. A slow drying time lets you handle the medium easily, even when attempting more ambitious effects. Water-based glazes are thinner and dry very quickly. Colorwashing and sponging techniques aside, they are unsuitable for most finishes. Water-based glazes are simply made up from colored acrylics thinned with water, or a water-based latex glaze, often with the addition of white latex to tint the color. Oil-based glazes consist of opaque glaze, available from good paint retailers, which can be diluted with a mixture of linseed oil and mineral spirits, or with turpentine. In both cases more opaque glaze in the mix slows down the drying process, and leaves more time for playing with the effects.

Start with a basic ratio of 50:50 if you are mixing opaque glaze with turpentine, adding more turpentine to thin down the mix, and the finished glaze, if preferred. When linseed oil and mineral spirits are used instead of turpentine, more mineral spirits will thin the glaze and shorten the drying time. Increasing the amount of linseed oil will result in a smoother, oilier finish. The exact proportions are a matter of personal preference, and some experimentation may be useful.

If you are happy with the consistency of the glaze, add the color of your choice, a little at a time. Any oil-based color can be used, but remember to mix specialist artists' oil paints carefully with a small amount of glaze to start with. This will show you whether the color is what you expect, and will prevent the mix from being lumpy.

TOP TIP

Photographs in magazines and books may appear to show exactly the effect that you want, but bear in mind that these are reproduced by a four-color process that is not necessarily an exact color match, particularly where metallics are concerned.

A selection of oil-based glazes showing the mixed-up version and the combed-out glaze.

Sponging and colorwashing

Two of the simplest, and most widely used, paint effects are sponging and colorwashing. Both of these broken-color effects work over the underlying base coat that has been applied to the wall, although sponging involves dabbing on additional color, whereas colorwashing creates effects and texture in a colored glaze.

Apply the larger sponge lightly to the wall, trying not to make the resulting pattern look too regular.

Reload the sponge as necessary, changing its position and adding more color in some areas.

When the first color is dry, dab on the second color with the smaller sponge until the effect looks right.

Sponging

Sponging is a very simple paint finish and the variations open to you with this technique are endless. Applied on a plaster, lined, or papered wall it should be water-based, but if you try sponging on a wood-panelled or cladded wall, use an oil base, such as low luster, because it will last longer. You will need natural or marine sponges for this technique. Select a large one that is easy to hold, and a smaller one in another shape to put on a second color or add patches of different color intensity. Pour your colored latex paint into a small tray or kettle, and partially immerse the sponge. Dab it onto a sheet of paper to remove any excess and to check the effect. If you are completely satisfied, dab the sponge onto the wall base color. Vary the angle and try to avoid making it look too uniform. When it is dry, add a second color with the other sponge.

Colorwashing

Colorwashing, also water-based, is similar in principle to waxed textured finishes. You can use this technique to create a rustic effect, with subtle color on a roughened surface. Similarities end here, though, because the wall must be sealed with two coats of emulsion as a base. Then the watered-down colors are brushed on, before being worked into the wall with a dry brush. Aging and distressing techniques can be applied if desired, using watery white to achieve a dusty, chalky feel. If similar colors are used on textured walls, contrasting colors used on smooth, flat surfaces give an entirely different result with almost the same technique. Latex the wall as before, brush on the colored glaze, and then use a very wide, dry brush to create long, sweeping strokes in a haphazard manner. The base coat underneath will show through.

Apply a base coat to the wall in the standard manner, using long, sweeping strokes.

Add a liberal coat of colored glaze. The best effects will be created by using a contrasting color.

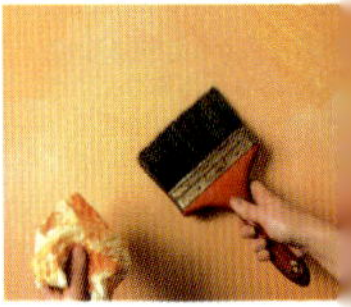

Using a dry, wide softening brush, work over the glaze in a random direction, using long strokes.

Stippling and rag-rolling

Two additional techniques are stippling and rag-rolling. Stippling with a brush is a one-off finish, which creates a pleasingly mottled appearance on a wall. Rag-rolling, which is also known simply as "ragging," can be built up in layers, provided that each layer is left to dry completely before the next one is added.

Brush the glaze onto the underlying base coat. The stippling action will remove any brush marks that show.

Hold the stippling brush at right angles to the wall and stab briskly at the surface.

Two-color finishes

Both of these techniques produce a two-color finish and are best used with oil-based glazes. Both require similar wall surfaces and give a pleasingly subtle result. Two coats of low luster are required as a base color in both cases.

Stippling

To achieve the best finish, stippling needs an even glaze on the base coat, because the aim is to remove all brush marks from the surface. A special stippling brush is best purchased specifically for this task, although you can experiment with any large, reasonably stiff brush.

The object of stippling is to hit the painted wall surface with the end of the bristles. The bristles must be reasonably dry, however, or you will simply put glaze back onto the surface, so unload your brush regularly by stippling onto a clean rag.

Stippling gives a rich, powerful finish. It is ideal for emphasizing bright, strong colors, so choose your combinations bearing this in mind. It needs to be done relatively quickly, so it is best to have someone else help you.

Rag-rolling

Ragging involves dabbing a dry, crumpled-up ball of cloth onto a glaze coat, to remove parts of it before it dries. As you roll the rag across the glazed surface, irregular patterns will be created. A design can be created using a variety of contrasting materials. Softer or harsher patterns can be made, resulting in quite different visual effects, depending on the fibers in the cloth.

Often these two techniques are combined, with a surface that has been earmarked for ragging being stippled first in order to remove all brushmarks.

Make sure you have plenty of rags and keep turning each rag to expose a clean surface as you work. When a rag becomes clogged with glaze, replace it. Work on small areas at a time; otherwise, the glaze may become too dry.

Brush the glaze over the base coat in a random manner, so that some of the base shows through.

Using a crumpled cloth, dab at the wall to remove some of the glaze while it is still wet.

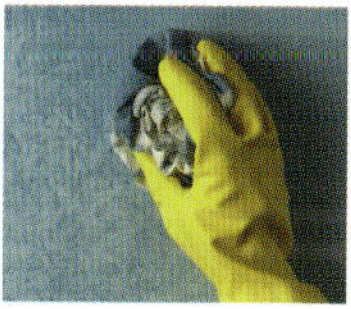

Vary the direction and change the rag as necessary, so that you end up with an irregular pattern.

Woodgraining and dragging

These techniques are variations on the same theme; woodgraining is merely an extension and amplification of dragging. However, dragging will show up any imperfections in the wall, so it is best kept for surfaces that are perfectly smooth. Woodgraining effects can look stunning in the right situation and will add interest to an otherwise plain interior.

A woodgrained blue wall with stenciling applied to the beams is offset by the simple table and ceiling in this dining-room. Woodgraining is often most effective when done on just one wall.

Both of these techniques involve pulling or dragging a dry brush through an oil-based glaze to create irregular linear patterns. Skilled decorators can achieve imitation wood finishes in this way, by raking long, narrow strokes with special straight-haired brushes called floggers. You can use any dry brush, however, and many irregular patterns and line widths can be achieved, depending on the condition and age of your brush.

Dragging through a wall glaze using a fine, soft brush results in a subtle fine-line finish. Adding a graining-comb finish to distort and offset these lines can give the appearance of exotic wood. This technique works well on furniture and wood panels.

To woodgrain, apply glaze generously over the base coat, working parallel to the grain on wooden surfaces.

Using a dry flogger, drag a series of parallel lines in the glaze to create the pattern of the grain.

Use a graining comb to manipulate the parallel lines and make interesting patterns.

To drag a surface, once you have applied the glaze over the base coat, draw a dry flogger over it, working from the top to about halfway down.

Then drag the brush upward from the floor, meeting at different points along the wall. Don't worry if the lines are not perfectly straight.

Dragging

Dragging is, in reality, the first part of woodgraining, but if you select an entire wall for this effect, only drag half the wall at a time; otherwise, the brush will overload because it picks up too much glaze from the surface. Always keep the brush as dry as possible—you may find this easier if you drag the second half of the wall upward from the floor, meeting in the middle. Lessen the pressure as you move through the join, and don't meet in exactly the same place as you move along the wall. Try to vary this by 12 in./30 cm or so.

Woodgraining

Using the woodgraining technique, you can make your surface look like the raised grain on planed lumber. Select your eggshell base coat carefully, for example, using a mid-yellow base showing through an orange glaze to imitate pine. Other combinations will give an appearance similar to other types of wood. Use a 50:50 mix in your chosen oil-based glaze and brush it on evenly. Any brush marks that are left visible must run in the final direction of the grain.

When you are satisfied with the even color, drag a dry brush through the glaze, leaving veins of base color exposed. The width of the grain effect will depend on the age and condition of the brush. Rubber rockers and graining combs can be used to imitate the peculiarities of a natural timber surface, such as the fibers, grain spirals, bands of paler tissue, and so on.

Other effects

A variety of effects involving oil-glaze graining and dragging can be achieved using manufacturers' paint-effect kits, consisting of base coat, top coat, and effect applicators. For example, you can create your own blue-jeans wall finish in this way. A denim-blue top coat is rollered over a dry, very pale blue base, and then dragged with a long-haired flogger brush, which can be used to create a denim jeans-effect, from ceiling and floor to the middle of the wall. Follow the kit instructions because a protective final coat may be needed.

On modern, smooth walls, a floor-to-ceiling denim effect adds a cool, unusual feel. If you prefer, the traditional blues can be replaced by other color combinations.

To create a denim effect, first paint the wall surface with a very pale blue base coat.

Then paint the surface with a denim blue, which should contrast well with the underlying color.

Drag a long-haired flogger over the wall from top to middle and bottom to middle to create the look

Spattering

Spatter effects, sometimes called speckling, are achieved professionally by using a spraygun fitted with a special decorators' spray head at very low pressure. The color is not atomized and hits the wall as a series of tiny splashes. You can imitate this finish by flicking single colors onto a surface with a brush, slowly building up the overall color.

Making a splash

For spattering you can use water- or oil-based paint. Oil will last longer, but a sealer can always be applied to emulsioned surfaces. Whichever you use, you need to carefully mask and protect the adjoining surfaces. By applying small splashes of red, yellow, and bright blue from separate cans in a dense pattern, you can make a wall look dark brown; only close inspection will reveal the secret.

Spattering can be applied to all kinds of surfaces, not just walls. Here it has been applied in a highly expressive way to a radiator. Remember to use heat-resistant paint suitable for this purpose.

Method

The technique consists of sharply tapping a paint-laden brush against an offcut of wood, directly in front of the wall. The size of the splashes will vary, depending on how near you are to the wall, and the quantity of paint on the brush. You can experiment on a large piece of scrap cardboard to get a feel for the technique. Flick bright yellow paint onto a white base, carefully building up an intense pattern of irregular splashes. Clean the brush and repeat with bright red, and then bright blue.

Although the paint on the wall is in reality a kaleidoscope of colored dots of varying shapes and sizes, viewed from across the room it will appear to be dark brown. This build-up of color is similar to that in a printing process, and you can try out different

Begin spattering by tapping the brush against a piece of wood to flick the paint onto the wall.

Start adding the second color, in this case red, in the same manner, building up an even coverage.

Finish off with a spattering of blue. When viewed from a distance, the finish will appear as a brown.

combinations. Spatter blue on a yellow base to make green. Try a black and white scheme using black and gray splashes to achieve a dull finish, and then liven it by adding white. If the combined effect is deemed unsatisfactory, you always have the option of adding another color. You can do this without waiting for the others to dry.

This technique is somewhat haphazard, the size and shape of the spatter effect being difficult to control. Experimentation with scrap cardboard is essential. If you find it very difficult, try dragging an old blunt knife along the bristle tips of a large wall brush. Hold the brush bristles down, and run the knife toward you. As the bristles spring back, paint is flicked onto the near surface.

Do not confuse this technique with multicolor finishes. These are special trade paints that achieve a spattered effect in one coat. Such industrial paints have pigment particles that remain permanently in suspension. They don't bind in the usual way, and as a result must be sprayed conventionally. Airless and hot sprays are unsuitable methods of application; neither are brush and roller an option. This is a special purpose finish which is best left in the hands of professionals.

You can create a soft focus effect in your home by using the spattering technique.

Depending on the color scheme you select, the effect can be cool or, as shown here, warm.

Marble finishes

Marbled paint effects are time-consuming and complicated to apply. However, careful consideration of the chosen surface, a suitable piece of marble, or picture, that can be used as reference, attention to detail, and sympathetic use of color in the rest of the room can transform any area in an attractive fashion.

Bathrooms and shower areas

Bathrooms and shower areas will benefit from a marble makeover, but be selective and don't overdo this effect. Smaller wall areas, bath panels, shower sides, and other places where tiles might be found are all suitable targets for experimentation. If you attempt to recreate the ultimate Roman bathing room, however, you may find the overall scheme a little intimidating.

Marbling is ideal for bathrooms, giving a feeling of opulence. With practice, you should be able to achieve very realistic results. Don't overdo it, though, as the effect can be overpowering.

Method

To begin, find a piece of marble to copy. A tile, for instance, in the appropriate colors, is a good starting point. If you intend to marble a bathroom wall, first ensure it is completely flat and in prime condition. Make good any defects, and coat the wall with oil-based low luster. Now brush on a contrasting glaze, using equal portions of opaque glaze and turpentine mixed with the artists' oil color that matches your scheme. You need only a thin coat, then add more or a different artists' color to the glaze. Apply this to selected parts of the wall, creating random areas of different color strengths. Blend these areas together by dabbing lightly with a soft cloth or natural sponge, or by stippling the surface. As this removes the glaze, it creates lighter tones in part. To create the marble veins in contrasting color glazes, use a small artists' brush and vary the width, sharpness, and direction of the veins across the wall. Complete the wall by adding more oil glaze to some of the veins, stipple more color onto selected areas, and lighten others until you are happy with the result. Let the wall dry completely, then apply at least two coats of clear oil-based varnish in satin or enamel, depending on whether you prefer a polished appearance or not.

With care, you can copy the veins and colors of marble in paint.

Begin by painting the wall with an oil-based low luster paint and leave it to dry.

Working on a manageable area at a time, brush on the colored turpentine and opaque glaze.

After adding a third color, dab a cloth into the glaze to blend the colors together.

Paint in the veins with a small brush. Vary their thickness and direction as in real marble.

Add more glaze as necessary until you are happy with the result. When dry, add a clear varnish.

Alternatives

As an alternative to an overall varnished finish, if you find a paneled pattern that suits the room, it is relatively simple to transfer the design to your finished marble effect wall using painter's tape to define the panel shapes. Adding different color tints to the satin or enamel varnish will alter or enhance the colors of panels making up a geometric shape. Several coats of tinted varnishes can be applied to the same areas, building up the depth of the design. Leave your geometric panel design to dry and finish as before with two coats of clear varnish. As an alternative to enamel, satin coat can be polished to achieve a sheened finish.

Varnish over paint

Building up a depth of finish, using several layers of varnish to give a "coach" finish on top of the color-tinted glazes and varnishes, protecting the geometric patterns created, is a technique not confined to marbling. Any wall finish can be overvarnished, thereby creating apparent depths in the finish. It is essential that the wall is in good condition.

- Prime the surface, roller on a flat color of your choice, and leave it to dry. Divide your wall into geometric areas, stripes, or hoops of horizontal stripes, or be more adventurous with squares or different sizes of interconnecting rectangles. Brush on clear varnish over the shapes you want to define.
- Use one coat for some, and two or three for others so that you build up a pattern of definition. Special paint finishes can work well if they are accentuated in this way.
- You could try using a metallic paint, such as copper, but remember to stir the paint throughout the operation. Varnish on top adds either a slight sheen or a spectacular mirror effect, depending on the number of coats you apply.

Varnished finishes have been popular throughout history, as evidenced by this beautiful lacquered cabinet from China.

Stamping and stenciling

Both these techniques are perfect for adding a unique character to your decorative scheme, an individual touch that defines the room as yours and yours alone. Symbols, simple cut-outs, silhouettes, abstract shapes, and caricatures can all be stamped or stenciled as a painted finish, in a continuation of the color scheme or as a complete contrast.

Stamping

Stamping involves rolling color onto an individual raised surface, a stamp, then offsetting the color onto a wall, forming a deliberate pattern or random marks. This technique is best suited to decorative borders and for framing larger areas of color.

Ready-made stamps, in a variety of designs, are widely available from artists' suppliers and decorating stores, and generally come in kit form with a selection of paints and a small applicator roller. You can, of course, make your own stamp, drawing a design or image onto foam rubber about 2 in./5 cm thick, and cutting around the external shape. The internal details can then be cut out and removed to a depth of 1 in./25 mm with a snap-blade knife. Try using your design to form a two-color creative border; use strips of tape to mask the edge of a wall stripe, and paint the stripe in a complementary color to the rest of the wall. Remove the painter's tape when the paint is dry. Roll the second color of your choice onto your stamp, and gently press it onto the wall stripe at regular and equal intervals, starting in the middle.

You can buy ready-made stamps for creating decorative patterns.

Latex is the best paint for stamping. Remember to roll color onto your stamp evenly, and try a test-pressing first to remove excess paint. Never dip the stamp directly into the paint.

Stenciling is a very effective method of adding decorative borders and paint features to a room. Either buy stencils ready-cut from a home center, or buy the raw materials and make your own.

Stenciling

Stencils, like stamps, are usually associated with edgings and borders, such as chair rails, or smaller decorative panels, but you could use this versatile technique over an entire wall.

You can stencil by brush or sponge, applying paints or crayons onto a surface, through shaped areas cut into a mask that removes areas of background, onto sections defined by painter's tapes, or through holes in paper and cardboard. Anything that partially masks your working surface can be referred to as a stencil.

Commercial stencils are available from artists' suppliers, either in a transparent plastic film or flexible waxed cardboard. Waxed cardboard is easier to cut and cheaper. Cardboard is opaque, so consider film if your design is complex, because you can see through it. Trace your design onto the stencils, making a different stencil for each color. To copy from an original, size it by using a photocopier and either use it as a mask or trace it down, using carbon paper or tracing paper from an artists' supplier. To ensure that the colors all fit together in the finished design, you will need

To form a two-color border, begin by masking off a stripe on the wall and paint it a contrasting color.

Complete the stripe with a darker shade to create a sunset effect and remove the painter's tape.

Draw the stamp design on cardboard, cut it out, and use it as a template for cutting out of a cork tile.

Brush or roll the desired color of paint onto the stamp, making sure it is evenly coated.

Press the stamp onto the colored stripe to create the pattern, recoating with paint as necessary.

to use a registration system to place the stencils one on top of the other on the wall. Either cut an "x" through all the layers when they are correctly positioned, one on each side, or cut notches in the sides. If you are using transparent film, you have the option of lining up the stencils visually.

Stencils can be used to decorate entire walls; for example, a patterned tile effect for a bathroom as shown here. The finished area is sealed with an exterior quality varnish to waterproof it. Decide on your tile design and size, draw it onto acetate stencils, one for each color, and mark the tile size as a black outline. Draw the tile size in grid form on the wall using a waterproof marker. Stencil the design onto the tile grid, completing the wall in one color before starting the next. Use the method of your choice, but for a large wall a stenciling brush and quick-drying stencil paint is fastest. Redraw over the tile grid with a waterproof marker, using a matching color, to indicate lines of grouting. A border can be easily added using painter's tape to stencil straight horizontal lines.

In this sunny yellow room, stenciling has been used to good effect to enliven the plain colored walls and outline the doorway. It is ideal for decorative framing and for use as a border.

Trace your selected design onto the stencil material, making a separate stencil for each color.

If you want to create a tiled effect, set out a grid with a waterproof marker and straightedge.

Apply the first color, taping the stencil in place and adding the color with a stippling action.

When the first color has dried, add the second in the same way, aligning the stencil carefully.

Murals and one-wall effects

Often used to decorate children's rooms, murals can also be considered as a way of decorating main living areas, too. By using a grid system to scale up the design, even large expanses of wall can be treated with great success.

Creating a mural

You may find inspiration for the mural in a magazine or newspaper or want to use an old photograph as reference. To draw or paint your chosen design onto a wall you will need to "scale it up" first. Scaling up can be done by drawing a grid of squares over the picture you want to copy. Use a tracing-paper overlay if you don't want to mark the original. Now draw a similar grid of squares onto the wall at the increased size, and copy the design over square by square. You must be accurate when transferring the marks, paying attention to detail where lines leave and enter the squares. If this appears too complex, technology is at hand. Specialist stores that offer a photocopying service can produce an enlarged image over several sheets of 11¾ x 16½ in. (297 x 420 mm) paper that can be stuck together. A feeder tray loaded with heavyweight tracing paper will produce an image that you can see through, assisting the positioning. Photocopy specialists may have color machines

To scale up a design for a mural, first of all lay a sheet of tracing paper over the picture you want to copy.

Draw a grid of lines over the reference picture you have selected. Then draw the same number of squares on the wall to the desired size.

Copy the picture onto the wall square by square, paying attention to where lines leave and enter the squares. Finally, paint in the colors.

that can reproduce an overhead visual on film from your image or design. This is then enlarged onto the wall via an overhead projector, and traced. Any of these methods can help you build up a series of images into a wall mural.

Combination images

Projected images can be used in conjunction with other, simpler paint techniques. A garden mural, for instance, may incorporate trelliswork diagonally masked out by 1 in./25 mm tape. Stipple pale blue and white latex into a sky effect, combining your stencil and colorwashing skills, or create an illusion of depth by washing over backgrounds with a thinned-out white latex, so they disappear into the mist. Painting in stronger colors to the foreground base will emphasize this three-dimensional effect.

Collage and montage

More accurately a paper finish, images from posters can be stuck onto painted walls to create a unique mural. Try cutting out figure images of a favored sporting team and positioning them on a grass green wall in playing formation to liven up the décor of a hobby or work room. Tramlines marking out playing areas can be masked out with tape, or backgrounds of spectator enclosures stenciled in, all adding to the graphic effect.

This technique can be used to produce a wide range of interesting and decorative effects. Make sure that the edges of the images are firmly stuck down; then, when the glue has dried, paint over them with one or two coats of varnish in order to provide a hard-wearing finish.

Murals need not be confined to children's rooms; they can make very effective decorative effects in your home's main living areas too.

In this case, the floor-to-ceiling garden scheme has even been extended to the window shutters with great success.

Images of sports stars, cut from magazines or posters, can be used to liven up a sports field mural.

Add "mud patches" to your green football field after masking off tramlines with tape.

When the paint has dried, carefully remove the painter's tape to reveal the tramlines.

Paint in the figures of spectators to give the appearance of a football game in progress.

Geometric art with a roller

Optical art forms that rely on contrast between light and dark areas in a patterned format for their visual effect, or on the interaction of the colored areas themselves, frequently have a hard edge. A more subtle approach is described here, with a vignetted or damaged edge letting colors bleed together, with a broken, less confrontational result.

Painted lines, squares, and rectangular shapes don't necessarily require a hard edge to form a geometric pattern. However, hard-edge paint effects can be achieved by masking the wall with tape into squares or diamond shapes, then stenciling, brushing, or rollering conventionally. The finished wall design may be harsh. If this is the case, a softer, more subtle broken edge is needed. For this you will need a foam or sponge roller sleeve used for creating patterned finishes, often with textured paints—a pile roller, for example, will not do here. Roller sleeves are available in 7 in./ 18 cm and 9 in./23 cm widths. The larger sleeve will roll out a slightly larger width, so check your requirements before selecting.

To create an oval paint effect, try the following. Using a measure, locate and mark the center point of the sleeve, then tie a length of string around the center, pulling it tight and cutting it close to the knot. Tie two more lengths of string around the sleeve,

Right: The soft edges of the patterns painted onto this living-room wall avoid the harsh effect that generally results from clearly defined geometric patterns used in decoration.

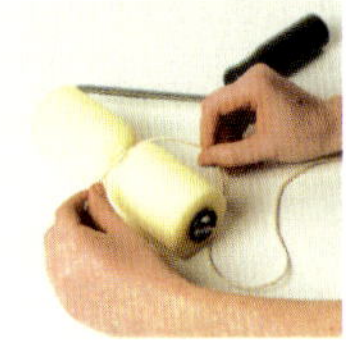

Find the center of the roller sleeve and tie a piece of string tightly around it at that point.

Tie more lengths of string around the sleeve at the center and ends to create two oval paint surfaces.

Roll a series of stripes onto the wall from floor to ceiling, touching in the edges with a brush.

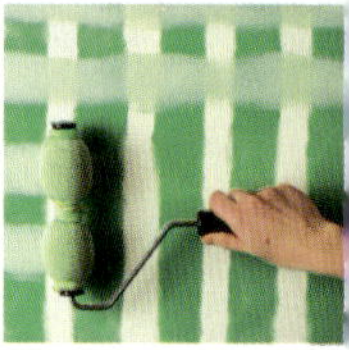

Apply another color to the roller and add a series of horizontal stripes to the wall.

diamond pattern can be applied o a wall with a small roller. The attern becomes more interesting if two colors are applied over a base color that is allowed to show through in places.

bout ½ in./12 mm each side of the center string, securing and rimming off as before. Tie some string around each end of the leeve, and your roller now has two oval paint surfaces to offer to he wall. Using a conventional short-pile roller for emulsion, roller he base or background color onto the wall and leave it to dry.

tripes

o create a stripe effect, run the roller onto the wall from the eiling to the floor, keeping it upright and parallel with the edge. he stripes go on two at a time, so try to match the gap between hem as you repeat the process. Don't overload the sleeve with aint; roll some off onto scrap paper, removing any excess. This vill also give you a preview of the effect. To finish off the stripe eatly where it meets the ceiling, cornicing, chair rail, baseboards r floor, use a fairly dry brush to touch the paint in. But be careful –too much paint on the brush will ruin the continuity by making he ends of the stripe stand out.

Hoops

Hoops can be designed using horizontal stripes. Make sure the roller uns parallel to the ceiling or baseboards, however, or the floor will appear to slope. By simply combining stripes and hoops you will create a pattern of squares, but the squares will be quite small, being the gap in the middle of the sleeve. If this design is for you, though, make sure the colors are applied in the right order. The small squares will be in the base or background color, and the dominant color will be the one with which you rollered the stripes and hoops.

Tiles and diamond patterns

Tiles and diamond patterns are created using smaller rollers, such as 4 in./10 cm long-handled radiator rollers with foam or sponge sleeves. Or you can use enamel paint mini-rollers. Roll out a sequence of 4 in./10 cm squares in level rows, lining up as accurately as you are able and leaving a tiny gap all around to represent the colored grout. Slight distortions and the inevitable irregularities are intended to resemble hand-glazed and individually fired tiles.

Rolling on alternate individual squares along the wall diagonal, that is at 45 degrees to the wall edge, creates a diamond pattern on a base color. It will help if you mark the diagonal first, so that the line of the first set of squares is correct. Use a taut piece of string held in position by painter's tape for this.

Because all these paint effects are rollered onto a new or existing wall base color, careful choice of the top coat can result in either a positive or negative pattern, since one of the colors will have a tendency to dominate the other.

One possibility in geometric art is to use a roller to create a series of colored squares like tiles. By leaving gaps for the base color to show through, you can simulate grouted joints.

PAPER FINISHES

The decorative styling and design features that are built into the modern dwelling differ in visual and practical ways from the basic amenities in the house that our grandparents lived in. A more time-conscious lifestyle, a greater reliance on electronics and labor-saving devices, the need for security, and an eye for fashion have all contributed to visual change in the home. One of the few things that has not altered, not even updated, is the use of wallpapers as the prime means of decoration. The versatility of the wallcovering, from cozy decorative feel to disguising poor surfaces, ensures its continued popularity.

Designer's notes

Selecting a suitable paper for a room surface, be it in a Victorian row house or a part-finished loft apartment, is an intimidating task. As multiples of choice do not usually simplify selection, it is a good idea to approach the pattern books with a clear concept; otherwise, you will face a bewildering array of shapes, colors, patterns, and styles.

The interior designer today is faced with more choice in wallcoverings than ever before. Hand-blocked, nineteenth-century designs can be bought, but most wallcoverings are descendants of machine paper runs begun in middle of that century. Factory production techniques, cost-effective paper runs, and new color dyes opened up the Victorian marketplace for wallpaper.

Just as paint-makers have introduced period colors to modern paint systems to allow for environmentally friendly historical colors, wallcovering manufacturers have reintroduced popular papers of the past. You can find simple Georgian hand-blocked designs and Regency stripes, as well as the familiar large patterns and floral designs of Victorian taste and the subtle, pale color combinations of the Edwardians.

The Victorian love of wallcoverings often ran to two different papers on a single wall, separated by a chair rail or paper border. Visually breaking up the wall height in this way can be very effective, provided the patterns do not compete for attention. A thin stripe and a bold, heavy stripe together, or a standard small-patterned paper on top of a heavily embossed one, can work well. Many embossed wallpapers are specifically made to be overpainted, and they are very hard-wearing on the bottom half of the wall. Consider, too, on a half-and-half wall, wood paneling or

Wallpapers offer a wide range of decorative effects, from exuberant floral patterns (left) to subdued stripes (below) and everything in between. Choose carefully to reflect the style of room you want.

Many wallpaper manufacturers offer ranges that duplicate Georgian, Regency, and Victorian patterns, letting you recreate the original look of rooms in a period property. Although more expensive than standard papers, they are worth considering.

paneling on the bottom half. It does a similar visual job while protecting the wall from knocks, and is a useful asset in entrance halls and corridors. If this combination appeals, try paneling the base of the wall with vertical tongue-and-groove (TGV) woodstrips finished with a horizontal shelf or chair rail. Then paper the top half in a subtle stripe that suggests a repetition of the joins in the TGV.

Visual tricks

Unlike wall areas of flat color, patterned wallcoverings use deliberate placement of designs and shapes to attract more, or less, attention. Visual illusion is caused by the arrangements on the surface area, not the area itself. Just as walls painted in different colors will advance or recede, papered surfaces use small patterns to create an illusion of space. Larger, more powerful designs can produce a highly dramatic impact. Place a sample of a delicate small repeat pattern next to a large colorful design, and you will see how this works.

When choosing paper, ask yourself the same questions about room sizes that you would if you were painting the walls. If your ceiling is low, heighten it with a vertical stripe. A hoop or horizontal stripe will appear to lower the ceiling and increase the width of the wall. A small patterned paper will increase the feeling of space in a small room. Using bold colorful motifs will make the wall area look smaller and nearer. Vigorous small designs that are good at hiding wall deficiencies are also easier to hang, because mistakes are disguised. A wall that is out of true unfortunately will be emphasized by symmetrical stripes. When hanging more than one paper in a room, consider which paper carries the overriding or dominant color, and use this color as a match or contrast for the woodwork paint scheme.

Wallpaper with vertical stripes can be used to create the illusion of greater wall height.

Choose a horizontally striped paper to make walls appear lower and wider.

Consider the design carefully: bold designs always work better on larger wall areas.

Papering the top half of the wall and adding wood paneling to the lower half can be very effective.

Use paper to create visual illusions: a large pattern will make a room seem smaller.

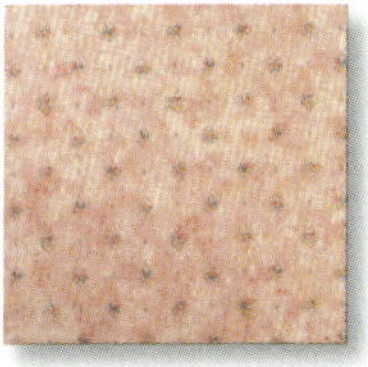

If you want the appearance of greater space, choose a small repeat pattern.

Basic skills: choosing wallcoverings

Be aware of the job you are asking your wallpaper to do, and consider your requirements. Perhaps its purpose is to be purely decorative, or it might have to disguise a badly cracked wall. It might get accidentally wet, in a bathroom area for instance, and so need to be water-resistant, or it may get dirty and you might have to be able to wipe it clean.

Certain paper types are intended for specific purposes. For example, heavy-duty wipe-clean vinyls are designed for use in kitchen areas, which are prone to steam and condensation. Your local decorating supplier or superstore will carry a range of all the popular paper types. But if you want something a little out of the ordinary there are specialist suppliers offering proprietary papers with period designs, hand-made papers, and hand-blocked or screened untrimmed rolls. If you are in search of a unique or unusual paper, start with the classified advertisements in the back of fashionable home interior magazines. If you are starting with pattern books, simplify the selection process by dividing the papers into two main categories: those that are made to be overpainted and those that are not. Wallcoverings intended for overpainting will usually, but not always, have a relief design, having either a textured finish like woodchip, or a raised surface pattern like molded or embossed papers.

Hand printing of wallpaper is an expensive process and is used for short runs only.

Wallcoverings that have a printed pattern that is not meant to be painted can be further divided, into washable (frequently ready-pasted) and nonwashable papers.

Liner paper

As the name suggests, this is used to line the wall, providing a sound, uniform surface prior to hanging top-quality decorative or heavy-duty embossed papers. It is useful for improving uneven walls and disguising recently repaired surfaces. It comes in various weights and can be easily painted.

Machine-printed paper

Multicolored and available in different weights and qualities, this is the most common wallcovering. "Pulps" are cheap papers where the printing inks sit on the paper surface. "Grounds" are more expensive machine papers where inks sit on a prepared surface, coated with a "ground" of color. These are both produced in bulk and are therefore more economical to buy.

Liner paper (left) provides a good surface for papering. Machine-printed papers (right) are the most common.

ɫand-printed paper

Vhether block-printed by hand or screen-printed through a frame, ɿis is more expensive because of the labor cost. Large-scale esigns and special colors can be incorporated on very short runs.

Voodchip paper

he cheapest of the relief papers, this has small wood shavings :hips) sealed between two layers of paper. The resultant rough extured finish works well on substandard surfaces, disguising racks and imperfections. It is sometimes called "oatmeal" paper.

ˈmbossed paper

Vith various registered tradenames, this has a relief pattern ressed into it when damp. A pattern is produced by pressure from n embossing roller. Color can be added simultaneously, or the aper produced with a white finish for overpainting. Damp mbossing, as opposed to dry, enables the relief to retain its shape etter when receiving paste.

′inyl paper

ılso available in heavy-duty, hard-wearing formats, vinyl paper consists of simple designs printed onto plastic or vinyl film with special inks, bonded onto a backing paper. It is tougher than washable paper, but more expensive. Some varieties need a heavy-duty wall adhesive. This paper can be difficult to remove, since the moisture of normal stripping won't penetrate the vinyl surface film. If you can lift a corner, it may be possible to peel off the top layer to leave the backing paper behind, which must be stripped in the normal manner. Otherwise, they must be scored to let moisture reach the backing—and this is a particularly laborious task.

Flock paper

Originally an expensive hand-made paper where a blocked adhesive print had wool or silk fibers dusted onto it, it is now available as a more economical machine paper. The elaborate design has a velvety, raised pile on a backing paper, and synthetic fibers are used to produce vinyl papers with a flock pattern effect.

Washable paper

Machine-printed designs with a film of protective, transparent plastic on top, this wallcovering is often found in convenient, ready-pasted form.

ɫand-block-printed papers are at he quality end of the market and ›ften recreate historic designs.

Woodchip sandwiches wood shavings between layers of paper to make a cheap relief paper.

Embossed papers have a raised pattern and are often supplied white for overpainting.

Flocked paper has a raised pattern formed from velvety fibers bonded to a backing paper.

Washable papers are protected by a thin plastic film and are often ready-pasted for easy hanging.

Vinyl wallcoverings provide a tough, hard-wearing surface, but need special adhesive.

Tools and equipment

Paperhanging equipment is not expensive or difficult to source, and many items serve other decorating purposes too. Only specialist brushes, a pair of paperhanger's scissors, single seam roller, plumb line, and paste table are unique to this job. The remaining multipurpose items will form a useful part of your household tool kit.

Drop cloth and goggles

If you are painting, access to ceilings or high wall areas can be simplified by the use of extension arms, or a simple stepladder. Paperhanging is a more difficult task. You need to be able to reach the top of the wall safely while carrying the pasted paper roll. For ceiling work you need a platform giving 8 in./20 cm head clearance that lets you hang an entire length without getting down.

A stable stepladder will suffice for the wall, but a sturdy platform is required for the ceiling. Use two scaffold planks tied together side by side across adjustable trestles, which you can hire. For stairwells, a combination of extension ladder, plank, and adjustable stair or multipurpose ladder will be needed. Cover the area with protective drop cloths, and use a retractable measure, spirit level and pencil to mark starting points and horizontals. You will also need a plumb line to line up your first roll, a bucket for paste, a stick to stir the paste, and some string stretched across the top of the bucket to wipe off excess paste from the brush. If your paper is ready-pasted, you will simply need a wallpaper trough filled with water.

Safety stepladder

Combination or adjustable ladder

Paste table

Adjustable height trestles and scaffold planks

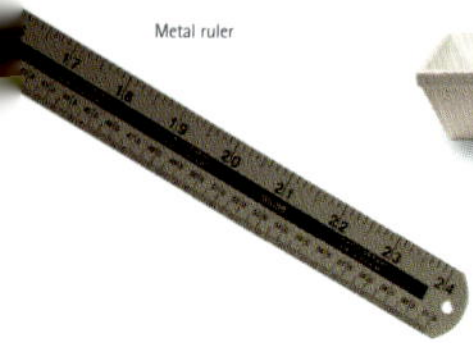

Metal ruler

Water trough for ready-pasted paper

Scraper, putty knife, dispenser, and joint compound

Bucket, sponge, and sugar soap

Long-handled fitch

You will also need:

- pasting brush
- folding paste table (which you could rent)
- paper-hanging brush
- paperhanger's scissors (12 in./30 cm)
- fitch (a small brush used to add extra paste to seams)
- seam roller (to stick seams after extra paste has been added)
- sponge (to remove excess paste)
- snap-blade knife
- gloves to protect your hands and the paper
- eye protection when mixing paste
- measuring pitcher to ensure paste is mixed correctly.

Measuring up

There are several ways to count up the number of rolls you will need to paper a room or wall, and one or two extra factors to consider. Use a roll of paper to measure all around the baseboard, and count up the number of full lengths, ignoring short lengths under windows and above doors. Now measure the room height, to see how many full lengths can be cut from each roll, allowing for pattern wastage. Now divide the first figure by the second, the number of full lengths by the number cut from each roll, to give you the total of rolls required. Part of a roll must be reckoned to be a complete roll. Or you can work out the surface area in square feet (square meters) (multiply height by depth) and calculate one standard roll per 16½ sq. ft. (5 sq m) or use the standard table for your wall height and length. The chart (see page 247) assumes the roll is 33 ft./10.05 m long and 20½ in./520 mm wide. Hand-made papers vary, so check the total surface area of the paper you are using, and adjust as necessary. The standard chart assumes an average door and window area per room. If you have large windows, reduce the quantity accordingly. Papers with a repeat pattern or design will produce more wastage as you line up, so add the pattern depth to the height of the room when calculating. Very large patterns will need an increase of one roll for every five.

Wallpaper stripper, misting handgun and all-purpose joint compound

When calculating the number of rolls for a ceiling, use the first method described above, measuring the length of the ceiling and working out how many of these lengths can be cut from a single roll. Using a roll of paper, count up how many lengths will be needed and calculate the total number of rolls. When the mathematics are completed, buy your rolls at the same time and from the same batch. A batch number is included for this purpose; slight color variations are possible between batch numbers. Your retailer can also supply the manufacturer's recommended adhesive, which may be heavy duty.

Protective gloves

Wallpaper scissors, plumb line, chalk line, snap-blade knife and seam roller

Above: Bucket and string, brush, mixing stick, sponge, and measuring pitcher

Stringed bucket, kettle and hook (for use when working on a ladder) and paperhanging brush

Spirit level

Preparation of surfaces

If your wall surface is not stripped plaster in good condition, you have a job or two to complete before papering. First, place drop cloths on the floor to collect debris and protect the carpet. You may need to strip off old paper, make good parts of the surface, wash down and key a painted surface, or simply seal and stabilise the plaster.

Previously papered finishes

Papered walls have to be taken back to the plaster. Leaving on old paper or vinyl backing leads to an unsatisfactory finish, because it may not bond well to the wall. Over-papering can cause it to lift away and form small air pockets. If the existing paper is vinyl or washable, it won't adhere. Stripping printed wallpapers is time-consuming and messy, but is not difficult. In older properties you may find yourself removing several layers of paper at once, and a great deal of patience is needed. The greatest danger is that when the last layer comes off, it pulls off old plaster with it, so try to avoid digging the scraper into the wall. Be very careful at this point; it may save you a lot of time spent filling and sanding later.

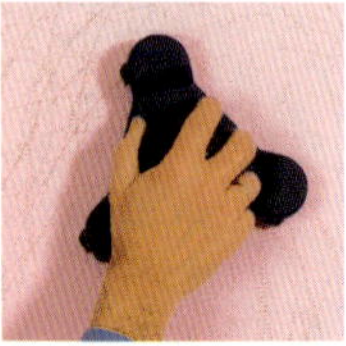

To aid penetration of the stripping solution, go over the papered surface with a scorer.

Working on small areas at a time, brush the paper with the solution and let it soak in.

Use a scraper to remove the soaked paper from the wall, taking care not to gouge the plaster.

A scorer has sharp wheels that cut through the surface of the paper, improving penetration of water.

Soaking or stripping with hot water

Hot water will penetrate and soak printed wallpapers, but to speed the job up, mix stripper, in powder or tablet form, with the correct amount of hot water in a bucket. To aid water penetration, run a spiker or scorer over the surface of the paper. Wearing eye protection and gloves, soak the wall, a little at a time or it will start to dry out before the scraper gets to it. Let the solution penetrate fully and then remove the paper gently with a broad-bladed scraper. On stubborn areas you will have to repeat the process. The scraper has a stiff blade, not to be confused with a flexible putty knife, so try not to scratch the wall surface. It's a good idea to clear up the mess as you work; otherwise, it dries out where it falls and sticks to the drop cloth and your shoes.

Dry-stripping vinyls

The two layers making up the paper can be separated fairly easily by carefully lifting the top layer at the corner, and pulling up and away from the wall to free it from the backing paper. It is inadvisable to leave the backing paper on the wall. It doesn't double as liner paper, so you should ideally strip it off the wall using hot water.

Scrapers

You can rent a steamer for major jobs.

Jsing a steamer

his speeds up the process. Steam enetrates the surface under the pad, lifting the paper away from he wall. You can hire a steamer fairly cheaply, but familiarize ourself with the machine before you start. Prime the reservoir vith hot, not cold, water, switch it on, and wait for it to boil. Wear rotective gloves, a long-sleeved shirt, and glasses or goggles. 'osition the steam pad on your starting point. Hold it for about alf a minute, then move along the wall to the next position while scraping off the steamed paper. The best results will be achieved by scraping with your writing hand and holding the steamer pad in your other hand.

steamer provides an effective means of stripping wallpaper quickly. With ractice, you can hold the pad to steam one area of the wall while scraping aper from a previously treated area. Remember that steam can scald you, o take care and wear protective clothing.

Wall furniture

Permanent wall furniture, such as a radiator, is best removed, if possible. Isolate the radiator from the water supply at the valves, drain the water into a shallow bowl, and lift it off the wall supports. If this is not possible, however, a long-handled radiator roller can be used to press the pasted paper into the problem area. Electric switches and outlets must be isolated from the supply before the faceplate screws are loosened, if this is necessary to strip away the paper behind. Curtain rails can be left in place, and valances need be removed only if they interfere with paperhanging around the window area.

Go over the wall looking for cracks and other damage. Mark them all so that you don't miss any.

Use the blade of a scraper to rake out all the loose debris and undercut cracks slightly.

Repairing walls

Once the wall is back to the plaster, you need to inspect the surface. Look out for cracks, holes, and deep scratches in the plaster surface as a result of the stripping, or because removal of the paper has revealed previous damage. All these imperfections will have to be made good. To avoid missing any when filling, mark them all clearly as you find them using a watercolor fiber-tip pen.

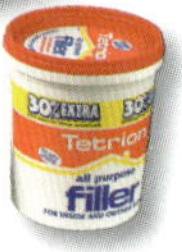

You will need a scraper, putty knives, a brush, joint compound and gloves.

To prepare the crack for filling, carefully rake it out with a scraper blade, so that no loose debris remains, and clean the damaged area with a dusting brush. Using a small paint brush, dampen the entire area with water so that your joint compound bonds with the wall plaster, and ensure that the wall does not draw too much water out of the compound too quickly, causing it to shrink and fall out. Mix up your compound, using a proprietary "decorators' pack." Following the makers' directions, try to achieve a smooth, but firm, consistency. Don't mix up too much at once; the makers claim a workable time of one hour, but this is less on a hot day. Fill the damaged area using a flexible putty knife, overlapping the edges slightly and leaving the joint compound raised proud of the surface. This allows for shrinkage when drying, and for sanding back. Make sure the compound is completely dry before you abrade the surface. Deep cracks will be dry on the surface long before they are dry all the way through. Sand back with the abrasive of your choice until the filled area is uniformly smooth and flush with the wall surface.

Decorators' packs and other general-purpose joint compounds are suitable for all peripheral wall damage. Deeper crevices can be filled if they are "layered." Apply a little at a time and allow each "layer" to dry. Don't attempt to save time and try to fill a deep crevice all in one go. The compound will be unable to bond properly and will slide out, forming a bulge.

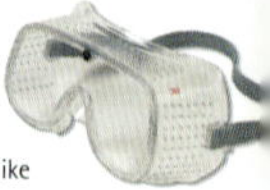

Safety goggles

Larger cracks and holes are best filled with plaster. You can buy small amounts, 11 lb./5 kg, of multifinish from your local builders' merchant. Don't assume plaster is like joint compound and apply it the same way. The mixing is the same, but that's all. Plaster is stronger and must be applied with a trowel, not a putty knife. Plaster surfaces are not meant to be sanded, either, so a flush, smooth finish must be your aim. Old wall surfaces will be very dry. If you apply plaster without a sealer, the wall will draw all the water out of the mix and the plaster will fall out. Splash a solution of one part PVA diluted with three parts water liberally in and around the damaged area, and leave it to dry, preferably overnight. Repeat this just prior to plastering. Not only have you sealed the wall, but the area is "keyed" and the plaster will bond better. Use a trowel to smooth the surface flush. If you are not confident that you can achieve this, leave the plaster just shy of the top surface, and complete the job with joint compound, which you can sand back when dry.

After raking out, use a brush to remove any remaining dust from the cracks.

Dampen the area with water to prevent the joint compound from drying too quickly and falling out.

'll the cracks, applying the joint ɔmpound with a flexible-bladed ɩtty knife. Press the compound well into the cracks and leave it slightly proud of the surrounding surface. Leave plenty of time for it to dry.

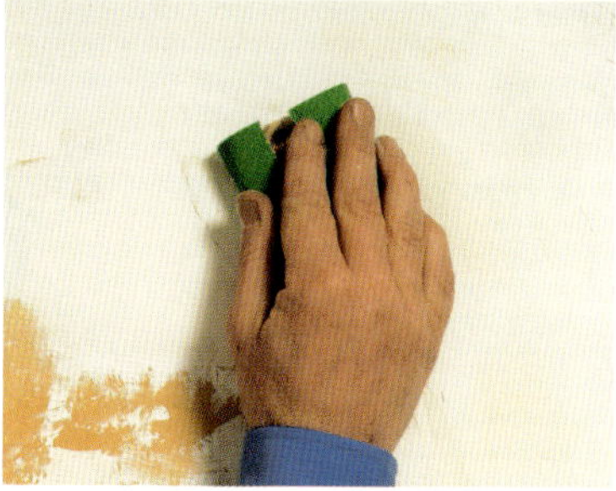

When the compound has dried, sand it flush with the surrounding surface using abrasive paper wrapped around a sanding block. You may need to add a little more compound here and there to finish the job.

ırge areas of damage are best paired with plaster, and you can ıy special packs for the purpose. First treat the area with a PVA solution to seal it and help provide a good bond with the new plaster.

Mix the plaster with water and trowel it into the hole. Use the trowel to strike it off flush with the surrounding surface, or leave it just below the surface and finish off with regular compound.

Cracks caused by movement around doors, or where baseboards eet the wall, particularly on the stairs, should be filled with a exible joint compound. This will allow for a certain amount of ɔntinual movement. Flexible compounds are available ready-ixed in tubes and are applied with a dispensing gun. Once dry, ɩey are easy to sand back.

Finally, as with all home decorating projects, it is important to consider the health and safety aspects. Remember that sanding filler will produce a lot of dust, so protect adjacent surfaces with drop cloths and wear old clothes. Wearing a dust mask and a pair of protective goggles is a good idea, too, in order to avoid irritating or damaging your eyes while you are working.

Washing, sealing, stabilizing, and sizing

The wall surface should be cleaned thoroughly, using a solution of sugar soap and hot water. Wearing gloves, sponge down the wall. Rinse it with clean water and let it dry overnight.

Old wall stains can eventually show through the wallpaper, so they need to be sealed with a coat of oil-based primer to stop them ruining your finish. If the stains are a result of an old (and cured) damp problem, oil-based primer or a damp sealant will prevent any further stains from appearing. However, if the patch is still damp to the touch, or you suspect that it is still active, you must investigate the cause of the trouble before proceeding. On no account attempt to seal over it, and don't ignore it. Consult a professional builder.

Stabilizing the surface results in an equal amount of suction on all parts of the wall, preventing problems caused by shrinkage due to patchy, uneven drying. Walls that are very dry, and therefore very porous, should have a thin coat of PVA adhesive diluted with water. Mix this up one part to five. When it has dried, run the palm of your hand over the surface. If white powder comes off onto your palm, the wall needs a second coat.

When the wall is ready, apply a size to the surface. A coating of size will let you manipulate the paper on the wall, enabling you to slide it carefully into position and line up the pattern. Without size the paper will stick to the wall immediately, and moving it on the surface will be difficult, often resulting in a tear. If you are working on a lined wall, size the liner paper just as you would a bare wall, before you wallpaper over it. A coat of thinned-down wallpaper paste can be used instead of size.

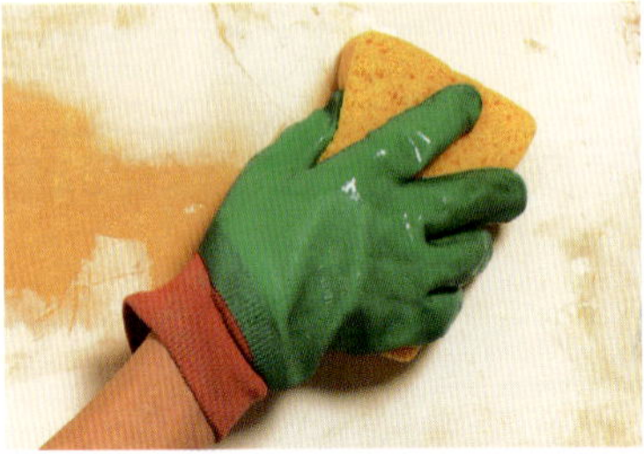

Wash the wall thoroughly using a solution of sugar soap and hot water. Rinse it well and let it dry completely.

Wall defects

While damp areas that are still active demand professional advice, areas of mold or fungus caused by moisture can be cleaned using fungicidal wash. Investigate the cause of the moisture before proceeding. It is most likely to be poor or nonexistent ventilation. mold containing live spores is present on the underside of the paper you are stripping, you must take precautions to stop the mold infecting the new finish. Wrap the old paper up and discard immediately, or preferably, burn it.

Treat the wall with a PVA solution to stabilize the surface and reduce the amount of suction, which could cause shrinkage problems.

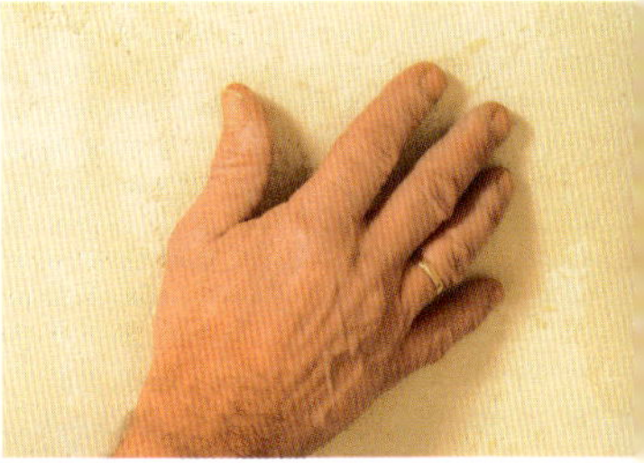

When dry, run the palm of your hand over the wall. If it becomes coated in white powder, a second stabilizing coat will be required.

Sizing the wall will make it easier to slide the paper into position. Mix the powder with water.

Brush the size onto the wall, making sure you cover it completely, and leave to dry.

Condensation produces damp patches on walls and encourages mold growth. Improved ventilation should provide a cure. Treat mold with fungicide.

Condensation encourages the growth of mold, particularly in older properties not built for today's central heating systems. Make sure you have adequate ventilation and air circulation. It is interesting that wall paints that "breathe," like distemper, are becoming popular again in older houses because they do not trap damp below the wall surface.

Fluffy white deposits on plastered walls are the result of soluble salts coming to the surface as the wall dries out. Called efflorescence, this surface problem can simply be brushed away, but it must be done with a dry brush. If you use water, the salt will dissolve, become reabsorbed into the wall and the problem will reappear later. If the wall suffers from flaking paint, either the finish cannot adhere to the surface because of under-preparation, or a damp area has been painted over. Once the cause of the damp has been determined, the wall area must be properly sealed.

Brown stains appearing on ceilings and walls are due to water penetration; they remain even when the cause of the problem has been solved. They may show through paintwork and light-colored papers, so cover with an oil-based paint to seal before papering.

Staining is caused by damp penetration and the cause must be found and cured before proceeding. Treat stains with an oil-based paint to prevent bleed-through.

Flaking paint occurs because it has been applied over a dusty, damp, or incompatible surface. It should be scraped off and the surface sealed before proceeding.

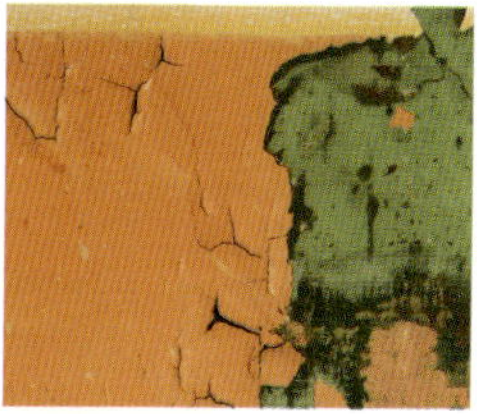

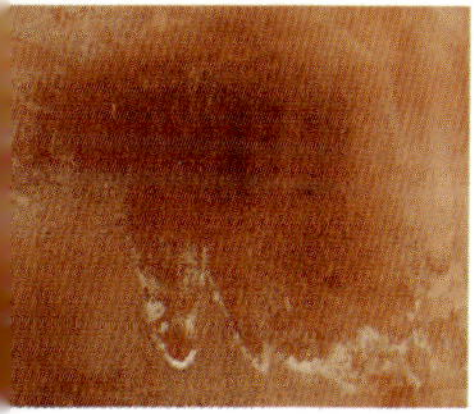

Efflorescence is caused by salts within the brickwork being carried to the surface as the wall dries. Dry brushing should remove it. Don't try to wash it off.

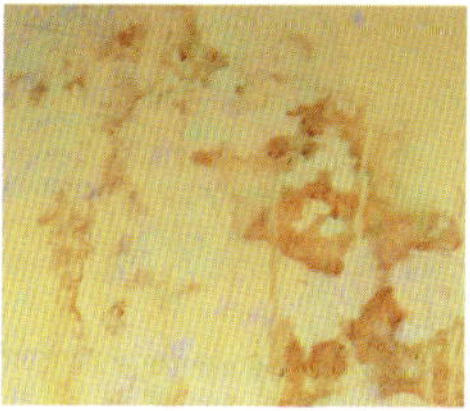

Damp patches that remain active must be investigated and dealt with promptly. Seek professional advice; don't try to cover up the problem, as this may make it worse.

Lining the walls

If the surface is still not ideal for hanging the patterned wallcovering directly onto it, you need to line the wall. Use a plain paper roll, about 1⅜ in./35 mm wider than the standard patterned roll. It is hung in the same way as the final paper.

Liner paper is available in several weights, either as an uncoated pulp or with a smooth finish. It helps to disguise wall imperfections, and some particularly rough areas can be lined twice. If you do this, make sure the seams are not in the same place, or hang the first paper vertically and the second horizontally. It is better to butt-join lengths at a room corner, rather than take a narrow strip the height of the room around the corner. If the walls are not square, there will be a slight, uneven gap where the vertical lengths don't quite meet. You can disguise this by smoothing a length of flexible joint compound into the corner.

You will need to take a narrow strip around a chimney breast. The breast face should be lined in the opposite way to the walls; if the room is lined vertically, then line the breast face horizontally. The walls may not be square, so line horizontally first and wrap the paper around the corner each time. The next vertical length sits on top of these overlaps, and you need to cut the paper from ceiling to floor 1½ in./36 mm from the edge, parallel with the corner line. Use a snap-blade knife and a steel ruler for this. Remove the overlaps after peeling back along the length, so that you do not have a double weight of paper, and smooth the vertical length back into position with the paperhanger's brush, to achieve a butt join.

Cross-lining—hanging liner paper horizontally and wallpaper vertically—is not mandatory. If lining a wall horizontally, start at the top; the widths won't divide into the wall height exactly and pasting on specially cut widths is easier at the bottom of the wall.

Lining a wall

Adding a liner paper to a wall before papering it is a good way of improving the surface and is essential when hanging high-quality papers. In some cases, it may be necessary to hang two layers of liner paper to disguise surface imperfections.

Hang liner paper horizontally so that the seams don't coincide with those of the wallpaper.

When doubling up layers, fold back the edges and tear them off later to prevent ridges.

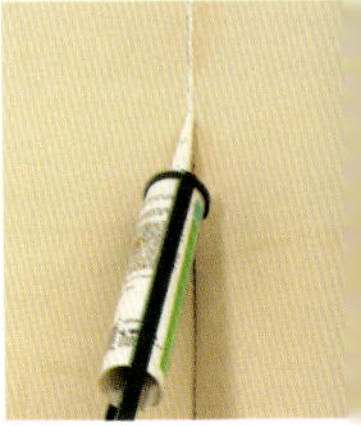

Butt-join lengths of paper at internal corners. If they don't quite meet, add joint compound.

Lining a chimney breast

Chimney breasts need treating slightly differently to the rest of the room because of the narrow reveals on each side. Horizontal lengths of paper should be hung on the face of the breast and wrapped around over the reveals and onto the adjacent walls.

Cut paper long enough to span the breast, cover the reveals, and lap onto the adjacent walls.

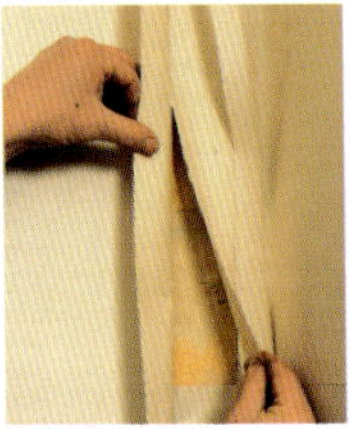

Overlap the next vertical length and cut down through both layers of paper, removing the waste.

Brush the edges of the paper down and they will meet in a perfectly butted seam.

Use a steel tape and waterproof pen to mark the paste table in 1 ft./30 cm increments. This will speed measuring the paper.

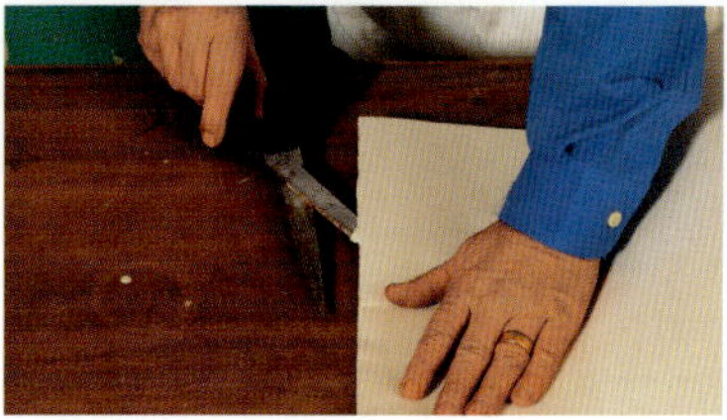

Allow for a slight overlap of paper on each length, fold the paper and use a blade of a pair of scissors to slice along the fold.

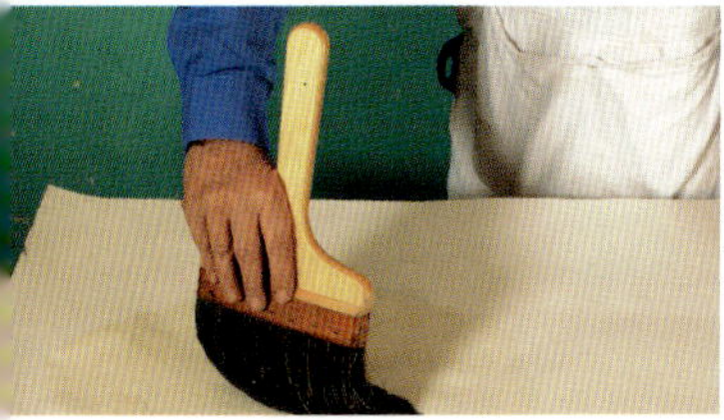

Lay the paper on the table and paste it, working out from the center. Overlap the edges of the table slightly to keep the table free of paste.

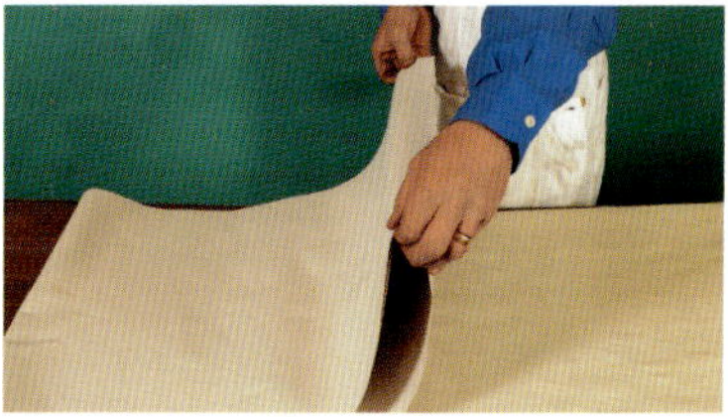

As you paste, gently fold the paper back on itself in concertina fashion to make the length manageable for hanging.

Using the paste table

- Set up your paste table in the center of the room.
- Paper lengths will be longer than the table, so make sure you have enough space at the ends. Working in a confined space is more difficult.
- Keep your buckets of paste and water under the table where they can't be accidentally kicked over.
- The paste table will double as a measure if you mark it out along the edge. Use a waterproof pen so that you don't wash the measurements off. Mark in increments of 1 ft./30 cm, depending on your preference.
- Keep the paper square on the table. This reduces the risk of inaccurate cutting when using the edge measure.
- Cut the liner paper, leaving a small overlap at each end for final trimming on the wall.
- Apply the paste evenly, starting at the center of the paper and working outward.
- Keep the table clean at all times. Washing down with a warm wet sponge and drying with a clean cloth, after pasting each length minimizes the risk of paste getting on the wrong side of the paper.

Papering walls

The key to successful paperhanging involves preparation, so that the bare surface provides uniform suction and manipulation (the final positioning of the paper on the wall) is easier. Never skimp on the preparation, because ultimately it will affect the final result, and although you have an expensive wallpaper, you may not have an expensive-looking finish.

Checking color

Printed wallpapers carry a surface pattern printed by machine, and variations in color can occur, even if the batch numbers are the same. Checking for color at the start is crucial; otherwise, the first time you will notice a color variation between lengths is when the wallpaper dries out in position, and then it will be too late. You cannot do this as the hanging progresses because when the paper is wet with paste, the color will be slightly different. Open and unroll the first length of each roll on the table. Set them out so that about a quarter of the length is visible, one behind the other: any color discrepancies will be obvious. Should you have any cause for complaint, return the rolls to the store.

When working with a repeat pattern, cut one piece to length and match others to it.

Line up the lengths of paper on the table and check that the pattern will match.

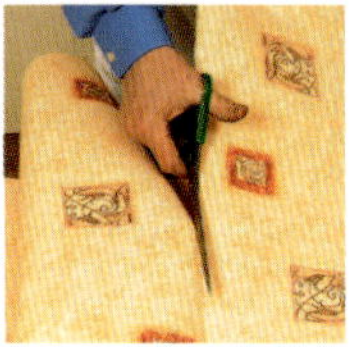

Cut each length with the scissors, allowing the repeat pattern height at top and bottom.

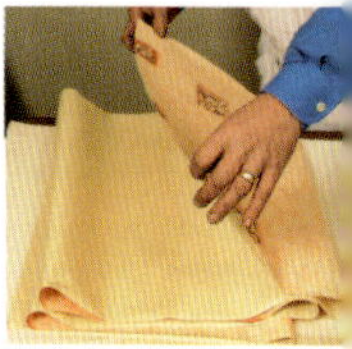

Pasted paper should be folded concertina fashion, pasted face to pasted face.

Cutting

Using the measuring guide you marked on the table when lining, cut the lengths required. If the paper is cut too short, it is useless; if it is too long, it is wasteful. Add on a small amount top and bottom for trimming in position. Cutting a repeat pattern to length is more difficult, because you have to match up the patterned design. The easiest way is first to cut a wall length with the repeat pattern height added on at the top and bottom. This lets you position the pattern and trim it to fit. Before any pasting takes place, cut several lengths at the same time, lining them up on the table and matching each to the previous length before cutting.

Mark your cutting lines in pencil on the face of the paper, using a long straightedge as a guide. As you cut each length, make a pencil mark on the top so that when hanging you don't inadvertently hang a drop upside-down.

Pasting and folding

Paste should be mixed according to the maker's directions, but do ensure it is not too thin; otherwise, sliding the paper on the wall during precise positioning becomes very difficult. Line up the paper's edge with the paste-table edge, and apply paste by brushing from the middle to the edges, which reduces the ibility of paste contaminating the face of the paper. If paste ; accidentally meet the patterned face, wipe it off immediately a damp cloth or sponge.

s you finish pasting an end, fold it over on itself as if you were ting a concertina, and carry on pasting the rest of the length. the remainder to complete the concertina. Set the paper aside t it absorb the paste before attempting to hang it. The ufacturer's data sheet will tell you how long the soaking time r your paper; usually this is ten to fifteen minutes. It's a good to write down the length number and the hanging time, and e this next to the concertina, ensuring it goes onto the wall at right time and in the right order.

nging the paper

most important length is the first one you hang. It must be nb vertical and in the correct place in the room. If the room a chimney breast, any repeat patterned paper must be centered t, so you need to hang your first length here. If pattern ering is not a requirement, start by dropping a plumb line to one side of the main window and work away from the major source of light. Starting with the first length centered on the chimney breast requires accurate measuring to each side. Subtract the width of the paper from the width of the breast, and halve the figure. Measure in this amount from either edge, and mark by drawing along a vertical spirit level. Line up the first piece using this guide, and paper the entire breast first.

To start at the window, drop a plumb line from ceiling to floor. If the frame is plumb vertical, start at the frame. If it is not, drop a line just less than the width of the paper away from the frame, mark the line at several points with a pen, and join up the marks using a straight edge. You will need to paper three sides into the last corner, return to your starting point and paper in the other direction to finally join in the window corner. This corner will best disguise a nonmatching join, as the wall contains the major source of light.

Having decided on your starting position, check to see whether the pattern is designed to be hung in a specific direction. This may or may not be obvious. Some designs appear to be truly abstract, but an initial impression can sometimes be wrong. When such patterns are hung as a complete wall, you may discover there is a definite top, and bottom, to the image. Time taken getting the first length plumb vertical, the pattern centered satisfactorily over the wall depth and trimmed equally at both ends, will be well spent because the following lengths can be positioned more easily.

When hanging the paper, begin at the top of the wall, brushing it into place with the paperhanger's brush and gradually unfolding the concertina as you go. Make sure that the first drop is aligned perfectly with the guideline, as this will affect the position of all subsequent drops.

a plumb line to establish rfectly vertical guideline for jing the first length of paper.

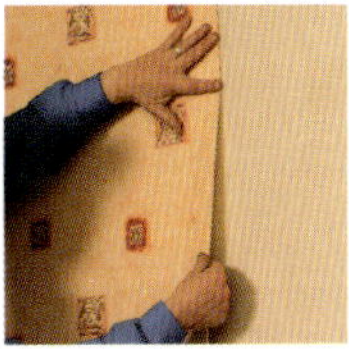

Carefully align the edge of the first length with the guideline. This is essential for a good job.

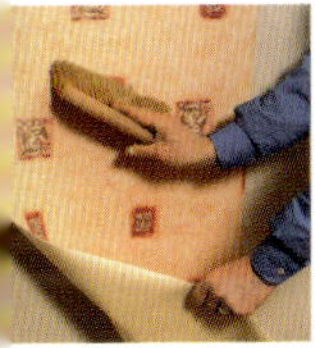

k down the wall, unfolding the ertina of paper and brushing it to remove air bubbles.

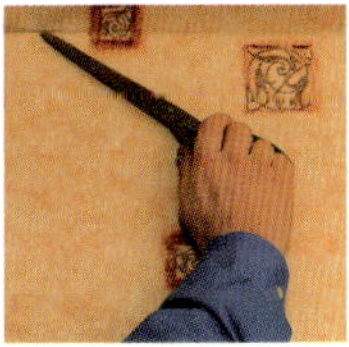

At the ceiling, crease the paper into the angle with the scissors, then cut along the crease.

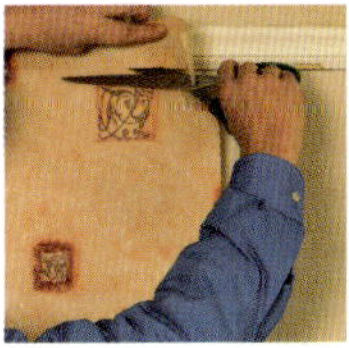

Make release cuts in the paper so that it can be fitted around, for example, crown moldings.

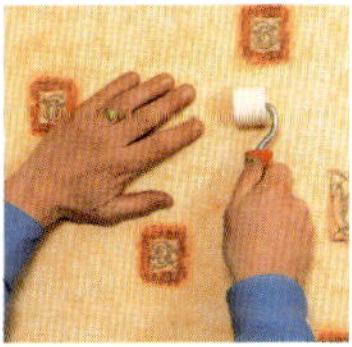

Use a seam roller to flatten any seams that have lifted, adding more paste if necessary.

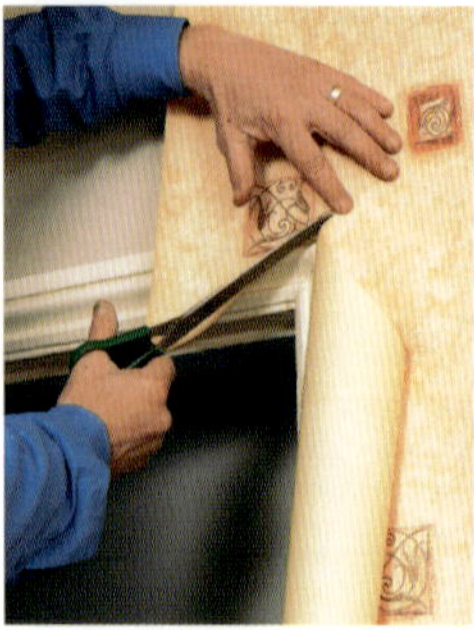

At the corner of a door frame, make a diagonal release cut and paste the paper onto the wall around the frame.

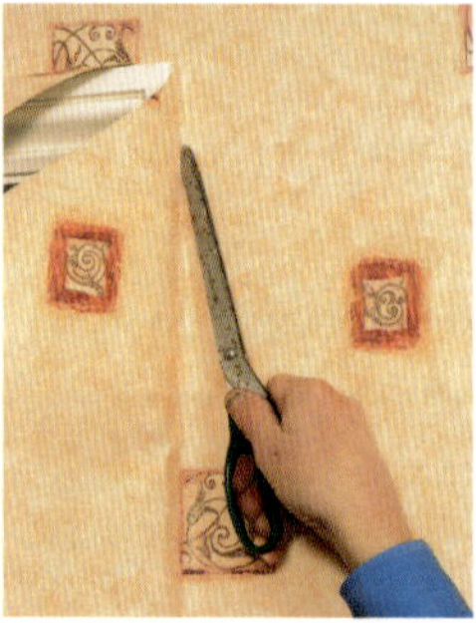

Crease the paper with the scissors, pull it away slightly, and trim along the crease to fit. Finally, brush it into place.

Wall obstacles

Hanging lengths against a straight wall is simple, so long as your first length provides a good template. Papering around obstacles such as window or door frames involves cutting a diagonal into the corner where the molding meets the wall. Now crease a cutting line along the frame edges with the scissor points. Be sure to take the weight of the excess paper when you do this or it will tear. Pull the paper away from the frame edge, and cut carefully along your crease line. Paperhanger's scissors are the best tool for this, but if you use a snap-blade knife, make sure the blade is sharp. You must keep it clean because paste drying on the blade will blunt it, and consequently tear the paper. The snap-blade knife is very useful for the intricate detail to either side of the mantelpiece, however. Drop the paper from the ceiling, and let it drape over th front of the fireplace. Using the paperhanger's brush, crease the paper int the right-angled join along the mantelpi and trim to each corner. You will need tc support the weight of the paper again, a smooth the side papers into position, making a series of cuts into the side molding details. Crease a cutting line around the moldings and the sides, and the sides with scissors. You may find the sharp knife is better for cutting around t edges of the detailed moldings.

Electrical fittings

To paper over a square surface fitting, indent the paper with a finger to mark t edges. Cut a hole in the center, cut diagonally toward all four corners, and bend back the paper to expose the fitting. Trim the paper sufficiently so that it will fit neatly under the faceplate, a isolate the fitting from the supply. Loosen the two screws and push the paper underneath. Alternatively, you can trim the pape to fit flush with the edges of the fitting. This will be your prefe method if the faceplate is not flush. Wipe any excess paste off electrical fitting with a dry cloth.

Pasting the wall

Some papers are made to be hung dry, directly from the roll, on a pasted wall surface. Mix up your paste, following the directio

At a mantelpiece, crease the paper into the angle with the wall and cut it to size.

At the sides, make a release cut in the corner and brush the paper onto the wall.

Use the scissors to make a series of release cuts around the detail of the fireplace surround.

Brush the paper into place, removing the slivers of paper with a sharp knife.

ɪn you encounter a light switch, drape the ɛr over the top and make diagonal release out from the center.

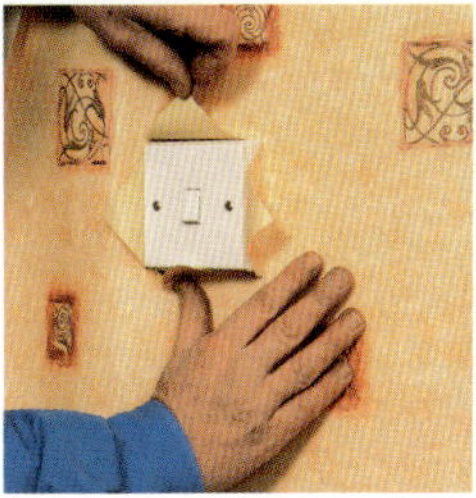

Fold back the paper flaps and brush the paper flat onto the wall around the switch. Turn off the power supply and remove the faceplate.

Slacken the mounting-box screws and pull the box away from the wall. Trim the flaps and brush them under the box. Replace the switch.

use a pasting brush to coat the wall. Paste an area slightly er than the roll width, and smooth it out evenly. Hang the er from the roll or, if you prefer, cut it to length and match the tern in the usual way first. A fitch is useful to re-paste seams if hang by this method.

ːpasted papers

yl or wipeable papers normally come pre- or ready-pasted. re is a dried coating of paste already on the back of the paper. manufacturer's recommended soaking time is given with roll. A water trough, usually supplied with the rolls, is used to k the paper, paste side out, which is then positioned on the l. Many patterns can be hung directly from the trough if it is ːed at the baseboard below the intended position, and moved ınd the room as hanging progresses. You still need the paste e, though, and when you are cutting and matching large gns, you may prefer to place the water trough at the side of table. This lets you check the pliability of the soaked length ɔre hanging by folding inward in conventional concertina style ːhe table. If you are satisfied that the paper is ready, carry it to wall as normal.

t is quite acceptable to apply your own paste to ready-pasted ers, treating them as conventional machine-printed papers. ıy decorators are of the opinion that self-pasting gives ːer control of the paper, especially during manipulation .he wall, and the data sheet supplied with the roll may ıowledge this.

Ready-pasted papers must be soaked in water. You can either place the trough at the foot of the wall and hang directly from it, or pull the paper onto the table and fold it in the usual way.

Papering a ceiling

Don't avoid this job just because it looks difficult; in many ways a ceiling presents fewer problems than a wall does, because there are no radiators, electrical outlets, or frames; a ceiling rose will probably be the only complication. Remember that a good working platform is essential and, if it's your first time, make sure you have a helper.

Do not feel intimidated by this task. The pasting, folding, and carrying technique used to position and brush paper onto a ceiling is the same as that used when covering a wall. In fact, a ceiling will have fewer obstacles to paper around. There are no doors, radiators, windows, or switches to make life difficult, merely a central light fitting, and not even that if you just have wall lights. The only difficulty is that working over your head, your arms get tired, particularly if they are supporting a long length of heavy pasted paper, so a second pair of hands is very useful. Of prime importance is a safe means of access that lets you reach the ceiling without having to stretch and to hang each length without continually having to move ladders.

Decide which direction you are going to paper in. You may think it's easier to paper the shorter ceiling width, but if there are two of you, it will be quicker to start with the longer lengths. Professional decorators will paper parallel to the window wall, or if there is more than one window, parallel to the bigger light source. This means that they will start at the window wall and paper away from the light.

Starting the job

Set up your working height platform underneath the proposed f length. Under no circumstances try to over-reach on a stepladd The best arrangement is two scaffold boards tied into position across two adjustable trestles, with a step-up stool at each end This arrangement gives access to the complete paper length as unfolded along the ceiling, and is stable and safe to use. The cornice or angle on the window wall will not give an accurate l for your first length, so measure out from each end of the wall 20 in./50 cm, and join these two points with a chalk line. This w give you your starting line, with a small overlap onto the windo wall for trimming off. Position the pasted concertina at the starting point, allowing for a small wall overlap, tightly against marked line so that each loop opens out as the length is pasted across the ceiling. Make sure each loop is brushed firmly into th correct place before releasing the next. A second pair of hands hold the pasted concertina simplifies matters considerably. If yo are working alone, support the folds on an unopened roll of pap Crease and trim the length and width to the cornice or wall ang

Papering a ceiling is not as difficult as it may seem, especially if you have someone to help you. Some form of access platform is essential, but otherwise the techniques are much the same as for standard wallpapering, and you will encounter fewer obstacles.

Use a chalked stringline to snap a guideline onto the ceiling for hanging the first length.

Have your assistant hold the concertina of paper while you align its edge with the guideline.

Work across the ceiling, one of opening out the paper while the other brushes it into place.

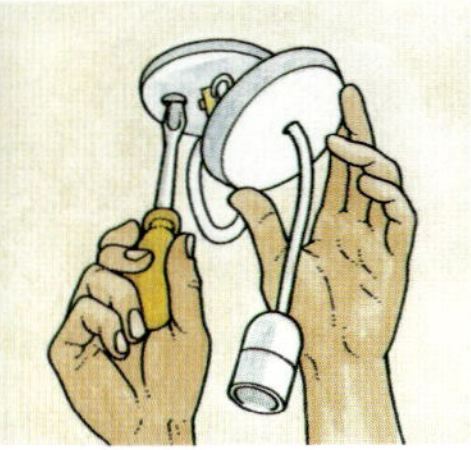

Before you begin papering, switch off the power, remove the light fitting cover and release the baseplate from the ceiling.

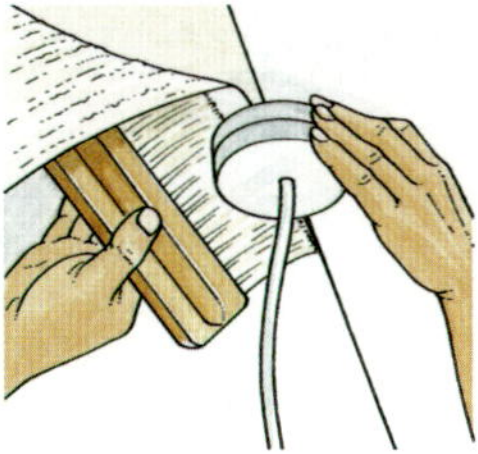

Let the light fitting hang on its cord and brush the paper onto the ceiling behind it. Then replace the light fitting.

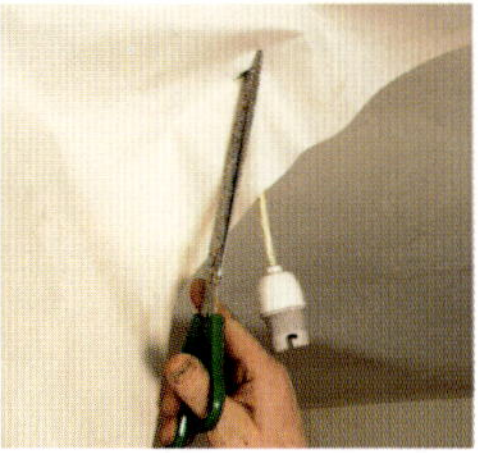

If you can't avoid the fitting being in the middle of a length of paper, work up to it and make a small cut in the paper at the center of the fitting.

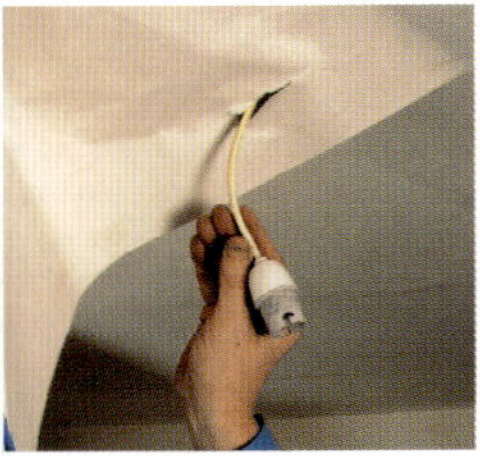

Pull the cord and bulb holder through the hole, taking care not to tear the damp paper. Brush the remainder of the length into place.

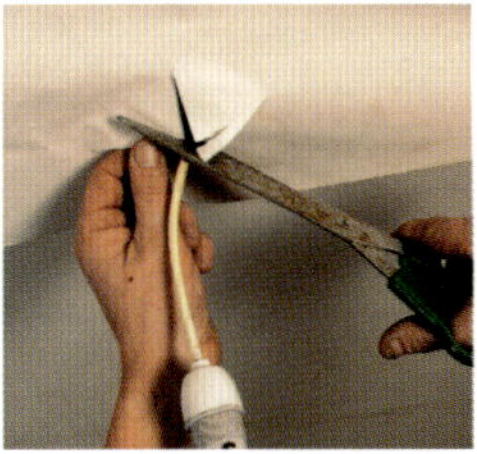

Make a series of release cuts out from the hole to the edge of the fitting. Brush the paper tightly into the angle.

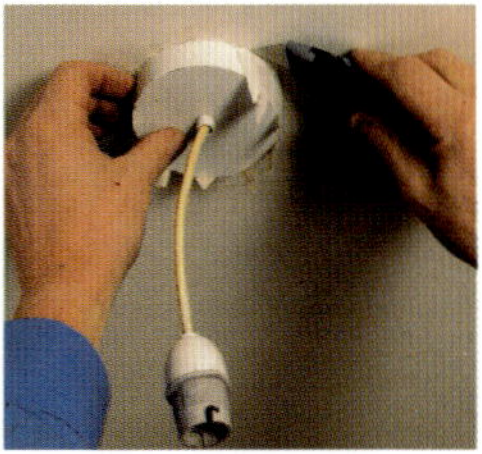

Finally, use a sharp knife to trim off the slivers of paper to leave a neat finish. Clean any paste off the fitting with a dry cloth.

This first length will be a difficult, time-consuming job, but having completed it, a marker will have been established on the ceiling, and the remaining lengths will be easier.

The ceiling light fitting

By measuring out from the window wall to the center of the fitting, it is possible to arrange the paper lengths so that a seam join runs through the middle. A larger overlap on the window wall may result, but it will simplify things in the center of the room. Either make small cuts in the edge of the paper, starting from the center of the fitting, so a cutting line can be marked with the point of the scissors and then trimmed off, or, if possible, remove the fitting. Switch off the power if you do this, unscrew the cover, and remove the retaining screws. The fitting can be left to hang from the wire for a minute or two while the papers are smoothed into position and the screw holes marked with a point. Replace the screws in their original positions and put back the cover. Should you reach the fitting with the middle of a length, mark the position on the paper where the wire will drop, and cut a small hole, supporting the paper as you do it. Pull the wire through and brush the remainder of the length into position. Now make a series of outward scissor cuts starting at the center of the fitting, so a cutting line can be marked at its circumference. Exchange your scissors for a snap-blade knife and trim. Wipe off any surplus paste with a clean, dry cloth. Never use a wet cloth on an electrical fitting for safety reasons.

Papering problem areas

Whether your problem area is a simple light switch or electrical outlet, or an intimidating stairwell where the drop is the height of the house, there is a technique to help you. Even difficult jobs are simplified if you approach them in the right way. However, safety must always be paramount when using platforms, so make sure they are quite safe.

Stairwells and landing areas

The biggest problem areas in your house will be the stairwell and landing, particularly in older properties where the stairwell drop is the entire depth of the house. There are no more difficulties in papering technique here than you have already encountered elsewhere, apart from the length of drop. Here a second pair of hands is needed to support the pasted concertina, or it will tear under its own weight as you hang it from the top. The real problem is one of access to the walls at a convenient working height. However, small, interlocking scaffold towers that will fit a stairwell are available for hire. As an alternative you can combine ladder, stepladder, combination (multipurpose) steps, and trestles with scaffold planks in an ingenious arrangement to let you complete the job successfully and safely. Set up your platform, using any variation of the examples shown here, with safety uppermost in your mind. Remove all stair carpets and underlays, and clear the area of all obstacles. If the ladder feet rest on a stair tread, nail or screw a batten support in place to prevent the feet from moving, and tie a soft cloth around both head ends where they contact the wall, to prevent marks. Double up scaffold boards to minimize sagging, and tie them to each other and to the supporting ladders or steps.

Survey the task ahead. Identify the edge of the longest length you have to hang and drop a vertical plumb line from the ceiling to

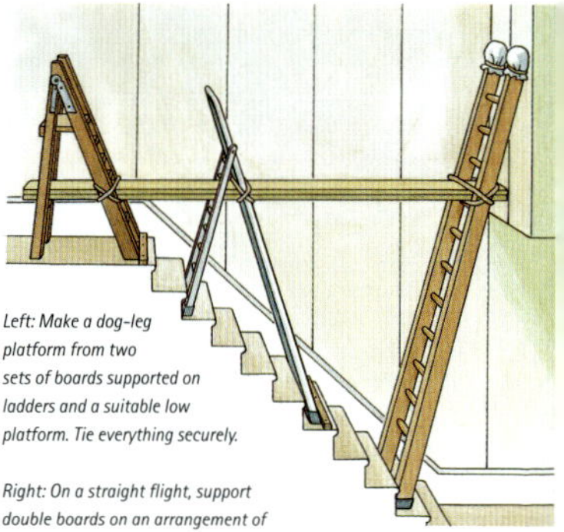

Left: Make a dog-leg platform from two sets of boards supported on ladders and a suitable low platform. Tie everything securely.

Right: On a straight flight, support double boards on an arrangement of ladders and stepladders.

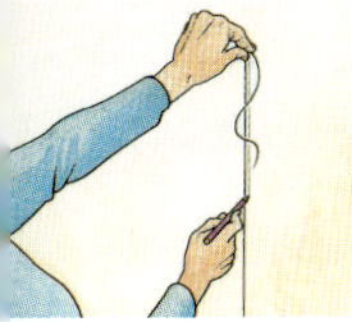

Begin by marking a vertical guideline on the wall with the aid of a plumbline.

Remember to allow for the fact that each drop will have a long edge and a short edge.

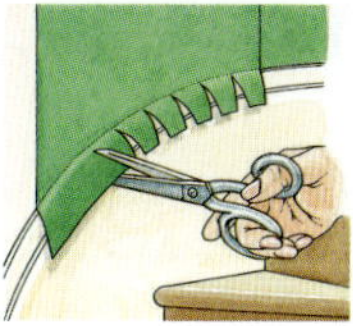

Make small triangular cuts in the paper to fit it neatly against a curved skirting.

Make a vertical cut beneath a banister, shape the paper around the rail and paste to the wall.

:he baseboard. Make a mark with a pen and a straightedge to establish your guide for the first length. It is crucial that this ength is correctly positioned and plumb vertical, because it will be a template for what follows. When you calculate a drop onto stairs, remember that the paper has two edges of different lengths; you must measure the longer edge, or the paper will come up short. For this reason it is better to paper up the stairs, not down, as a mistake in calculation can be re-sized farther up the wall. It can even be the next length if you are not matching a pattern and the stair baseboard rises consistently.

One or two difficulties, usually unique to the stairwell, will have to be overcome. For example, the baseboard and the strings are likely to be shaped, and the banister rail on top of the balustrade may be joined to the wall on the landing. If your baseboard curves around at the top of the stairs, then the paper must curve as well. Make a series of triangular cuts butting up to the baseboard, and smooth the paper around the corner. If the banister does not butt to the wall at the edge of a paper length, cut from the bottom of the length parallel with the side so that the two strips can fit each side. Make a series of small cuts from your initial slit outward, then shape the two pieces around the banister with the paperhanger's brush and trim carefully with the scissors.

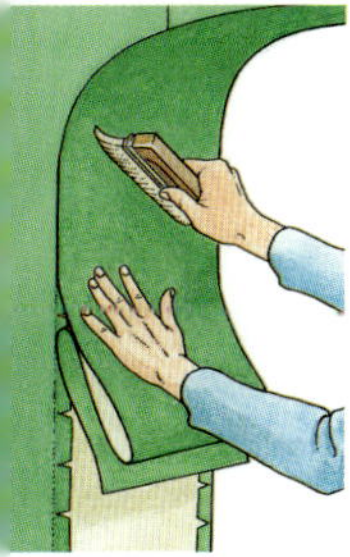

Take a small margin of paper from the face wall onto the arch, then paper the arch itself.

When papering an arch, cut two strips of paper that will meet in the middle; otherwise, the pattern will be upside-down on one side. Strong patterns will make the seam more obvious.

Arches

It is not really possible to match a pattern into an arch. Papering the inside of the arch is done in two sections, one from each end with a straight butt join at the arch center. The best approach is to take the patterned paper from the face wall around the corner into the arch, trimming to leave about 1 in./25 mm overlap. A sequence of small triangular cuts in the paper edge will let you wrap around the curve. Paper the inside of the curve with a one-piece heavyweight liner paper. Cut it flush to the facing wall. Paint the liner paper in a matching or opposite color.

Special effects

Use a matching or contrasting (by color or pattern design) border strip, as a decorative dividing line between different papers, as a paper chair rail on a half-and-half wall, as an outline to emphasise a window recess, or as a simple mitered frame around a serving hatch to add an attractive and stylish feature to your home.

Patterned borders can enliven newly papered walls.

Patterned borders

Borders can dramatically change the look of your newly refurbished room. Small patterned wallpapers with an overall base color can have the effect of that color emphasised or muted by a border. Small rooms that need plain, pale walls to make them appear larger can still have a decorative effect in miniature. Apart from the obvious color and decorative qualities, placing a border or frieze at the ceiling/wall junction will appear to lower the ceiling, and bordering a window will make it look larger.

To save expensive mistakes, try positioning the border with painter's tape first, so that you can study the effect. When you have determined your border position and height, use a spirit level and pencil (not a pen because it may show through the design) to draw a line around the room. Take care to maintain a dead level; nothing looks worse than a sloping border. If the ceiling or baseboard has a pronounced slope, don't add a border anywhere nearby, as this will emphasize the slope even more.

Wallpaper manufacturers produce some border designs to complement a range of their own papers, and you can select both at the same time by looking through the pattern book. There are several widths available, and two application methods. One involves using backing paste like conventional wallpaper, and the other is self-adhesive. You simply peel off the backing paper to press down the self-adhesive type. But take note; it is not designed to be repositioned should you place it incorrectly. Printed borders applied using wallpaper paste can be manipulated on the wall just as wallpapers can, but beware of paste getting onto a nonwipeable paper because it can stain the face. You can always wipe clean water-resistant coverings with ease, but you require a special adhesive, available from your decorating store, to stick the border onto vinyl or wipeable finishes. In all instances, if you use a seam or small roller to flatten the border onto the surface, protect both border and existing paper with a tear sheet of liner paper, and roll on top of that.

Mitered corners

These are simple, provided your border angles are square. Even if the window you are outlining is slightly out of true, measure and

Mark the position of the border, using a tape measure and pencil. Make light marks only.

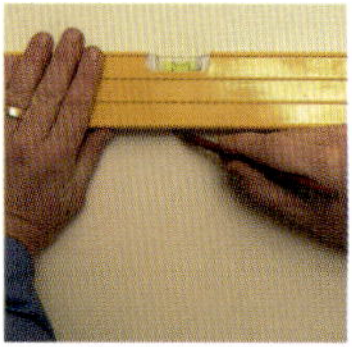

Using a spirit level, mark out a continuous horizontal or vertical guideline for the border.

Apply paste to the border, folding it concertina fashion in the same manner as normal wallpaper.

Brush the border onto the papered surface, aligning it carefully with the pencil guideline.

draw a positioning line in pencil that has 90-degree corners; do not follow the window shape. Paste up the top horizontal border strip first, followed by either vertical, adding on 2 in./5 cm or so at each end. Overlap the lengths at 90 degrees, then draw a guide line from corner to corner, using the 45-degree angle of a set square. Cut through both strips together with a sharp snap-blade knife, and carefully peel away and discard the waste pieces.

Matching a bold, obvious pattern at each angled join will not be possible, so you could consider smaller, intricate, or more abstract designs that will serve to camouflage rather than to emphasize any discrepancies.

Paste on the horizontal and vertical borders so that they overlap at a right angle.

Using a steel rule and sharp knife, make a diagonal cut down through both border strips.

Pull back the ends and remove the off-cuts. Finally, brush the ends back for a neat mitered seam.

Paper dividers

Some of these do the same job as a chair rail and can be used for a purely decorative effect, acting as a border to separate two different designs or styles of paper, or they can have an important function. Running a paper divider up the stairwell at the same height as the banister rail lets you replace the bottom section of paper (and the border), while leaving the top part intact. As the bottom of the wall is more likely to suffer human traffic damage, and the top section is the one that causes all the difficulties, this can save much time and money. In a divided room, hang the two different papers together, completing the bottom paper run first, butting up to the guiding line around the room. Overlap the top paper by the exact width of the border. Now hang the border on top, using the paper join as a base guideline. However, if the lower part of the wall is to be covered by a vinyl paper, you will need to overlap this onto the upper paper, and use the join as a top guideline. The reason for this contradiction is that ordinary paste is not an effective adhesive on vinyl, and when running the border you must use border or overlap adhesive.

Patterned borders have many uses, but they can be particularly effective when used to create a chair rail effect. In this case, they match the height of the banister.

WOOD, BRICK, AND TILE FINISHES

Repainting existing wood finishes and hanging a new paper on the walls of a room are cosmetic changes, and, although a facelift results, the area is not radically altered. Removing the plaster to reveal and emphasize original brickwork, using hand-made tiles or wood panels on complete or half-and-half walls, or building paneled shelving and storage into a recess, have a much more far-reaching effect. The nature and "feel" of the room are changed, because different materials have been brought together in exciting new combinations.

Designer's notes

Changing the feel of a room space by using new materials, building in a purpose-designed storage solution, or uncovering or paneling wall areas require you to accurately assess your constructional capabilities. As always, a scale drawing of the scheme is a good first step, before starting on any minor or major construction work.

Changing the color of your walls or repapering a surface to upgrade the appearance of an internal area are really cosmetic alterations. Cosmetic paint and paper alterations utilize the existing features in the room, and any decorative change they make is on the surface. If you decide to physically change an area of your home, then you must progress from decorative techniques to basic carpentry and building work. Spare a few minutes, initially, to consider space and how it is perceived in a room. Any form of clutter, particularly on the floor, will make a room look smaller. Simple steps such as racking magazines, putting books onto shelves, and tidying up generally may create the feeling of spaciousness you desire. Coordinated seating arrangements and plain flooring, rather than a mix of mismatched chairs and brightly colored rugs, can give an ordered, somewhat geometrical feel, which assists the impression of spaciousness. This aspect becomes more important as property becomes increasingly expensive. Families are often forced to accept smaller living areas and need to maximize the available area and yet create a spacious feel. Everyday clutter needs storage space in closets and shelves, so that the main room area can be free from obstruction. If you are able to create this space without altering your room dimensions, however, and thereby make good use of previously "wasted" areas like alcoves, you have the ideal solution.

Coordinated seating and a plain floor will help to create the impression of space and order.

torage solutions

ɔ not think of a storage solution as several shelves, cabinets, or osets in a room; think of your solution as an integral part of your ᵋw scheme. Not only can you achieve a matching décor, but you ın visually disguise the true function of any storage unit that atches and continues the line of the wall surface. Even one ɔnstructed from different materials will instil a sense of geometric ʳder, provided it does not interrupt the wall line.

Other possibilities include half-wall units, preferably floor-anding, with the ceiling line recessed, letting the top half of the ᵋcess be paneled, tiled, or taken back to the brick. This , visually speaking, little more than a practical development of alf-wall finishes, where the chair rail divides two different ᵋcorative effects, or where the bottom half of the wall is clad for ʳotective purposes. Shelving utilizing the top half of the wall, ith the floor line interrupted, is also possible, but somewhat self-ᵋfeating as anyone using the floor space is in danger of banging ıeir head. For this reason the area underneath tends to become a ıore obvious and unsightly storage area itself, so you might as

Left: In a kitchen, make the most of available space with built-in storage cabinets.

Above: Free-standing, half-wall-height cabinets can be used to good effect in alcoves.

well include it in the plan in the first place. As always, a sketch or drawing of the intended scheme is a good first step because it will let all interested parties voice an opinion on its viability. Measurements should, of course, be precise. A storage unit that does not house certain items because they are too big for it is no use at all.

Once you have worked out the kind of storage you need, consider whether you will buy it ready-made or build it yourself. There are many storage systems and items of furniture on the market, but to make the most of the available space, you may be better off constructing something that meets your needs exactly.

Using color with different finishes

Which base color is most suitable to match a pine wood finish in a bathroom? How can you emphasize the subtle colors of a local stone? Which wood finish best complements hand-made tiles in earth colors? The answers—you will not be surprised to discover—indicate that natural materials have their own color associations.

In sketching out your scheme for consultation, consider the effect the raw materials could have on the finished room decor. Woods, whether solid planks or veneered manufactured boards, can be varnished or oiled to enhance as well as protect their color characteristics. Wood colors like dark reds, oranges, browns, and yellows will look their best alongside green and blue schemes. They are at their most familiar and friendly too, because we associate trees with green fields and blue skies. Any natural materials that you use in your own environment will have color associations that are dependent on their source, and you should consider these, without feeling restricted by them, when making color decisions. An obvious example is to place pine paneling on the bottom half of a yellow wall. Because pine is predominantly yellow the colors wil match well, but the impact will be lost and the cost of the raw materials wasted. Far better to take the darker green of pine needles, or the mid-brown of a pine cone as your contrasting colo for the top half of the wall, thus emphasizing the yellow textures in the wood.

A color scheme that lets the lumbers be the focal point is essential if you decide to use sawn, unfinished lengths (i.e., not planed), for a rustic, more traditional look.

If you strip off the plaster to reveal a wall made of local stone, as opposed to brick, find out about the soil in the area. Is it red, sandy, or brown in color? A tint of the local color will be a natural

Left: Combining exposed brickwork and woodwork can produce a charming country kitchen feeling.

Above: You can achieve a Scandinavian look by incorporating plenty of pale varnished woodwork

xposing rough-sawn ceiling joists y removing the plasterwork can roduce an eye-catching ceiling. Team it with sturdy wooden furniture to create a harmonious decorative scheme.

A chimney breast will often be the focal point of a room. You can emphasize it by stripping off the plaster to reveal the brickwork. Exposed wooden lintels can also make dramatic statements.

artner for the stone, and the finished scheme will be pleasing to he eye. Back-to-the-brick finishes are focal points. Mixed yellows ontain subtle colorings that will be wasted if they are juxtaposed vith vivid or abrasive color. The scheme will be more successful if ou use white as a base mixed with a hint of the brick coloring as : lets the brick finish tell its own story.

Jsing colors with wall tiles

he way that you consider colors when they are used with wall iles must generally differ from considerations made for wood and tone because the clay of the tile is not in its natural state. Original tiles are available that use earth oxides, for example, or les that have a mat finish on pale blue clays, but these are hand-rafted exceptions. Commercial mass manufacture has introduced n extra process, a colored glaze fired onto the surface of the riginal clay. Colors created in this way can be matched or ontrasted in the same way as painted walls, because nature's olors have been superseded. Blue and white may have come to be egarded as the classic tile colors through the years, but they are ot the original colors of the raw material. Consequently, unless ou source a hand-made tile from a specialist limited-edition vorkshop, your color scheme will be manufactured. This lets all inds of decorative patterns and designs appear on a tile, more uitable, perhaps, for smaller wall areas.

Backsplashes above and behind basins and sinks, bath panels, and shower areas are ideal places for tiles. They are practical, being waterproof and easily cleaned, and in a confined space need not dominate the room. Pick a wall color to match a specific hue within the tile for a coordinated room scheme, or note the overall base color of the tile and pick its opposite on the color wheel for your wall.

A tiled backsplash behind a kitchen counter provides a wonderful opportunity to make a statement with color while taking care of the need for a hygienic, easily cleaned surface.

Basic skills: wood

The strength to weight ratio of wood makes it the most versatile of constructional materials, as well as the most attractive. Your lumberyard holds wood stocks and manufactured boards in specific sizes, and before you start to draw up and price a project you need to find out what they are.

Measuring up

A sketch of your construction project serves as more than just a discussion piece. When you add accurate dimensions, it becomes a working drawing, letting you calculate how much lumber you will need, and what sizes you should buy.

This is not quite as straightforward as it seems because the nominal dimensions of lumber—such as 1 x 4—are not the actual finished (planed) dimensions. The length doesn't vary between actual and nominal sizes, but the width and thickness do.

The actual size of a 48 in./1220 mm long 1 x 4 is 1 x 3 x 48 in./ 19 x 95 x 1220 mm. In general, if you figureon a reduction of ⅛ in. on all sides, you'll be close to the actual size.

Buying considerations

The raw materials you purchase can be placed in one of the three following categories: hardwoods, softwoods, and manufactured wood. Hardwood, such as oak, beech, and birch, is cut from deciduous trees, is less readily accessible and can be very expensive.

Good lumberyards will usually stock mahogany, but again, price may be prohibitive. Softwood is cheaper and is stocked by all lumberyards. Redwood, spruce, and yellow and white pine are all fairly common, and they may be simply sold as "softwood," and no by individual name. Pine may be the exception, however.

Flush siding is machined from softwood with a tongue on one edge and a matching groove on the other, and is thus easily joined together for paneling. Sizes will vary, but ½ x 4 in./12.5 x 101 mm is popular. Fir and cedar tend to make good choices for tongue-and-groove boards.

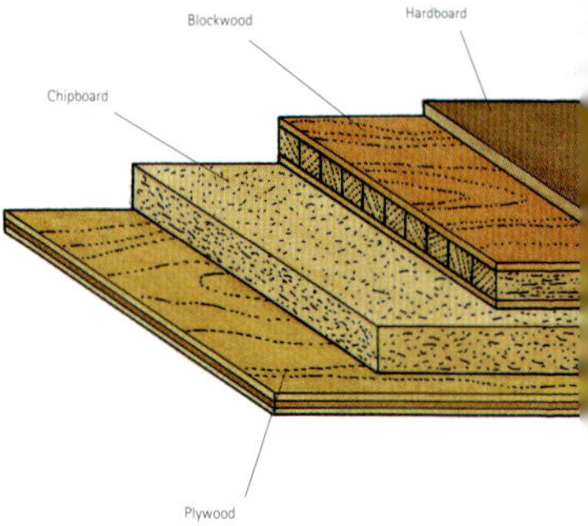

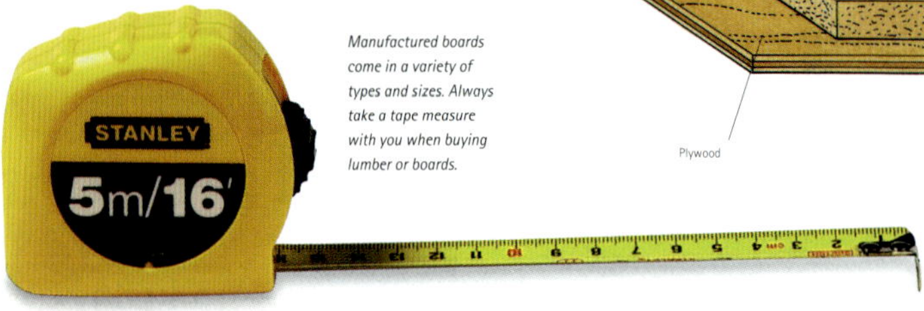

Manufactured boards come in a variety of types and sizes. Always take a tape measure with you when buying lumber or boards.

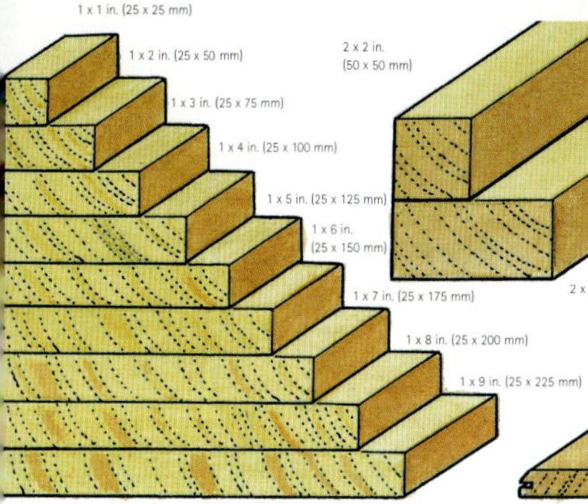

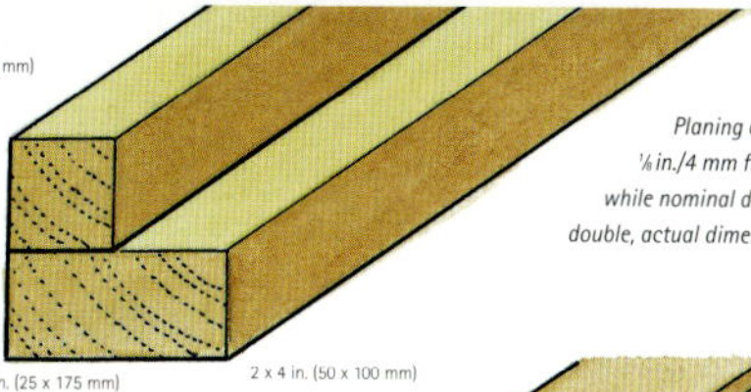

Planing can remove up to ⅛ in./4 mm from each face, so while nominal dimensions may be double, actual dimensions may differ.

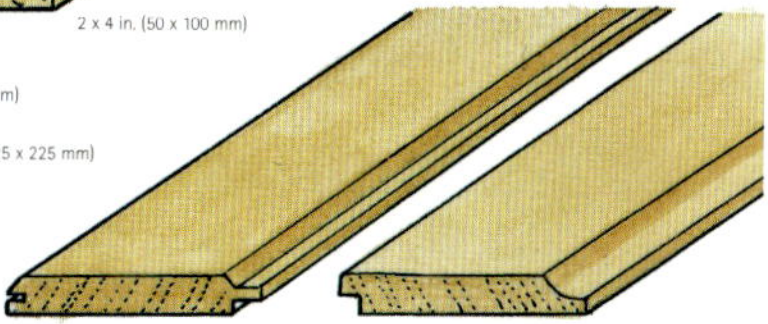

Softwood is sold in a range of standard sizes. However, the quoted size 's the original sawn dimension, not the finished size.

Paneling boards may be tongue-and-groove (left) or shiplap (right).

Plywood consists of thin layers of wood (real or manufactured) lued together so that the grains alternate at 90-degree angles vith real wood veneer on one or both outside faces. Lumber-core lywood is made in a similar way, but the interior consists of trips of scrap wood. This can lead to different cutting resistances uring the same saw-cut, and this type is not as popular as eneer-core plywood.

Plywood is usually supplied in:

- 8 x 4 ft./2440 x 1220 mm panels
- in ¼, ⅜, ½ and ¾ in./6, 9, 12.5 and 18 mm thicknesses.

The top layer of veneer, or facing, varies. You can buy birch-, eech- or oak-faced boards, one- or two-sided, and the price aries according to quality.

Other manufactured boards are available, such as chipboard or particleboard), which is used as an underlayment for ountertops, and oriented strand board (OSB), which can be seful for subflooring.

'hoosing and cutting

umberyards stock their material in nominal sizes, thickness x vidth. When you draw up a plan for the job, a knowledge of tandard sizes will be invaluable.

Select linear wood carefully; try to avoid knots and look for boards cut from the center of the log. (These have growth rings that are closer together than those on the rest of the stock.) Look down the length to see if it is distorted, bent, warped, or twisted. If it is, reject it.

The lumberyard will usually be willing to cut the boards to your exact lengths, but it is better to pick pieces that are slightly longer than you need, which you can cut to the exact length on site. This lets you cut off any ends that were damaged in transit or that show shakes (splits along the grain, caused by uneven shrinkage) and splits in the end grain.

When buying long boards or odd-size lumber, make sure the yard has a machining service. They may charge extra for this, but your boards will be professionally cut to the right size, saving you time and trouble.

If you are starting a big job, or if you are re-using old boards and need to do a lot of cutting to fit, consider hiring a dual-purpose "flip-over" saw. This machine cuts to length and miters on one side of its table, and, when rotated, cuts as a conventional table saw on the other side. Not only can this save on cutting charges at the lumberyard, but it will let you resize materials as you need them.

Tools and equipment (basic)

It may be true that "a bad workman blames his tools," but it is also true that first-class results cannot be attained with substandard and inaccurate equipment. Always buy the best tools that you can, maintain and look after them, because in most cases they are an investment that should last a lifetime.

TOP TIP

If funds are limited, always buy several hand tools rather than one power tool. They will let you tackle a far wider range of jobs and will help you develop useful manual dexterity. When you've assembled a good kit of hand tools, add powered examples.

Cheap and badly made equipment is a bad investment. High-quality hand tools will enable you to produce first-class results, and will last a lifetime if you look after them. Poor work, inaccurate fixings, and amateurish finishing are all you can realistically expect from badly made tools. Do not attempt a job without the correct tool, either. Improvising takes longer and puts current and previous work at risk.

Ensure guidelines are level with a spirit level and mark them with a high-quality steel straightedge. Use a retractable steel tape to measure larger boards and linear lumber, and a steel rule for smaller dimensions. Square up with a try square or engineer's square, and mark miter cuts with a combination square. A good-quality combination square will include a detachable steel rule and a spirit or carpenter's level. Nonstandard angles can be measured and transferred using a sliding bevel. Cutting lines for boards should be made with a carpenter's pencil, but a marking knife must be used for small cuts and wood joints. Keep a conventional pencil and a general-purpose snap-blade knife in your kit as well. Saw wood across the grain with a crosscut saw; when sawing with the grain use a ripsaw. A panel saw is, in effect, a smaller crosscut saw, used for cutting boards. The more stable-bladed backsaw cuts large wood joints. Smaller or restricted-access cuts need a small backsaw.

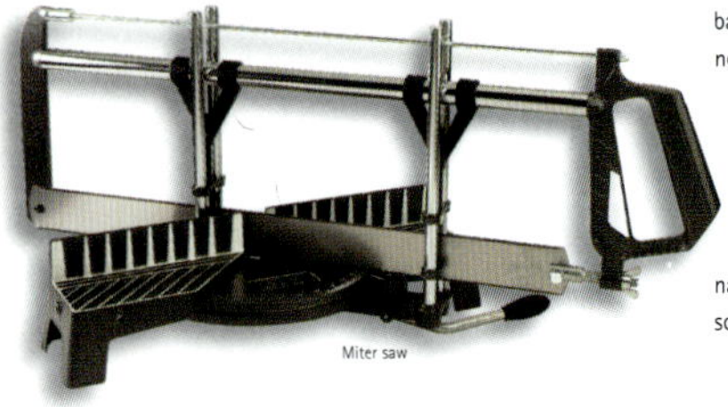

You can cut holes in panels with a keyhole saw. Make right-angled cuts on the bench supported by a bench hook, and cut mitered angles in a miter box. Sink brads and molding pins with a ball-peen hammer, pull out pins using a curved claw hammer or pincers. Counterpunch pin heads below the surface with a nail set or punch. Use an awl to make starter holes for small screws, and a tee-handled gimlet for threaded pilot holes,

remembering that the correct bladed screwdriver is needed to drive screws. Large woodscrews require a drilled pilot hole. To do this, use an awl and twist bits, or a self-starting auger bit in a hand drill or brace. A countersink will ensure the screwhead is below the wood surface, and a plug cutter will produce neatly chamfered plugs to fill screw holes. Combination drill-drivers that are powered by mains lead or rechargeable battery can combine these jobs, particularly if fitted with a combination screwsink. Any power driving into masonry will need a drill-driver with a hammer action.

Rabbet waste wood can be removed with a mortise or firmer chisel, driven by a wooden mallet if necessary. Keep sharp chisel blades in their protective plastic casings; if they are blunt or chipped, sharpen them using an oilstone.

Always secure the workpiece with a C-clamp or bar clamp, and use a sash clamp to hold glued joints until dry. Small pieces of waste wood can be positioned to protect the workpiece from cramping indentations. Smooth edges using a jack file or smoothing file, and keep all edged blades sharply aligned. Along with chisels, drill bits and files can be sharpened. Your local hardware store will be able to provide this service.

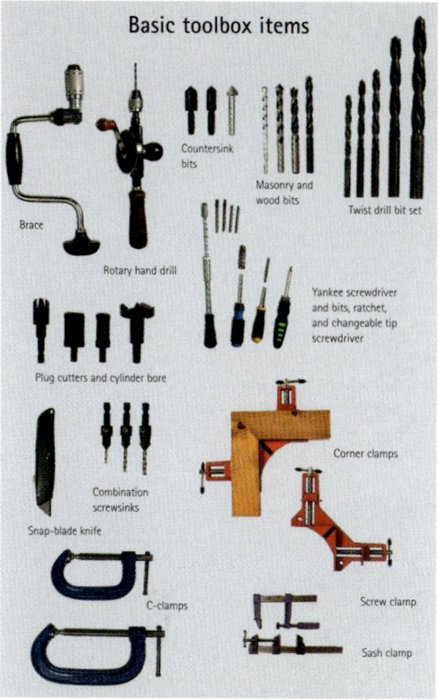

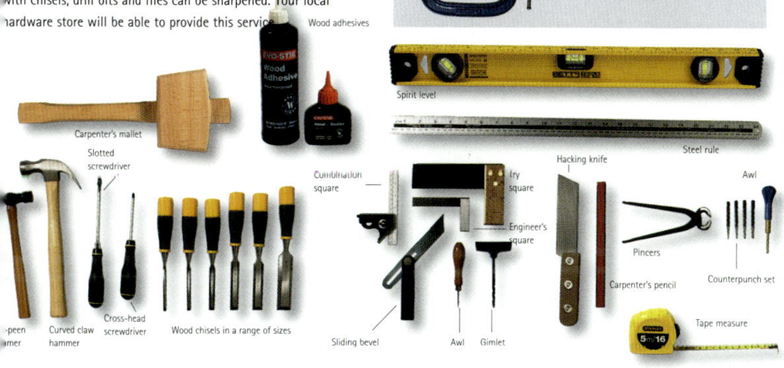

Tools and equipment (advanced)

Cheap versions of drills and saws are on special offer in every large home center. But don't be tempted—inaccurate, badly made power tools merely do a poor job faster. Buy a brand name with a good reputation, and go for the top of the price range. You can be sure that it will be worth it.

Mains-powered jigsaw

Power drills

The drills found in most basic tool kits are an electric hand drill and possibly a small cordless drill-driver. These small portable power drill/screwdrivers have become very popular due to their reasonable price and ease of use. They will help with many small jobs around the home but will be found wanting if you attempt to tackle anything heavy-duty. Even the professional-quality drill-drivers are intended to penetrate primarily only wood, plastics and wallboard. Drilling into masonry is left to the hammer drill, which is basically a drill-driver with a hammer feature for driving into brickwork.

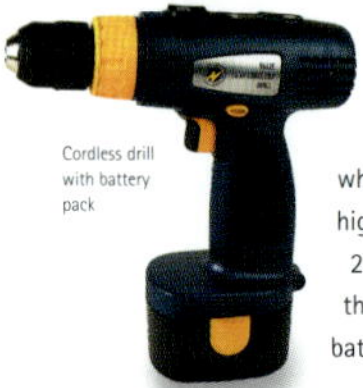
Cordless drill with battery pack

Cordless drills are rated by the voltage of their battery-pack: drills for home use are often 9.6V or less, while professional hammer drills for high performance in concrete will be 24V. A good cordless hammer drill for the home tool kit would have a 14.4V battery pack, and a drilling capacity of ½ in./13 mm in masonry and 1¼ in./32 mm in wood. The price is high, though, and a compromise may be adequate. If you already have a drill-driver, you could extend your capability by adding a traditional top-quality electric (nonportable) hammer drill at considerably less cost.

Mains-powered hammer drill

Power saws

Two basic types of power saw are available: the jigsaw (or saber saw) and the circular saw. The jigsaw will cut curves and irregular shapes, while the circular saw cuts in a straight line. The jigsaw has easily interchangeable blades that are designed to cut different materials, and a tilting baseplate for cutting bevels. The saw cuts with a powerful reciprocating motion, and better models have an orbital-action blade. Variable speed control is a real advantage. Try to find one with a knob handle so that you can use both hands. The circular saw also has changeable blades, but it is a more complicated tool; it usually comes supplied with a tungsten-carbide-tipped blade for cutting both hard and soft materials. The

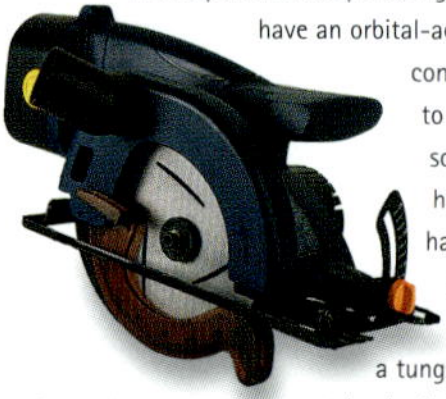
Cordless circular saw

TOP TIP

Always adopt a safety first policy with powered equipment. Wind leads around handles when not in use and never let them trail across the floor. Store tools in their carry cases or in a locked cabinet, out of the reach of children.

Belt sander

lepth of cut can be adjusted, and the baseplate tilts for cutting angles. A blade diameter of 7¼ in./ 185 mm is ideal. Make sure your saw comes with a guide fence or ripping guide. Miter saws are hinged circular saws that are mounted on a swivel turntable on a mountable base. The saw cross-cuts and swivels up to 45 degrees for cutting various angles. Better models have a fence clamp, adjustable debris guard, and a dust bag.

Power sanders

Orbital sanders are sanders used for fine surface finishing. A rectangular base holds the abrasive paper, and is driven in an oscillating motion by a motor, thus "orbiting" the sanding surface, usually in a ¼ in./ 6 mm diameter. The abrasive paper can be changed quickly, from medium to very fine grades for the ultimate finish. All-purpose random orbit sanders come with a supply of quick-fit perforated sanding discs. The standard size is 5 in./125 mm, and a dust extraction bag is also provided. Detail sanders that use triangular sanding surfaces allow access into tight corners and confined

Palm sander

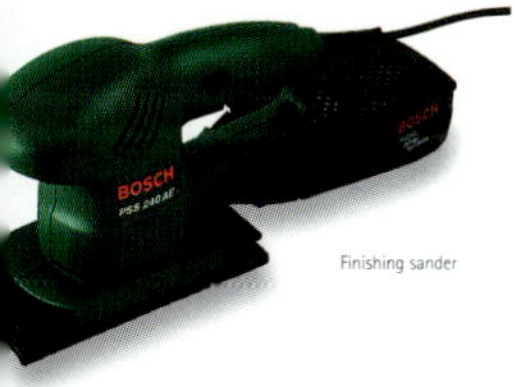

Finishing sander

spaces. Profile sanders have soft rounded heads for other types of detail work. Belt sanders are used primarily for heavy-duty abrasive work, such as leveling surfaces, rounding off corners, and reducing the width of lumber. An interchangeable sanding belt moving at a continuous speed removes wood stock very quickly. A 3 in./75 mm belt is a good width—the belts are available in coarse, medium, and fine grades. Better machines have variable speed control.

"Snip-off" miter saw

Routers

An electric plunge-type router will cut a rabbet, channel a groove, or cut a mortise. The router bit is driven in a clockwise direction, plunged down into the wood through the hole in the center of the base, and carefully guided from left to right, cutting into the workpiece. Variable speed is a real asset, giving more control. This tends to be a feature of only the more expensive machines, however.

Plunge-type router

Electric planes

You can shape linear lumber to fit against uneven wall surfaces with an electric plane. It can be used to rabbet, chamfer, bevel, and smooth. It is faster than a hand plane, so beware of removing too much wood—you can't put it back! A blade width of 3¼ in./82 mm and a cutting depth up to ⅛ in./ 3 mm is adequate for household projects. Make sure yours has a setting gauge and a fence.

Electric plane

Bench planes

Basic wood techniques

The basic requirement in cutting wood to fit is accuracy. Ensure that you measure, mark, and saw the wood carefully. You don't need excessive strength, but you do need patience, a stable workpiece and a sharp saw. Drilling also needs a secure workpiece, a marked starting point, and a sharp bit. In neither case should undue force be necessary.

Measuring and marking

Remember the woodworker's basic rule: measure twice, cut once. Measure at right angles if you are measuring across a board, and parallel to the edge when measuring along its length. Don't let tapes sag or kink. Mark cuts to be made across boards with a carpenter's pencil, and cut on the waste side of the line. Blow away sawdust if it obscures the line as the saw moves through the piece. If you use a circular saw, remember to calculate for the width of the blade. Mark cuts across the grain with a marking knife, and cut on the waste side of the marked line. Simple halving wood joints are marked accurately by using one half as a template to mark the other, so you only need to measure the one half. If you mark a miter, use a combination square at 45 degrees, then transfer the wood to a miter box or saw.

If you need to cut at a right-angle to an edge, use a try square and pencil to mark the guideline.

Using a marking knife to mark cutting lines severs the surface grain, preventing splitting.

When marking out angled miter cuts at 45 degrees, use a combination square.

To make an accurate mitered cut, place the wood in a miter box, which has slots at 45 degrees.

Cutting

The first rule of cutting is to have a stable workpiece. Any movement or slipping of the wood causes inaccuracy and is potentially dangerous. Secure your board with cramps when possible, supporting any overhang on a trestle or something similar. Adequate support is also needed for long sections of timber, but shorter pieces cut on the bench can be stabilized by a bench hook.

When making cuts with a large hand saw, whether cutting across the grain (cross cutting) or along the grain (ripping) of lumber stock or cutting manufactured board, hold the saw at an angle to the workpiece throughout the cut. Establish the cut with backstrokes first, and then cut using the entire blade length, with your index finger pointing along the top edge of the saw. This will help keep the saw straight and aligned with the cutting line. Keep just to the waste side of the line; if you center the blade on the line, your finished piece will be too short. You can always plane or sand the sawn piece back to the line.

Backsaws have a rigid back, so the blade is stable when you make a cut. Establish the cut as before, but as you progress, gradually lower the blade until it is cutting horizontally through the workpiece. Don't cut all the way through the wood, as the grain will tear and splinter as the blade breaks through on the

;ecure the wooden)oard with a clamp before 'ou start to saw.

When cutting smaller pieces of wood with a backsaw, stabilize them on a bench hook.

Establish a saw cut by holding the blade at an angle to the edge and pulling back a couple of times.

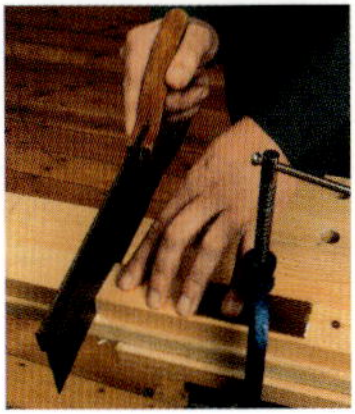

Cut with the backsaw blade horizontal, cramping the work to scrap timber to finish off.

ınderside. Stop the cut just before completion and cramp the vorkpiece onto a scrap piece of wood. Now continue the cut :hrough into the scrap to achieve a clean finished cut.

)rilling for screws and dowels

'his is a very simple technique for joining wood pieces, provided /ou use the correct size of bit. To insert a screw, you first need to Jrill a small pilot hole (to guide the screw thread), then a hole the ;ame diameter and depth as the screw shank (the shank clearance ıole), and finally the countersink (to take the head below the wood ;urface). Some screw types do not have a shank, because the :hread is continuous, so the shank clearance hole can be dispensed with. Always drill a pilot hole, however; otherwise, the screw is ınlikely to run straight and may bind so much when you insert it :hat it becomes impossible to turn. A finishing hole is essential for ı countersunk screw; otherwise, the head will end up slightly)roud of the surface. Countersunk heads can be filled before painting. As an alternative, use a combination screwsink that will drill a pilot, shank, and counterbored hole at the same time. Insert the screw and fill the hole with an anchor of the same wood cut to the size of the hole with a cutter. Drilling holes to join wood pieces with dowels needs a self-starting auger bit with a rubber depth stop. Adjust the rubber ring to indicate the correct depth of hole if you are using fluted dowels. If you intend to drill completely through the wood, cramp it to a scrap piece of wood. Drill straight through to the scrap, minimizing damage as the auger bit leaves the hole; otherwise, you risk splitting the grain. You must be sure to use the correct sized auger bit. If you buy a pack of fluted dowels, however, the bit is usually supplied in the kit.

Examples of tools and equipment are shown below, and they are as follows: a number 12 masonry drill and wall anchor fixing used to screw a number 8 screw into the wall; a number 8 combination screw sink and number 8 CSK screw for wood; and a $^3/_8$ in./7 mm slotted driver blade fitting a number 8 CSK screw.

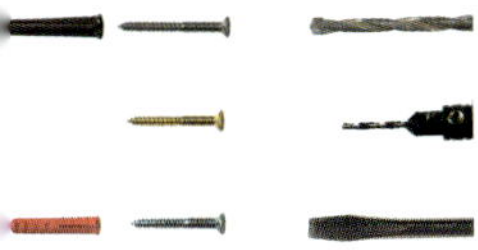

(Top to bottom): Wall anchor fixing and number 12 masonry drill; number 8 combination screw sink and screw; wall anchor fixing and slotted driver blade.

Drill large holes with a self-starting auger bit. It has a sharp point to allow easy centering of the bit on the hole position.

A rubber depth stop can be attached to the bit and adjusted so that you can drill holes to an accurate depth.

Advanced wood techniques

Joining wood pieces together is an art form in itself. If you don't feel confident about tackling the more difficult joints, start with a simple halving joint. Accuracy is everything in producing good wood joints, so it is a good idea to practice a little on an off-cut first.

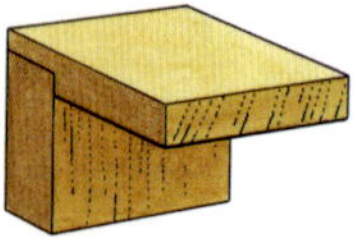

Rabbeted right-angle joint

Simple wood joints are not difficult, provided you measure and cut accurately with correctly set, sharp tools. Use a marking knife, not a pencil, and use one half of the joint as a template for the other to ensure a tight fit. Joints and housings that are identical, but cut from separate wood lengths, can be clamped together and marked for simultaneous cutting to ensure uniformity. Cut the wood precisely and assemble it "dry" to check the fit, remembering that a loose joint has no strength. Do not rely on excessive amounts of wood glue acting as a filler in a badly crafted, ill-fitting joint.

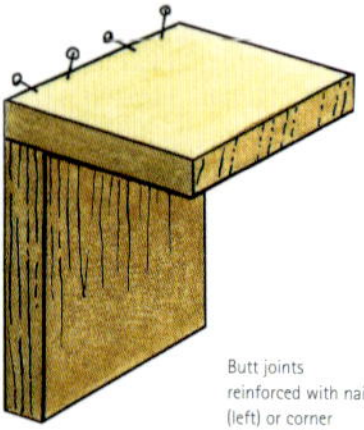

Butt joints reinforced with nails (left) or corner blocks (right)

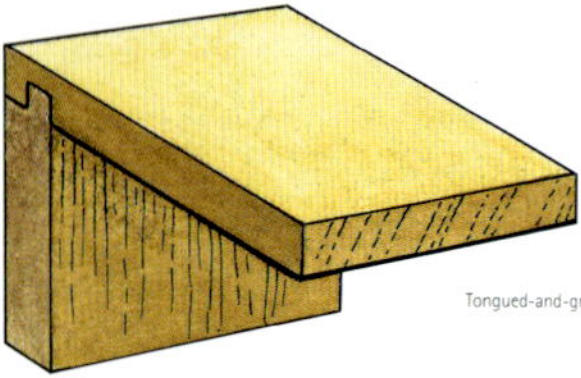

Tongued-and-grooved corner joint

Use dowels to reinforce any of the following joints:

- butt joining, L-joints, and block reinforced joints
- tongue-and-groove joint (for panels, bought pre-machined)
- halving joint
- rabbeted joint
- 45-degree miter joint
- bridle joint/open mortise-and-tenon.

L-shaped butt joint

T-shaped butt joint

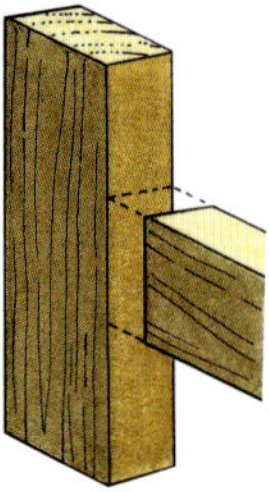

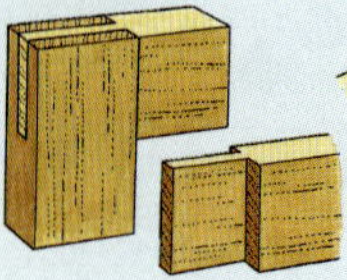

Bridle joint/open mortise-and-tenon

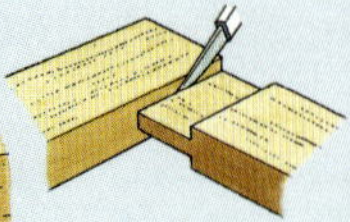

For accuracy, mark one half of a joint from the other.

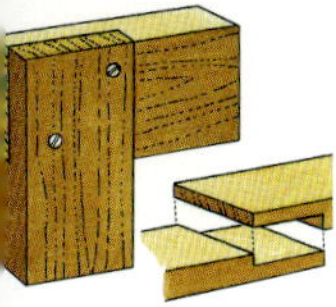

'alving or lap joints can ıake right-angled and ıline connections.

For an exact fit, clamp the pieces together and cut them both at the same time.

Clamp each piece to the bench and begin cutting down the grain at an angle.

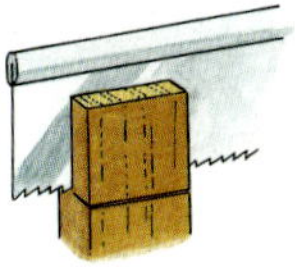

Finish the cut with the saw blade parallel to the cut across the grain. Check the fit of the joint.

TOP TIP

Removing waste wood from a cut housing is simplified by making several parallel cuts side by side to the housing depth with a small backsaw. You will find it much easier to remove slivers of waste wood one at a time with a ¼ in./6 mm chisel than to try to chisel out the housing in one piece with a larger blade.

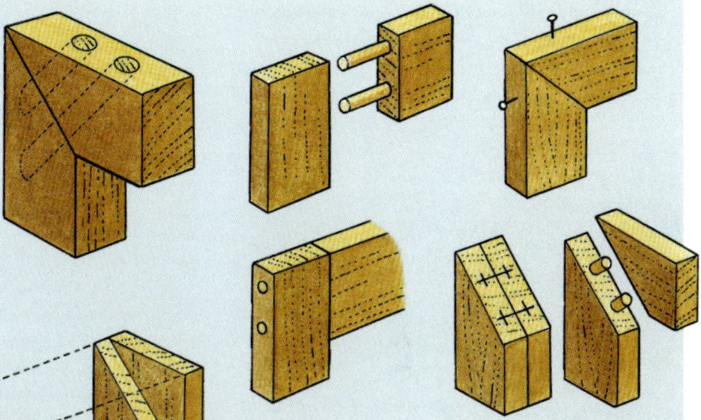

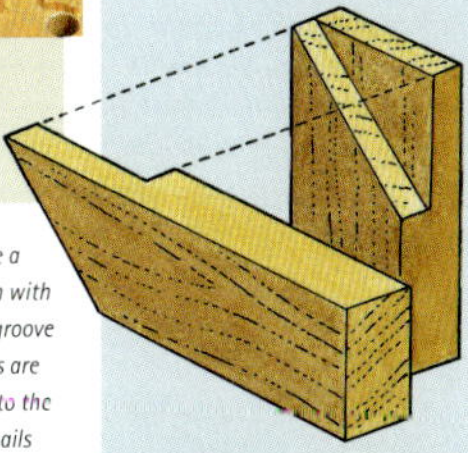

3oards sold for paneling have a imple machined joint system with ı tongue on one edge and a groove n the other. When the boards are ıssembled, the tongue fits into the ıroove. They are secured by nails lriven through the tongues.

For strength, glued butt joints should be reinforced. One method is to drive nails through one piece into the other. However, wooden dowels are far better and can be concealed within the joint in blind holes. If visible, their ends should be trimmed flush with the wood. If hidden, careful marking out is necessary to ensure the dowel holes coincide exactly.

Wall fixings and hardware

Wall fixings and hardware are now so widely available that your hardware store and even the local general store will have a selection on sale; there is no need to visit the home center. The difficult task is discovering the type of wall you are trying to fix into, and trial and error is just about the only way to find out.

To attach constructed wooden pieces to a wall, or to start a "built-in" project with wooden cleats on the wall surface, or simply to put a screw in the wall for a mirror or bathroom fixture, you will need the appropriate wall fixing. This involves selecting an anchor to receive the screw; the type of anchor will depend on the original construction of your wall, usually whether it is solid or cavity.

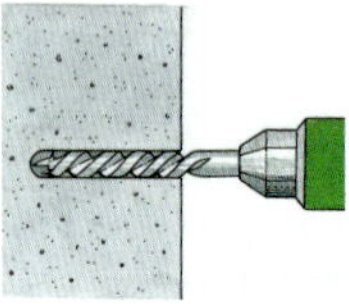

When you are using wall anchors, you need to drill a hole of the correct size and depth for the anchor in the wall.

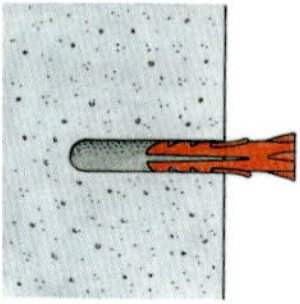

Push the anchor into the hole until it is flush with the surface. It is important not to hammer it, as this may distort it.

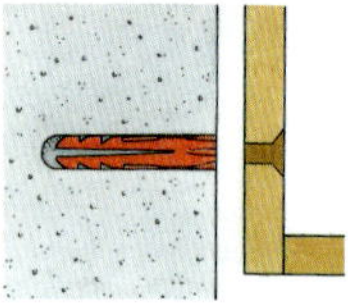

Hold up the fitting to the wall and align the screw hole with the wall anchor. You can then insert the selected screw.

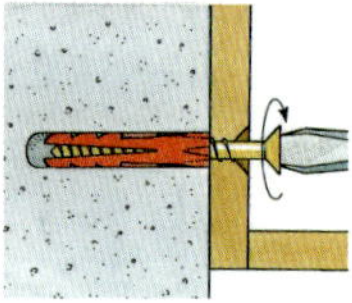

Tighten the screw. When the screw enters the anchor, the latter will expand, gripping the sides of the hole tightly.

Solid walls

If your wall is solid, all you will need is a simple nylon or polypropylene wall anchor. This type of anchor has grabbing lugs or pointed teeth to stop it turning in its hole as you insert the screw. You will need to predrill a hole, and you must be very accurate in lining up and marking.

You will find that the drill, anchor, and screw sizes are all related. Anchors sold in packs have the required drill size and recommended screw shank acceptance size pressed into the plastic center strip.

Frame fixers are long-shanked screws in their own sleeves and do not need previously marked and drilled wall holes, letting you drill through the wood directly into the masonry. The anchor is fitted directly through the wood piece, and, as the screw is tightened, counter-rotation lugs open out to grab the wall. The sleeve is designed to eliminate distortion of the wood during tightening.

Some forms of frame fixer are designed to be hammered home, which speeds installation. A screwdriver may be required for final tightening and to remove the screw so the framework can be removed.

For a really heavy-duty fixing in solid masonry, an expanding bolt should be chosen. It works on the same principle as a wall anchor, the segmented steel body of the fitting expanding in the hole as the bolt is turned with a spanner. Removing the bolt leaves the body of the fixing in place.

Cavity walls and wallboard

Anchors designed for these walls are to be pushed through a hole in the wall until the petals or arms reach the cavity and can open out to spread against the back of the wall as you turn the screw.

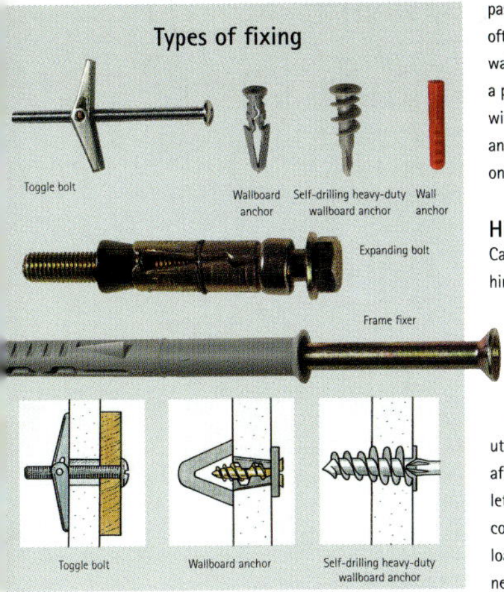

hey are simple to insert, but not very strong. Heavy-duty expanding ixings, which consist of a metal sleeve around a central bolt, will ake more loading. The sleeve fits the hole precisely and expands utward when the bolt is tightened, gripping the sides and back of he hole. Spring toggle bolts have metal wings that are pushed hrough the hole into the cavity and spring open. Then, as the bolt is ightened, the wings grab the back of the wall. This fixing has a rawback in that the hole must be quite large, because the wings pass through it, but the open wings spread the load effectively. It is often recommended for walls of low structural strength. Self-drill wallboard fixings are anchors with a screw thread. You simply make a pilot hole and insert them with a screwdriver until they are flush with the wall surface. After this you can treat them as you would any wall anchor. A screw is supplied with the anchor, but longer ones of the same type will be needed for cleats.

Hinges and catches

Cabinet doors and shutters built in to your new room will need hinges. Butt hinges, which need to be recessed to fit flush, are the most common and are available in every size, format and finish. Flush hinges are designed for lighter load-bearing duties. Their advantage is that they are designed to screw to the surface, and no cutting in is necessary.

Small matching cabinet doors that are fiddly to align often utilize concealed adjustable hinges, adjustments being possible after the doors are hung. These hinges were primarily designed to let doors not inset into the frame to open at right angles in confined spaces. Some concealed adjustable hinges are spring-loaded to keep the doors closed. For other hinge styles, you will need to fit a catch. Magnetic door catches are easy to fit, usually being an enclosed magnet case screwed to the cabinet, which attracts a small metal plate fixed to the door.

More difficult to fit, because it requires completely accurate positioning, is the automatic latch. This excellent device lets you open the doors if both hands are full, and makes handles and knobs unnecessary. The mechanism is cased inside the cabinet, and the latch lever is lined up on the inside of the door. You simply press the outside of the closed door to unlatch it, and it swings open.

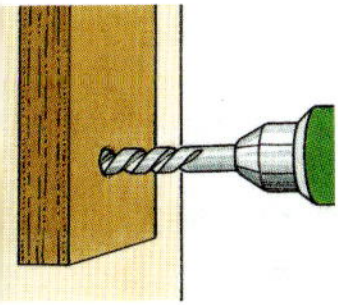

Frame fixers let you hold the wood framework in place and drill straight through into the wall.

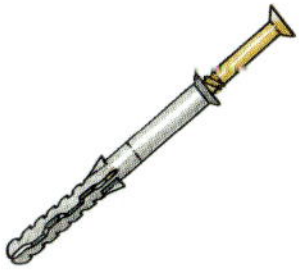

The fixer comprises a long, heavy-gauge screw and long expanding plastic anchor.

Pass the fixer through the wood into the wall so that the end of the anchor is flush with the frame's face.

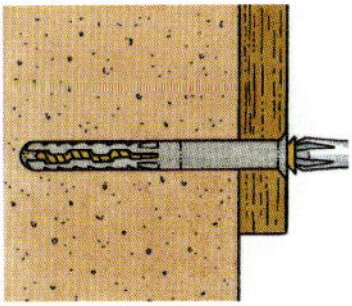

Tighten the fixer's screw to expand the anchor and secure the frame to the wall in one operation.

Screws, nails, and adhesives

There are an amazing number of screws on the market in all types, sizes and finishes, with slotted- or cross-heads in countersunk, raised, and round-head form. Nails, too, come in many different types and sizes for specific purposes, while there are plenty of glues to choose from to meet your home improvement needs.

Screws

Despite the confusing array of types, hold onto the basic principle that screws are used to draw together and join two previously separate items. This may be two pieces of wood for permanent fixing or it may be holding a cleat against a wall by gripping the inside of an anchor, or simply holding hardware, such as hinges, against a wooden surface.

Of the types you may find in your local hardware store, slotted screws have been used in carpentry for many years, manually driven by a matching bladed screwdriver. Screws with cross-heade slots, like Phillips, require a matching cross-headed driver, and many users claim that this type of driver is less likely to jump out of the slot.

Cordless drill-driver users rely on cross-slotted screws, partly fo this reason, and partly for speed. The length and "grab" of the thread varies. Conventional woodscrews have a shank, the diameter of which determines the size number (e.g., 6 or 8). Cross-heads have a continuous thread that can be quite pronounced wit a high 'grab', and are often similar in appearance to self-tappers. The head can be countersunk, intended to be driven below the work surface, unless a screw cover is used.

The other head shapes are domed (round), often used with washers and when the screw may be removed periodically, and raised, when the head is set in a cup for decorative effect.

Screws can be steel or brass; brass may look better, but steel is stronger. Steel screws may be stainless, bright, galvanized, zinc-plated, or chrome-plated for protection against rust.

Screws

Whether you need a screw for a strong hidden fixing or one that can be exposed as a decorative feature, you'll find what you need.

Use the correct blade size for the screw head. A blade too small for the head will damage the slot and jump out; a blade too wide will damage the workpiece as the screw is inserted.

Modern nails and pins

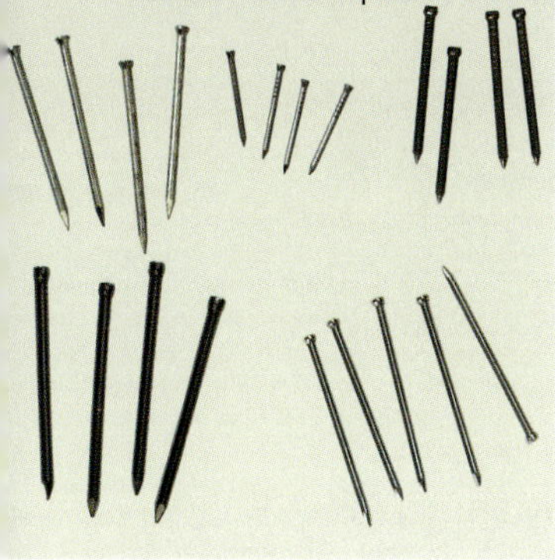

lails, brads, pins, and tacks

lodern nails, brads, pins, and tacks are the distant relatives of and-forged nails produced in the smithy; they had tapered, sharp-ornered bodies or shanks. These original fasteners held better than oday's machined round nails, because the sharp shank cut hrough, as opposed to spreading, the woodgrain. Buying cut floor r floorboard nails is as close as you are likely to get to a piece of istory, however, as today's manufacturers prefer to offer hundreds f different types and sizes of round nail.

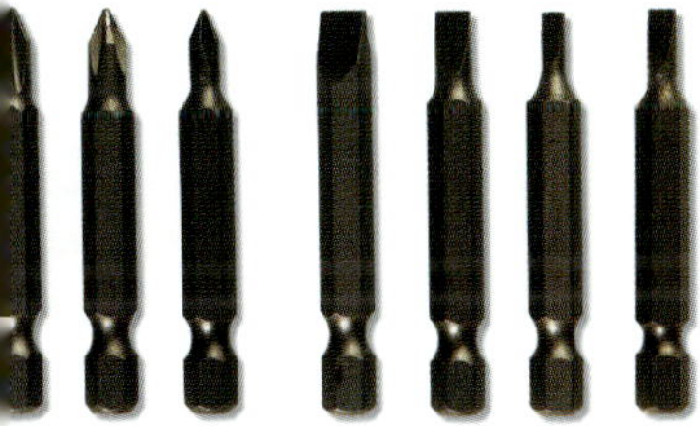

Interchangeable driver bits

Nails have different heads, lengths, and thicknesses (gauges), and you will find that the reference name usually describes the use. For general use about the house, a toolbox could contain round or finishing nails, 1½ to 3 in. (40 to 75 mm), oval brad or lost-head ovals 1 to 4 in. (25 to 100 mm), and a selection of brads and molding pins (available in small boxes). Hardboard nails, masonry nails, and wallboard nails, all self-descriptive, can be bought for more specific jobs.

Glues

Wood glues, particularly when used in conjunction with pins or screws, will give a very strong joint. Jointed surfaces must be supported, either by screws, C-clamps, sash clamps, or similar, while the glue dries, usually overnight. Both waterproof and nonwaterproof glues are available in handy sizes, starting with mini-packs and 4 fl.oz/125 ml containers with easy-to-use applicators, up to 3 quart/5 liter professional packs. Moldings are sometimes glued to the wall surface with a rapid setting, fast-grab panel adhesive. This is a high-strength gap and filler adhesive. It is usually available in a tube, which comes with a dispenser similar to a skeleton gun.

Wood adhesives are available as waterproof and nonwaterproof.

Cut floor or floorboard nails

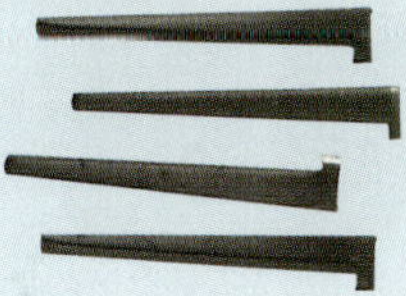

Cut floor (floorboard) nails have sharp-cornered bodies designed to cut through the woodgrain.

Wooden moldings

Wooden panel moldings provide a finishing flourish to offset a sometimes functional piece. For this reason, they have long been used as decorative features on built-in room units, doors, and cabinets. Moldings can line recessed panels, provide a decorative edging to shelves, and hide screw heads around fixed frames and room panelwork.

Softwood moldings

Most wood moldings are routed from softwood. Baseboards and picture and chair rails will all be familiar, as will door and window frames, and they can be found in a multitude of shapes and designs. Period styles with ornate patterns or more austere, modern chamfered lengths are available to suit or match any room. A few basic examples are shown here. They vary in molding detail from supplier to supplier, so you need to buy from the same source.

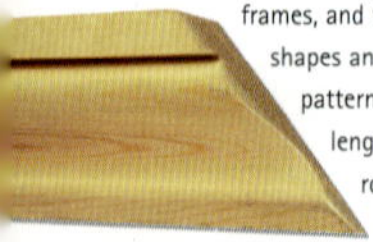

The growth in the refurbishment market has led to some period designs being available "off the shelf," but you will need to find a specialist supplier for more unusual and imaginative designs. Some suppliers may be able to match your existing molding if you provide them with a sample. Panel moldings that give a finishing touch to plain surfaces and decorative pine strips for smaller areas like cabinet doors can be found at most home centers and good lumberyards.

Hardwood moldings

Hardwood moldings are for edging the outside of boards and the inside edges of cutaway panels, where the layered sides of the board would otherwise be visible. Boards with a hardwood veneer can thus be edged with a matching strip, and oiled or varnished. Small hardwood moldings in ramin or mahogany can be employed as decoration for cabinet doors, as contrasting finishing lengths on panelwork and frames, or as internal edging on right-angled corners.

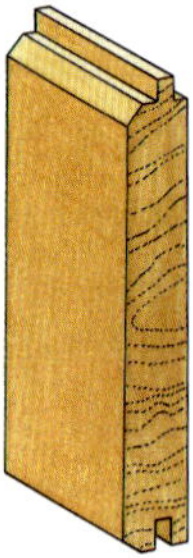

Tongue-and-groove

Shiplap

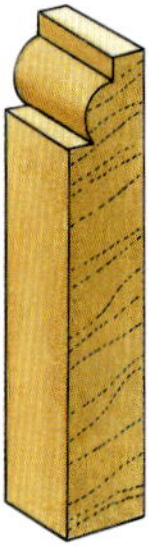

Torus baseboard

Splayed baseboard

Ovolo baseboard

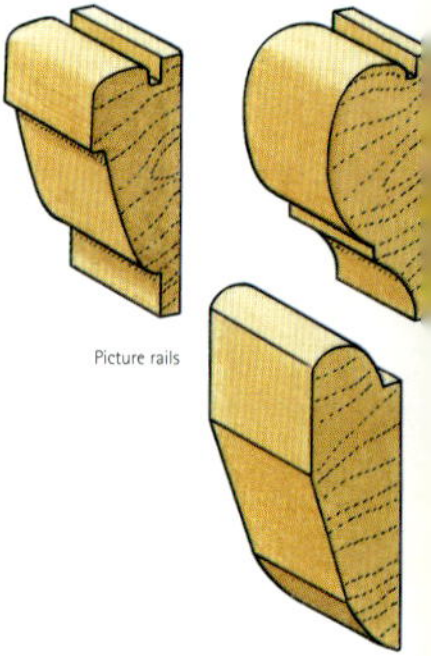

Picture rails

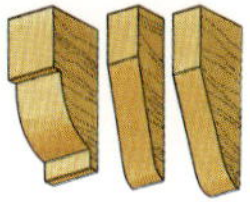

(From left to right): ovolo crown molding; splayed and rounded crown molding; chamfered crown molding.

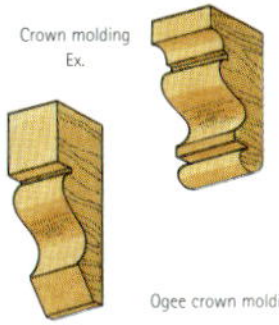

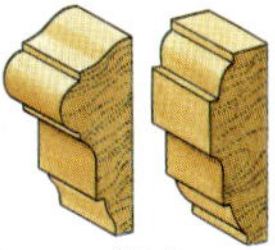

Chair rail

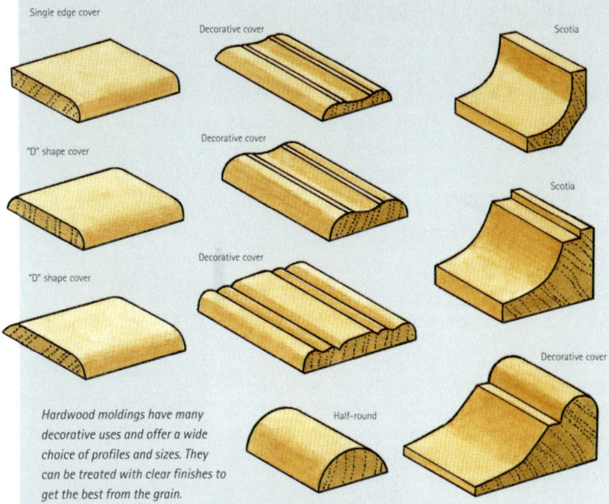

Hardwood moldings have many decorative uses and offer a wide choice of profiles and sizes. They can be treated with clear finishes to get the best from the grain.

Left: Chair rails tend to be chunky to withstand knocks from chair backs and other furniture.

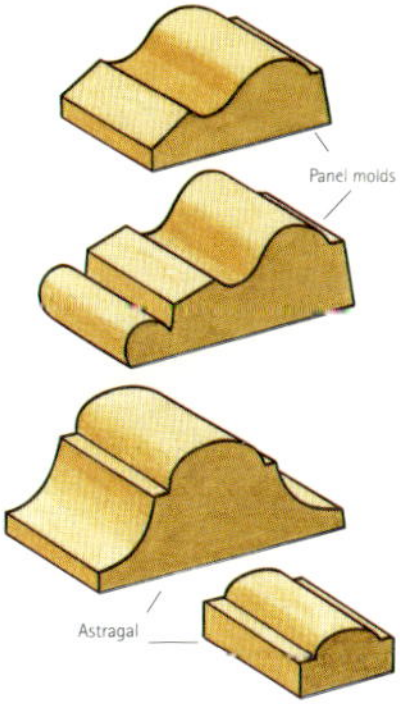

Wall paneling

Wood has a unique way of altering the look and feel of a room. As a natural material, it has an aroma all its own and a visual elegance second to none. Whether you opt for vertical or horizontal paneling, pick an appropriate finish, not only to go with the room décor, but to enhance the natural beauty of the wood itself.

Prepared lumber lengths for paneling a wall can be bought from home centers, usually in shrink-wrapped bundles priced per foot/meter. Traditional paneling is intended for interior use only. Exterior siding, such as clapboard, can be used outdoors. Alternatively, buy your wall paneling from your local lumberyard. Both tongue-and-groove and shiplap will be priced per running foot or per 30 cm units.

Before buying specific lengths, be sure you know whether the paneling is to run horizontally or vertically. This way you will minimize wastage when cutting to size on site.

Wall surface

Before you start any planning, examine the wall that you plan to panel. If it is damp, even very slightly damp, the paneling will exacerbate the problem and fungi will form on the reverse side of the wood. Simply fitting vents will not solve the problem. You will need to cure the damp at source, and will require professional advice. Whatever the state of the wall, a coat of wood preservative is recommended.

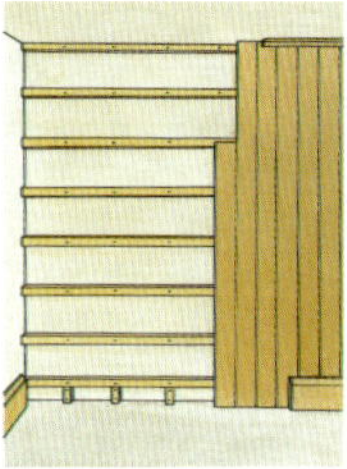

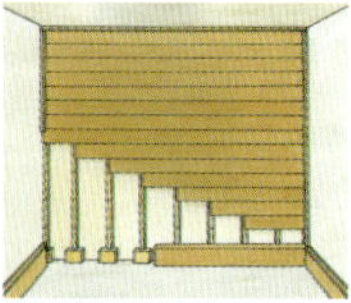

When paneling walls, boards can be run vertically and horizontally. The supporting cleats always run in the opposite direction.

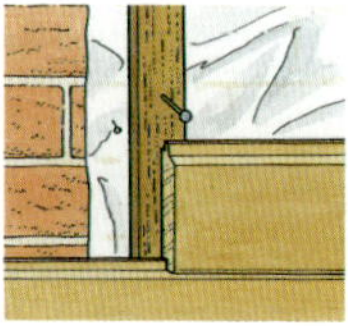

On an external wall, trap a damp-proof membrane behind the cleats, then add the boards.

The ends of boards should reach halfway across the cleat to ensure adequate support.

Wood paneling should be pinned to softwood cleats fixed to the wall. An ideal size for the cleats is 2 x 1 in./50 x 25 mm. These must be horizontal for vertical paneling, and vertical for horizontal paneling. Fix the cleats to the wall, approximately 18 in./ 460 mm apart, using the same spacing for the fixing points. If you are driving into bare masonry, you can use masonry nails. Plastered surfaces, however, require anchors and screws; countersunk 2 in./50mm number 8 are ideal. The framework of cleats must be in a true vertical plane. You can check this by placing a spirit level on the uprights and on a long straightedge held across the horizontal sections. If the wall is very uneven, pack out the wood with strips of cardboard or thin plywood.

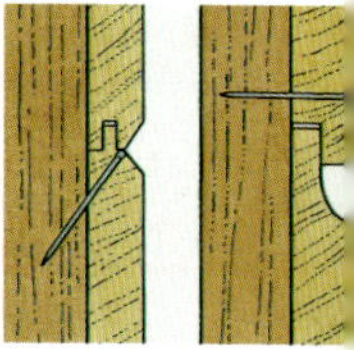

Tongue-and-groove boards should be "secret nailed" through their tongues, shiplap through the face.

aseboard

/hether you retain the baseboard or not is your choice. If the new aneling is intended to fit flush from ceiling to floor, then the xisting baseboard merely becomes part of the cleating because it is ie same depth. If the baseboard is part of the new scheme, owever, then it must be carefully pried off. Position a cleat so that ou can nail the baseboard back in position to complete the job.

ertical paneling

entering vertical lengths on your chosen wall requires precise athematics. You need to measure the visible width of the wood rst. A popular size is 3½ in./90 mm. Divide this figure into the wall ngth. If you are lucky, the paneling will fit exactly or fall very ightly short, leaving a slight opening of the fit between tongue id groove to take up the space. Otherwise an equal amount iould be taken off each end, effectively centering the wood ngths on the wall. If this does not worry you, or the paneling is ontinuing around the corner, simply start at one end. With the xception of the very first piece, which is pinned through the enter of the face, TGV paneling should be invisibly pinned through ie tongue, the groove in the next length hiding the fixing. This eans that whichever end of the wall you start, the groove must utt to the wall. Shiplap starts the same way round, but is fixed irough the face of the wood, just before the lap. The pin needs to be punched below the surface and the hole filled. The first length must be plumb vertical. If the wall is not, plane the wood to fit. Build up the paneling with successive lengths until you reach the end of the wall; the end piece may require planing to fit in the same way as the first piece. If the paneling fits flush, a decorative panel molding around three sides will complete the job. If not, nail the baseboard back into position on top of the paneling.

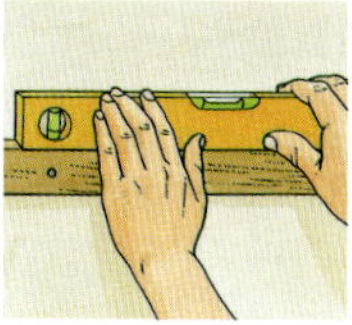

When attaching horizontal support cleats to the wall, check with a spirit level that they are accurate.

At switch and outlet positions, nail a framework of cleats to the wall around the mounting box.

When you reach the switch or outlet with the boards, mark them and cut them to fit around it.

Screw the faceplate to the mounting box so that it overlaps the cut edges of the boards.

/ooden wall paneling is a versatile eans of providing a room with a unique look. You can stain it or paint it to suit the style you want.

Horizontal paneling

The same principles apply to horizontal paneling. Start with the groove against the ceiling line, using a spirit level to ensure it is straight. If not, and the ceiling is slightly bowed, plane the length to fit. Retaining the horizontal level line, pin the lengths down the wall to the floor. The final piece must be cut or planed lengthwise to fit flush, and panel moldings added to finish. Alternatively, you could stop just below the level of the baseboard. In this case, pin short off-cuts onto the remainder of the cleating, down to floor level, and reposition the baseboard, nailing through the off-cuts onto the cleats.

Plywood paneling

This kind of wallcovering gives you an opportunity to explore the concept of paneling further, either by matching the veneered surfaces and the woodstrips, using a stock such as beech, or by using a mix of different woods to make up the wall area and running different water-based stains into the grain.

Plywood ¼ in./6 mm thick can be found in a variety of finishes, from fairly crude exterior grades to one-sided, hardwood-veneered interior panels. You can buy sheets of 8 x 4 ft./2440 x 1220 mm and have it machine cut to size. Alternatively, you can purchase smaller panels of 6 x 2 ft/1827 x 607 mm or 4 x 2 ft./1220 x 607 mm. The smaller sizes are made for home improvement purposes and are consequently more expensive, but usually have a good veneered finish. The concept is to produce a wall that looks like old-fashioned paneling, but at a fraction of the cost. This style is very effective in study rooms and home offices, giving your home-based business center the appearance of a traditional library.

Positioning and centering

Sheet paneling must be pinned into position on cleats, in the same manner as TGV lengths. This time, however, the cleats must form a horizontal and vertical grid, making an identical grid to the finished panel work. The reason is that when the finishing strips are pinned through the veneered sheet onto the wall cleats, all board joints will be hidden under the strips. The grid you choose can be to any dimensions that suit your purpose or the wall effect you desire, provided the cleats and finishing strips line up and the joints are concealed.

Cleating

Attach 2 x 1 in./50 x 25 mm cleats to the wall, using 2 in./50 mm number 8 screws and countersinking. Masonry nails can be used if the wall is bare brick. Vertical cleats must be positioned so that

Although plywood is a very functional material, with a bit of imagination and effort, it can be transformed into stylish wall paneling.

ainted paneling offers a simple nd effective means of concealing lavatory tank.

neir centers coincide with the oints between boards: for xample, a board machine cut ft./2440 mm/8 ft. x 607 mm vide requires a cleat enterpoint 2 ft./607 mm from he starting wall edge. The orizontal cleat centerpoints re the same, and the ft./2440 mm edge will fall in he middle of one. You will eed to decide whether your aneling design should be entered on one wall, or could urn one corner to partly clad he next. Whatever the imension of the vertical cleat spacing, replicate it exactly when ositioning the horizontals, so that the finishing strips which onceal the joints form a pattern of a square.

inishing

Vhen the cleat grid is complete, check the system for accuracy by olding up a board, making sure the joints will be covered. Mark he position of the grid on the face of the board with a carpentry encil. Apply panel adhesive to the cleat grid, and pin the veneered sheet into position with ¾ in./18 mm brads, punching flush with the surface. Position the remaining boards. Following your marks on the surface, draw the grid again to act as a guide for the finishing strips to make up the squares. Glue and pin the strips into position using 1 in./25 mm molding pins. Some 2 x ½ in. /50 x 12 mm vertical strips with butt-joined horizontals will give a square, right-angled finish, but it is worth attempting a molded panel finish. Try a finishing strip size of 1 x ½ in./25 x 12.mm centered over the cleats, butt-joined as before, forming squares. Select a small decorative panel molding, no larger than 1 x ½ in./25 x 12 mm, and cut and miter to size to fit the inside angles of each individual square. Glue and pin at an angle into the cleat with ¾ in./18 mm molding pins.

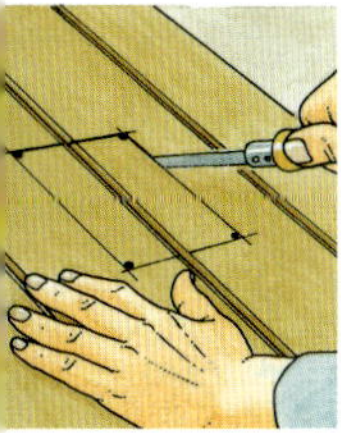

o make a cut-out for a switch, drill small hole at each corner and join hem with a keyhole saw.

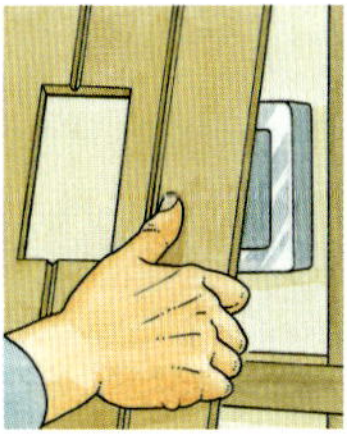

Fit cleats around the switch mounting box and hold up the panel; pin it in place.

Wall fixings

Wall switches and outlets that are not proud of the wall surface must be replaced with surface boxes. But first, isolate electrical fittings from the supply before working on them. Fix cleats in a square around the box, and measure the position of the box relative to your panel and its dimensions. Mark this with a pencil, then drill a pilot hole in one corner. Cut out the shape with a keyhole saw, and secure the panel, ensuring that the cut hole fits over the surface box. Fit the cover plate, so that it overlaps neatly.

Adjustable room-height shelving

You can customize your shelving to suit your individual household requirements with this entirely versatile scheme. Constructed simply from the same wood stock, it can form part of a paneling project, or be fixed directly to a decorated wall surface. Any varnished wood finish can be used to match a room scheme.

If planned and measured accurately, different cleat grids fixed to a wall can serve as a secure base for a variety of projects. Using this grid, a shelving system can run at right angles to the vertical paneling and can perform functional or decorative duties. An advantage is that all wood stock is the same size, 2 x 1 in./50 x 25 mm, so you can buy in bulk from a lumberyard. The system has been devised to support 5 in./127 mm wide shelves, but, if this is too wide, it can easily be revised to accept 4 in./100 mm shelves that will still hold paperbacks and decorative objects. Simply cut the slot-in shelf supports to 4 in./100 mm rather than 5 in./127 mm. Any number of shelf uprights can be incorporated into this versatile scheme, depending on the length of the shelves that will complete the wall. Reckon on one support for every seven TGV uprights, if using 3½ in./90 mm paneling, which gives a support every 25 in./630 mm. Aim to space out and fix the wall cleats (see vertical paneling project, page 114). Plug the wall even if you have bare brick, because of the weight the uprights might have to take. Use number 8 countersunk 2 in./50 mm steel screws, butting short horizontal lengths between the floor to the ceiling shelf-support cleats. All cleats should be 2 x 1 in./50 x 25 mm, which is the same size as the shelf-support pieces.

Shelving supports

This system employs two sizes of vertical support, screwed to the face of the wall support, creating a gap, into which the horizontal pieces that will support the shelf are slotted. For each upright you will need wood pieces cut from the same stock 5 in./127 mm long positioned starting from flush top, leaving ¾ in./18 mm dividing gaps as you progress down the length. These pieces are secured by center drilling 1½ in./38 mm from the bottom edge, and screwing through to the upright using 1¼ in./32 mm/number 8—raised—countersunk head brass screws and seatings. This gives a screw finish resembling a brass stud. A second layer of support pieces is needed only where the shelf supports are to be slotted in; 3 in./76 mm pieces are thus screwed flush with the top of the designated 5 in./127 mm pieces by center drilling 1½ in./38 mm from the bottom edge in exactly the same way as before. Slot in

This versatile adjustable shelving system can be installed on its own or as part of a wall cladding system. It is constructed from simple 2 x 1 in./50 x 25 mm softwood cleats.

the shelf support horizontals, which are also 5 in./127 mm pieces, to check the fit in the slot and to see if they hold a spirit-levelled shelf correctly. When you are happy with everything, sand all the pieces lightly to remove sharp edges and any splinters. For added strength, you can glue as well as screw the pieces together.

Finishing the wall

Now that the shelving system is complete, invisibly pin the TGV uprights to the horizontal cleats. Seven should fit snugly between the uprights. You may need to file to fit wall edges. The join at the TGV can be expanded slightly to take up a minor shortfall. The wood can be varnished with the finish of your choice, as can the shelving uprights and support pieces, and a baseboard added if desired. Finally, the shelf supports can be slotted into place. The shelves are intended to be cut from 5 x 1 in./127 x 25 mm lumber, to the length of your wall. However, shorter cut lengths in groups or seemingly random positioning can be equally pleasing to the eye in this versatile scheme.

Lay out the 5 in./127 mm long pieces of wood on the wall support cleat. It is advisable to space them with the shelf cleats in order to ensure a tight fit.

The next stage is to cramp and then screw the sections of timber to the support batten. For this you should use countersunk-head brass screws and screw seats.

Attach the 3 in./76 mm lengths of cleat to the first lengths in the same manner, flush with the top edge. You should use countersunk-head brass screws and seats as before.

Finally, check the fit of the shelf support battens in their slots. It is important that the fit is exact; if the shelf supports are loose, the shelf will not be stable.

Wood ceilings

Wooden ceilings look wonderful, particularly in older houses, cottage-style properties, and unusually shaped rooms. Converted lofts with roof windows as a natural light source and interestingly shaped shadow areas can show off quality lumber to great advantage. And you can either paint the wood or use a natural finish to show the texture.

Shiplap or TGV matchings can be used on ceilings, in much the same way as they are on walls. Cleating supports are used as before, and light fittings should present no difficulty. Varnished wooden ceilings can have a crown molding surround, similar to a cornice, and even a ceiling light fitting cut to a plain circle or a wavy-edged design with a coping saw. The ceiling will appear, and in fact be, lower. The wood finish will advance toward the eye, and physically it will be 1¼ in./32 mm closer, that measurement being the depth of the lumber.

Two difficulties you may encounter are locating the joists (hidden ceiling beams) to which you fix the cleats, and the fact that all the fixing work goes on over your head.

To locate the joists, measure accurately from the floor above. If it is the loft, and the wood beams are exposed, your task is straightforward; otherwise, you must lift a floorboard. Note the direction of run, measure the distance between joist centers, and draw the positions onto the ceiling. If you are unable to reach the joists from above, the only solution is to tap the ceiling with a screwdriver handle and listen for the sound to change from a hollow ring to a solid tone. When you think you have found a joist, probe with an awl to check. Decide which way the TGV is to run, and hold up a first cleat length (cut to size) at right angles to that direction. Mark the drilling centers with an awl, and drill the cleats on the bench to accept 3 in./76 mm countersunk number 8 screws. Mount the cleats on the ceiling, and invisibly pin the TGV through the tongues as described above. You will need to isolate the light fitting from the electrical supply and remove it. Cut a hole in the wood and thread the wires through, reassembling and repositioning on the finished side of the wood length. Cornicing or crown molding, if desired, should be wall-mounted, butting up to the new ceiling.

When teamed with exposed roof beams, a TGV ceiling provides an interesting decorative feature.

Adequate support for the boards is essential, as their combined weight will be considerable.

In this loft room TGV runs at right angles to the rafters.

Storage units can be incorporated to make the most of the space.

oft areas

xtending your living space up into the roof is a reasonably conomical proposition compared with alternatives like ground xtensions, conservatories, and moving to a bigger house. Although ›ft conversions must be left to a qualified builder, the decorative nishing is in your hands. Consider a wood finish for the inside of ne loft. TGV fixed horizontally across the rafters not only trengthens the entire roof structure, but also gives a natural, elaxed feel to the area.

Have your builder tackle all structural work, leaving the roof rea as a shell. The roof needs to be lined inside by ³⁄₈ in./10 mm hick wallboard first. Use a board with metallized polyester on one ide as an insulator, which should face the rafters. Mark their

Iake a feature of the board fixings y using screws and screw washers ather than nails.

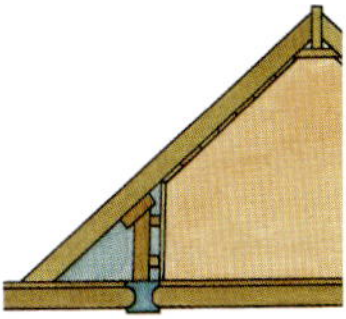

Boards can be fixed horizontally across the rafters and vertically to cleats attached to the studs.

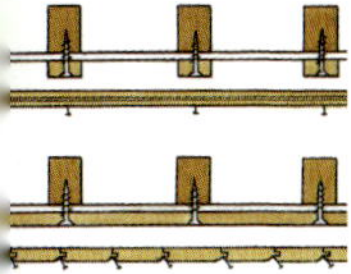

stablish the direction of ceiling oists before deciding on the nethod of cleat attachment.

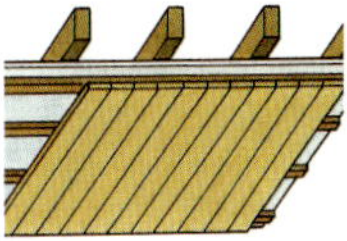

Regardless of the direction of the boards, the support cleats must always be at right-angles to them.

›ositions in pencil as you go. Fix it in place with wallboard nails, sing as few as you can get away with. With the insulation in lace, line the roof area with TGV, starting at the apex and working lown to the short vertical support studs tied into the rafters. Fix he wood with 1½ in/38 mm number 8 brass screws with screw washers. Screw them through the insulating plasterboard to the marked rafters. These screws have the appearance of studs, creating an almost marine feel. Loft window recesses can be lined with wood, and chamfered or decorative crown molding can be used as an internal lining border. The short vertical support studs hide the eaves storage space.

To provide access, a small door needs to be made up to fit, preferably in the same style as the TGV paneling work. TGV can be run horizontally each side of this access. If the insulation is continued on the inside of the rafters down to joist level, inside the eaves' space, then invisible pinning directly onto the studs is best. However, if the studs carry the insulation, then you must screw the TGV into position as you did on the rafters.

Wood paneling is an excellent means of providing finished wall/ceiling surfaces in lofts and can make use of much of the roof support structure. It is also ideal for lightweight partitioning.

Loft floor

If you intend opting for this type of wood finish, it is a good idea to ask your builder to fit a chipboard floor. A natural fiber woven floorcovering is the perfect finishing touch, fitted so that the floor is not seen. This solves the problem of wood overkill, which would result if wood were used to floor the loft, and because chipboard is a great deal cheaper than wooden floorboards, this option is economical too. Make sure you have access to underfloor services, however.

Basic skills: brick

An exposed brick finish on one wall, often the chimney breast, adds a new visual dimension to a room. The bond appears as a geometric pattern, and can be at its most effective complementing natural wood paneling, or a flagstone or tiled floor. But first it is a good idea to get to know the kinds of bricks available.

You don't need a bricklayer's skills when decorating or refurbishing the rooms of a structurally sound property. However, a knowledge of brick types and their use, pointing, and applying mortar is useful. It will also help if you can recognize bonds (bricklaying patterns) and the different types of mortar joints you could use, should you decide to take a plaster or wallboard wall back to the brick. Although the same basic principles apply to walls constructed of stone, the irregular formation of a stone wall requires only that you examine the quality of the construction and check the gaps and crevices that need filling.

Bricks

You may encounter three types of brick as you investigate what your house is made of.

Facing bricks

These are well made, and they often have a textured finish that allows their use as an exposed internal wall.

Common bricks

These have no special finish, and are intended to be covered, usually by plaster. They can be identified by their mottled pinkish appearance.

Engineering bricks

These are super-smooth and are often used as waterproof, nonabsorbent foundation courses due to their density and strength.

If you think an exposed brick wall will add to the character of your room, investigate the type of brick and the bond pattern before starting work, because normally only an outside or load-bearing wall will be suitable. Carefully remove a small patch of plaster from the wall, using a flooring chisel and mallet to reveal the bricks. If they are consistent with the rest of the house, the bond is uniformly well laid, and the mortar is it a regular depth, the wall is suitable. If you find pink common bricks that are badly laid and inconsistent with the house finish, stud walls where brick debris is laid between wooden uprights, or lightweight, perforated, or dense solid blocks, do not proceed—this wall was never meant to be seen. Your only option is to repair the exploratory hole in the plaster and rethink your plan.

Removing plaster

Assuming your wall is suitable, remove the plaster with a flooring chisel as before. This is a dirty, dusty process, so wear protective clothing, eye protection, and a dustmask. At the top of the wall carry down lumps of plaster if you can, but don't drop them. Try to remove smaller pieces directly into a garbage bag. This will keep the amount of dust to a minimum. Remove the baseboard and clean up around the base of the wall. A cornice needs care; cut in with a small flooring chisel directly underneath and proceed very carefully; a stable molding (one that is not cracked) should remain in position as you remove the plaster below it, even though you will damage the bottom curve slightly. Repair and smooth off the bottom edge of the molding as soon as possible. It will be ultra-absorbent, so a solution of water-diluted PVA should be applied, wetting the edge. Leave this to dry, repeat the process, and carefully smooth off with multifinish plaster. It is not a good idea to use joint compound in this situation, because it isn't strong enough.

Glass bricks can be used in external and internal walls as a means of letting light pass through, but without the clarity of a normal window. They are normally square in shape.

The parts of a standard brick

The various faces of a brick have specific names. The stretcher face is the long side; the header face the end; the frog is the recessed upper face; and the bed face is the flat bottom. Bricks are laid frog-up, although the top course may be laid frog-down in a garden wall to provide a flat finished surface.

Cleaning down

As the plaster repairing the cornice starts to dry, wash the wall down with warm water, beginning where the plaster ties the cornice into the brick, achieving a smooth line. Continue down the wall, washing away the surface dust to reveal the state of the brick pointing, and leave the wall to dry out. If the wall is absorbent, or the surface of the brickwork is flaky or floury, brush on a coat of masonry stabilizer. This solution has an unpleasant, sticky finish. Always wear gloves and protect your eyes from splashes.

Pointing the wall

Now you have revealed the bare brick face of a plastered wall. At best the mortar joints will be roughly and haphazardly finished, and probably recessed slightly. For this wall to become a "display" surface, it needs pointing and shaped, decorative mortar joints. Pointing compresses the original mortar and waterproofs the brick joints when used on an external wall. For an internal wall compression and angular decoration are the aims.

Preparation

Assuming you have washed down, and stabilised the surface if necessary, make room for the new pointing by raking out the old, crumbling mortar to a depth of 1in/25mm. You will need a cold chisel for this, preferably a plugging chisel with a slanted head, sometimes with a groove cut into it, to clear out the waste faster. You may find a highly useful tool known as a seaming or chasing chisel or seam drill. If you use a chasing bit in a power drill for this task, particularly if it has hammer action, take care not to damage the brick corners because any damage done to the bricks now will spoil the effect of displaying the wall.

Mortar—proportions and mixing

Knocking up a mortar mix may seem simple, but accurate measuring is vital. Proportions are designated by volume, not by weight, so use a bucket. Don't be tempted to "measure" by using a spade as a yardstick; this is only guesswork because sand and cement will not "sit" on the spade the same way. Avoid the use of dishwashing liquid instead of a plasticizer. A liquid plasticizer is a liquid air entraining admixture that forms air bubbles in the final

The four main types of bond

English bond
The courses of bricks alternate stretcher-on and header-on.

Flemish bond
Bricks in each course alternate header-on and stretcher-on.

Header bond
Bricks in every course are laid header-on, the wall being a full brick wide.

Running bond
Bricks in every course are laid stretcher-on, the wall being half a brick wide.

Left: Raking out with a plugging chisel.

leasure out the correct amounts of and and cement. Accuracy is ssential for strong mortar.

Adding plasticizer to the mix will make it more workable and prevent cracking as it dries.

Turn the ingredients over dry until they are mixed completely. Form a crater in the middle of the pile.

Gradually add water to the crater and mix well. Take care not to make it too sloppy.

The mix is correct when it holds ridges formed by chopping the spade across it.

Fill the vertical joints first, using the tip of the pointing trowel to form a neat profile.

Finish off by pointing the horizontal joints, creating your preferred decorative profile.

nix. These bubbles are spaces nto which the water expands, topping cracks appearing. 'lasticizers are available from uilders' merchants in multiples f 1 quart (1 liter). Add to your and and cement mix in the uantity specified on the ontainer. Traditionally, ydrated lime was used as an dditive. It made the mix more vorkable and smoother, etarded the setting time, and prevented shrinkage. Lime is still in se, but plasticizers that do the same job have become more opular. Use soft sand, also called builders' sand, and regular ortland cement in a mix of 5½:1, plus plasticizer, if you buy eparate ingredients. Otherwise use a dry ready-mix and add lasticizer, or a dry masonry mix (containing plasticizer) and add and. Carefully measure the correct proportions, and blend the dry nix well, using a 10 in./25 cm bricklayer's trowel. You will need bout the same amount of water as cement. Add the correct mount of plasticizer, and pour half the water into a crater in the niddle of the dry mix. Mix from the outside inward, slowly filling n the crater, adding more water as absorption takes place and urning the mixture several times. When you can chop firm, mooth fillets into the surface with the trowel, the mix is ready.

On the hawk

Jse a small brush to dampen the recessed joints with water. Attend to only a small area at a time or the joints will dry out. Put ome mortar on a hawk (plasterer's square board), select a slither with the pointing trowel edge, and draw it into the vertical, then horizontal joint. Flush pointing is finished with the side of the trowel; vee or struck pointing with a backward sliding action of the trowel point; concave pointing with the trowel handle or similar, and recessed pointing by pressing a sized length of wood into the joint. For internal joints, concave pointing shows off the bricks to advantage, and flush pointing is a good idea if the brick edges and corners are damaged. Recessed pointing should only be attempted on brickwork in near-perfect condition, and weatherstruck finishes are, as the name implies, for external walls.

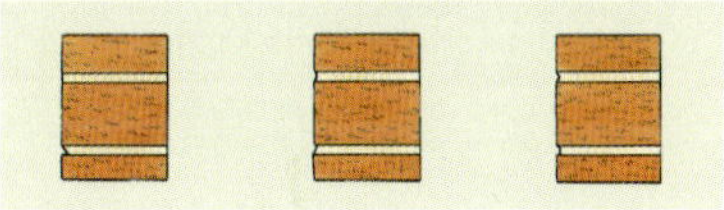

Top joint: flush pointing
Bottom joint: struck pointing

Top joint: concave pointing
Bottom joint: weatherstruck pointing

Top joint: vee pointing
Bottom joint: recessed pointing

Tools and equipment

Tools for brickwork and wall surfaces can be categorized as implements of either destruction or construction, in the form of breaking and shaping tools, such as brick chisels and masons' chisels, measuring and mixing tools, and application and finishing tools. A few may already be in your general tool kit, but most will have to be bought specifically for the job.

Remove old plaster or render with a bolster or mason's chisel, driven by a mallet weighing at least 2½ lb. /1 kg. Lesser weights will cause vibrations, making the chisel difficult to control. A crowbar will be needed if a fireplace has to be taken out.

Chop out old mortar with a plugging chisel. Clean the wall with a large paint brush and wet the joint areas with a small paint brush. Measure out your materials in a bucket, or a small plastic container depending on the required amount, mix them with a bricklayer's trowel on a mixing or spot mortarboard, and carry smaller amounts to the job on a bat or hawk.

Ensure the wall is plumb and level with a spirit level and plumb line. Use a pointing trowel to insert slivers of mortar and finish joints. Render or plaster larger areas with a plasterer's trowel, use a straightedge for leveling the floating coat, and obtain a flat finish by polishing the area with a wooden float. Damp down the wall and splash water on the trowel with a brush.

TOP TIP

Always consider your personal safety before starting building work. Bags of sand are heavy and must be lifted correctly, the legs taking the weight, to reduce the chance of a back injury. Wear protective shoes or boots, safety glasses to keep flying debris and dust out of your eyes, a dust mask, gloves, and knee pads, which are invaluable if you are spending time scrabbling about on the floor knocking up mortar.

Buying materials

Buying in bulk is generally more economical than buying small amounts because storing items for future use reduces the unit price. Materials that degrade, however, become a liability. Cement bought in a 55 lb. (25 kg) pack is not economical if you have to throw three-quarters of it away, which will happen if it gets even slightly damp. A cement binder sets by water action, and must be completely dry when mixing starts.

Storing badly sealed, partly used packs on concrete floors, in cellars or in outbuildings is pointless. A better proposition is available from home centers, in the form of dry ready-mixes, sand and cement prepacked in quantities of 11 lb. (5 kg), and multiples thereof. Be sure to pick the correct pre-mix.

Bricklayers' mortar mix contains the soft sand you need for pointing. A sand-and-cement mix for general use, like flooring screeds, will contain sharp sand, which is not suitable. Plasticizers to add to the mix come in powder and liquid form. Usually the liquid is easier to measure and use, and is available in quart (liter) containers.

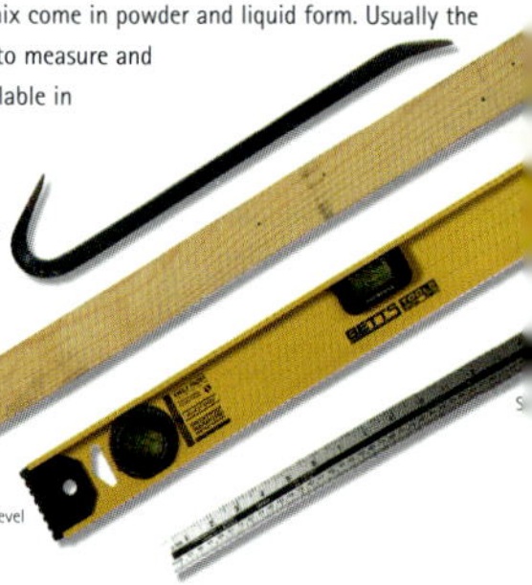

Basic tool kit

Plastering

You may never need to plaster an entire wall in your property, but a knowledge of basic techniques is useful. Different plaster types and their uses, preparation and application onto a wall are not trade secrets, nor is the use of the hawk and trowel. Practice can improve your technique and make smaller "patching" jobs and improving parts of a wall surface easier.

Preparation and plaster types

Absorbent old brick walls draw water out of a plaster coat too quickly, resulting in severe cracking. Absorbency can be tested by brushing on water. If it disappears immediately, it is a high-suction surface. If it sits on the surface or partly runs off, it is a low-suction surface. For jobs around the house, coating the wall with water-diluted PVA will seal and stabilize the surface. Walls should be damp prior to plastering, and smooth surfaces must be roughened or "keyed." Mixed plaster is applied to the wall surface in two consecutive coats. First, apply a thick backing or floating coat, known as bonding. Follow this within two hours by a thin skim coat, known as the finish. Don't confuse the finishing skim with thistle board finish, which is a single skim coat for use on wallboard partition walls.

Remove all old plaster by hacking it off with a hammer and flooring chisel. Wear eye protection to guard against flying particles. This is a very dirty and dusty process, so protect adjacent surfaces.

Test the suction of the wall by brushing on water. Choose a plaster to suit.

Nail timber cleats, known as "grounds", to the wall to provide a guide to the depth of plaster.

Mix the plaster with water in a bucket; a mixing attachment in an electric drill speeds the job.

Practice lifting plaster from the hawk until you are happy that you can do it well.

lold the hawk close to the wall nd scoop the plaster from it nto the wall with the trowel.

Spread the plaster up the wall, keeping the lower edge of the blade pressed in.

Key the backing coat by scoring the plaster surface as it begins to set. Spread on a thin finish coat (a thinner plaster), working from the bottom of the wall to the top.

/lixing

ı a bucket, mix equal amounts f water and plaster. Crumble ny lumps, and wait while the laster absorbs the water. Stir vell. The backing coat should be tiff. The finish should be hinner, and easier to work. mpty the bucket onto your pot board and knead the mix ıto ridges with a plasterer's rowel. The bonding should hold he ridges, but the finish should be slightly too liquid to do so.

Look for any gaps, hollows and imperfections in the surface and fill with more plaster.

)n the hawk

'osition the hawk under the spot board, and push some plaster nto it with the trowel. Hold your trowel at right angles to the awk, and push the plaster mound away from you, while tilting the awk upright. Scrape the trowel up the surface and off, loading he plaster onto the trowel ready for application onto the wall.

)n the wall

he required depth of plaster is usually marked out on the wall by vood cleats, called grounds, stuck or nailed to the wall. Cleats hould be about ½ in./12 mm thick, and spaced roughly yard/meter apart. Plaster between them and, when the bonding oat has partially set, remove a cleat and reposition it farther long the wall. Continue the plaster up to the cleat, repeating the rocess until the wall is covered. Start the plaster at the base of he wall, hold the hawk against the right-hand wood ground, and scoop the plaster onto the wall, with the bottom edge of the trowel on the cleat, tilting up. Push the trowel up the wall slowly to unload the plaster, spreading it evenly. Subsequent plaster loads can be spread parallel to the first, keeping to the same thickness throughout, until the whole area between the grounds is covered. A straightedge resting on the two grounds will scrape off excess plaster. As the backing coat sets, it needs to be keyed to accept the finish coat. You can do this by scratching the surface lightly with a couple of nails hammered through a wood off-cut.

Skimming

The finishing coat comprises thinner plaster. This is spread onto the wall from bottom to top in a thin coating. Work an area you can easily reach in one arm movement, trowelling evenly. Return to the starting position, and apply a second, thinner coat over the top. Cover the wall in this way. Dip the trowel blade in water, hold it at an angle to the surface, skim off any splashes, and leave it to harden. Polish the wall to a flat finish with the trowel surface.

Wall tiles

If you think wall tiles are suitable only for kitchens and bathrooms, think again. There is now a tile for every purpose and situation, be it decorative or protective. There is an amazingly diverse choice, and you can stick tiles on tables and cabinets, in alcoves, and on storage shelves.

Ceramic tiles have been used as wall decoration for centuries, as these classical designs show.

Choosing wall tiles

The history of tiles can be traced farther back than the birth of Christ, to the eastern Mediterranean and beyond. Early techniques of ceramic decoration were carried from the shores of this sea to North Africa and Western Europe, where an important center was established in the Netherlands. Stone, marble, and glass, particularly in mosaic form, were features of Roman buildings, and many of their decorations are preserved on historical sites today.

An interest in this history has led many independent designers to experiment in limited editions of distinctive hand-made tiles. Now tiles for wall decoration and protection can be chosen from an array of glazed and unglazed ceramic, glass, iridescent glass, mirrored glass, mosaic, stoneware, relief, metallic, and cork.

Small independent workshops have abandoned the familiar sizes too: just about any dimension and proportion can be found or ordered. For example, a tile range of 3 x 6 in./7.5 x 15 cm is available, which was inspired by London subway stations. A happy compromise between the old imperial 4¼ in. (10.8 cm) and 6 in. (15 cm) square choices is found at 5 x 5 in./13 x 13 cm. As a consequence, it is a better idea to select tiles before working out areas, as hand-made designs can differ in their dimensions.

Whatever tile size you favor, you will find that the border tile, glazed over two edges, and used at the edges or corners of the wall design, is no longer made. Today's universal tiles or square edge tiles have at least two edges finished and glazed, so that they can be placed either in the middle of a tile run, or at a corner. These tiles were often called field tiles in the past and were fitted with spacing lugs at each edge. Now, they have either a universal joining system based on beveled edges, which butt at the base, or are squared up and require separate spacers. In both cases the resultant surface gap is then filled with grout.

A backsplash behind a washbasin is the ideal first project in tiling. By combining tiles with different patterns and colors, you can creat an eye-catching decorative featur that is practical too.

Practical and decorative uses

Kitchen areas, bathrooms, shower and backsplashes are traditiona places for tiling. A vast range is available today to replace or upgrade your existing finish. Don't neglect other areas, though. Handcrafted tile sets complete with a choice of matching or contrasting border tiles and a ceramic chair rail will give a traditional welcome to your visitors in the entrance hall.

Windowsills and casings that receive a lot of light will look better if you fix tiles that do not reflect it. Try a finish quality similar to stone, containing muted, subdued colors with an almost satin-like sheen. Stoneware tiles are also suitable for work surface ı kitchens; they can often provide an attractive alternative ɔ dreary mass-produced worktops. Their slightly uneven ɹrface causes imperfection in color and variation, which reaks up large areas visually. In a food preparation area, owever, you will need a waterproof adhesive and a special rout, for hygienic reasons.

ilass tiles

n smaller areas of wall, such as backsplashes, wafer-thin metal esigns that are sandwiched between layers of glass give a articularly unusual light effect, with the colors in the metals

'iles are perfect in a kitchen, ɔroviding a hard-wearing, hygienic ɹurface for walls and worktops.

Use them on large areas such as walls or backsplashes behind basins and work surfaces.

ppearing almost lost inside their tile. Glass is transparent, so the le adhesive must be evenly applied on a good, flat surface. If you se a notched spreader, the ridges will show through.

For partitioning off small areas without reducing the light ɜvels, try glass blocks. They can be bought as a kit, which includes pacers, reinforcing rods, and mortar. The last can be colored to ppear as a grid.

It is important to remember, however, that glass blocks ɜnd to be heavy and will therefore need to be positioned on a substantial foundation. They cannot be built onto a suspended vooden floor.

Cork tiles

Cork has been around a long time, mainly as thin floor tiles. However, it is unsuitable for flooring because it is easily damaged by heels and heavy furniture. It will serve well on a complete wall surface, though, or as part of a half-and-half wall. Thick cork tiles (about ½ in./12 mm thick) make a good studio or home office pinboard. You can apply them to form a square or make a shape out of the tiles, then edge them with mitered wooden cleats.

Contemporary tiles

Tools and equipment

A number of items needed for tiling will be used for other jobs and so may be in your tool kit already. Some of them are "homemade," such as the tiling gauge or marker. Starter kits available from home centers may supply all you need for small tiling jobs and the more expensive items, like tile-cutting jigs, can be rented.

Starter kits

If you are contemplating just a simple tiling job on a straight wall, it may only be necessary to buy a tiling starter kit, comprising:

- a tile snap cutter and nipper
- a tile edge sander
- adhesive spreader
- tile spacers
- a grout spreader and finisher.

More advanced kits are available; they include:

- tile-cutting machines that incorporate a measuring guide
- angle jig, which works with universal or square-edged tiles.

Ceramic tiles are cut by simple "pencil" scorers, fitted into a tile cutting guide if required, or by a heavy-duty cutter and nipper with a tungsten carbide wheel. In both cases the scored tile is

Tile cutter

snapped over a match or thin edging strip. Cutting machines with measuring guides and heavy-duty cutting machines capable of cutting tiles up to $\frac{3}{4}$ in./18 mm thick are ideal for large jobs. Tile files will keep the edges smooth, and a tile saw with a tungsten carbide blade will cut in any direction. This will prove essential when pipework must be tiled around. Tile nippers nibble out odd shapes and sizes. Space and plan using tile spacers, a tile gauge and marker cleats, a spirit level, a retractable steel tape, a pencil (for the wall), waterproof pen (for the tile), and hammer and masonry nails to attach the battens. Painter's tape will be useful for holding insert tiles (like soap dishes) in position while the adhesive sets. Adhesive and grout are supplied in ready-to-use plastic containers, often with the required spreader. Use water-resistant adhesive and grout where tiles may be splashed, but in shower stalls and sunken bathtub surrounds a waterproof adhesiv and grout are needed. Worktops need a special two-part epoxy resin grout if they are to be used for food preparation. If one is nc provided with the adhesive, you will need a notched plastic spreader. For large areas, use a notched trowel. A grout remover, flexible spreader, and finisher will complete the job. Keep a supply of cloths for cleaning and polishing to hand at all times.

Tile scorer, pencil, and waterproof pe

Retractable rule

Tile saw

Tile spacers

Spirit level

Adhesives and cloths

Motorized tile cutter

Cork tiles do not require any pecial tools for cutting. A sharp raft knife, steel straightedge, nd accurate measuring are all hat are needed when using in/12 mm cork. A special ready-to-se water-based adhesive with a notched applicator binds the tiles the wall. Wooden cleat frames used as a decorative border for hese tiles also protect the vulnerable outside edges from damage. inished lumber ½ x 1¾ in./12 x 42 mm can be bought in acks, and will fit the edge depth. You will need to miter the orners to fit. Secure the cleats to the wall with 1¼ in./30 mm umber 8 countersunk head screws. You can easily disguise the eads by overlaying the same lumber size ½ in./12 mm to the nside, overlapping the cork edge, and pinning or gluing it into osition. If you are using cork floor tiles on a wall for a decorative ffect, you can apply polyurethane varnish as a sealing finish, or mply leave them unsealed.

Heavy-duty snips and cutter

Notched spreader

Bucket

Cloths

Sponge

Tile side nippers

Masonry nails

Curved-claw hammer

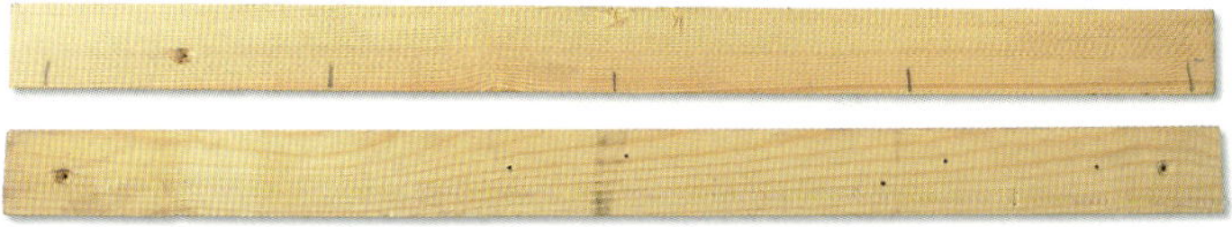

Homemade tiling gauge and cleat

Basic skills: preparation

Grout lines between tiles form very obvious geometric patterns and are often emphasised by colored grouts for decorative purposes. For this reason you need to be sure that the patterning will fit square to the walls. Thus accurate measuring and marking out are vital, for nothing looks worse than sloping tiling.

Preparing surfaces

As with all decorating jobs, the eventual finish will only be as good as the preparation, so examine the surface carefully. It must be flat and sound, and clean and dry without being too absorbent. Bare plaster surfaces are ideal, but if they are porous, they will draw moisture from the adhesive very quickly, and the tiles will become loose. Brush on a coat of stabilizing primer or a diluted PVA solution. If the plaster is unsound or cracked in part, then it must be filled. Rake out all loose material and brush the surface down well. Coat the area with diluted PVA as before, to stabilize the cracked edges, before making good the damage. New plaster must dry out completely, and an entire wall should be left for about six weeks before a stabilizing solution is brushed on.

Man-made boards present no problem, provided their surfaces are sealed and dirt, grease, and fingermarks are cleaned off. Wallboard is likely to be found as a wall surface. If you are erecting your own, use the rougher side of the board as an outer surface because it will provide a better "key." Smooth, man-made worktops will need abrading by hand or with an orbital sander.

All sound, previously painted surfaces need is a "key" for the adhesive, but flaking paint must be removed. Never attempt to tile on top of wallpaper, no matter how well it appears to adhere. You must strip the surface and treat the bare plaster as described above.

Previously tiled surfaces are a good base for new tiles, but, as usual, the surface must be sound. Stick down any loose tiles, and clean the whole surface thoroughly. It is not necessary to fill small cracks or defects because the new adhesive will span any gaps. Bare brick and rough concrete walls will be uneven and need to be treated as you would floor surfaces. You need to level the surface using a cement render and then set the tiles in a thick bedding adhesive.

Tiled surfaces are traditional for bathrooms. In this instance oblong tiles have been laid with an overlapping bond much like brickwork, rather than the usual grid layout.

stimating, marking, and setting out

ne number of tiles needed to cover a wall area depends on their imensions. Manufacturers issue tables showing the number of tandard sized tiles needed to cover a specific area. For example, 2 tiles of 4¼ x 4¼ in./108 x 108 mm are needed to cover a square ard, 86 of them to fill a square meter. However, with the vailability of limited edition and hand-made tiles of varying sizes n the market, it is a much better idea to make your own alculation from a homemade measuring gauge.

Select your tile and two lengths of (straight) wooden cleating. Aark out the tile positions on the cleats with a pencil, emembering to include the grout lines, for the horizontal and ertical rows. If your chosen tile is square, then one tiling auge will suffice. Place the gauge against the wall and count ne number of tiles in each direction, then multiply the

Aark a guide line for the horizontal upport cleat a tile's height above he baseboard.

Check the adjoining wall for plumb with a spirit level. If it is vertical, you can use it as a tiling guide.

orizontal number by the vertical number. Always add a few xtra tiles to guard against mishaps, such as breakages and utting errors.

Now that you have worked out the numbers, consider your next nove carefully, because it is crucial. Tiling must start in the correct osition on the wall, and lines must be level and plumb, not ecessarily following baseboards or door frames. Set out and mark he wall area using the tiling gauge to plan exactly where omplete tiles will lie, and where you will need to cut to size. On a lain wall, start in the middle, but if the wall has a window or a oor, it is a good idea to center the tile layout on the opening, so hat the pattern formed by the tiles does not make the room seem nbalanced. Move the starting point if necessary.

When you have decided on your starting position, check the walls for square with a spirit level and plumb line. If the baseboard is a true level, it can be used as a starting point; otherwise, nail on a support cleat so that it is level, its top edge just under a tile height from the baseboard, or from the floor if the baseboard is not part of your plan. That way you can accommodate any unevenness in the baseboard or floor by cutting tiles to fit the gap between it and the first row of whole tiles.

At the tile vertical line nearest to the corner, nail a vertical cleat; place a loose tile at the right-angled join to confirm accuracy. These cleats support the tiles while the adhesive sets. Use masonry nails to fix the cleats in place, but don't knock them all the way in because you will need to pull them out later with a claw hammer and remove the cleats. The remaining gaps are filled with cut tiles.

Otherwise, nail a vertical cleat to the wall in line with the last whole tile position before the corner.

Check the baseboard with a spirit level; if truly horizontal you can use it as a tiling guide.

Otherwise, nail a horizontal cleat to the wall as a support for the first row of tiles.

Check that the two cleats meet at an exact right-angle by holding a tile in the corner.

Basic tiling

Tiling is not a difficult skill to master, but if you've not done any before, it's a good idea to start with a small, simple "squared-up" area, such as a wall splashback behind a basin. When you are happy with an elementary project, you will have the confidence to move on to a more taxing job involving corners and cuts.

Basin backsplash

The easiest way to get used to tiling surfaces is to start with a basin backsplash. All you have to do is center the tile design over the basin, and make sure that it is level.

Measure up one tile height from where the basin joins the wall, and mark a level line with a pencil—don't assume the basin is square or level.

Use your tile gauge, resting on the pencil line, to find the center, and mark the tile grid on the wall. Then nail on a support cleat, with the top edge butting the pencil line. Cover the marked area with adhesive (a notched spreader is usually supplied with the tub), applying firm pressure against the wall. You need to make even, equal ridges over the tiling area, so that the tiles sit uniformly when positioned. Use a twisting action of the wrist to press the tiles into place, separating them with small plastic spacers. Leave the adhesive to set for 24 hours.

Lever off the support batten and complete the last row of tiles. You may need to adjust the tile size slightly with the tile file if the basin is not level. The final step is to apply the grout. Use the flexible spreader supplied to push the grout between the tiles, pulling the spreader firmly across the face of the tiles. Gently scrape off the grout left on the surface of the tiles. Run the grout finisher along the joints to smooth them off, achieving a consistent appearance. Clean the tiles with a damp sponge. Finally, polish with a soft cloth.

Tiling a wall

If you have completed a basic tiling job, the only difficulties you are likely to encounter with an entire wall involve accurate setting out and tile cutting. Measure, mark, and set out your grid on the wall in such a way that cut tiles appear at the end of the wall, not in the middle, under a window or over a door. Other obstructions, such as bath panels that are to be incorporated into the overall design, may designate a starting point of a different height; a complete row of tiles looks better at the top of the panel rather than at the bottom. If your wall has a recessed window ledge, a

Working on a manageable area at a time, spread adhesive on the wall with a notched trowel.

Place a row of tiles along the cleat, then add the second row, pressing them firmly into place.

To ensure uniform grouting gaps, insert plastic cruciform spacers between the tiles.

Check periodically with your spirit level that the rows of tiles maintain a horizontal run.

ɔw of cut tiles will look better next to the window frame rather ıan butting the main wall surface.

When a basin or sink is positioned under a window, you must onsider both. If the gap between basin and sill is not an exact umber of tiles, the cut row butts the sill, not the basin. The first ne of tiles on the sill is still a complete line, however. Don't be empted to try to match two tile halves over a corner by tarting the sill with the cut row, because the grout lines will ecome too fragmentary.

The rule is always to attempt a symmetrical layout around doors nd windows. Narrow tile strips hat have to be cut to fit one ide of a frame only will stand ut visually, the grout lines mphasizing an off-center rrangement. Center your ayout over a door, using an naginary vertical line drawn hrough the middle, and fix uide cleats around the frame, o let all complete rows be set n place first. Cut tiles can be ositioned later, once the dhesive has set and the upports have been removed. ollow this procedure for a ingle window, but if you have wall with two openings side y side, imagine a vertical line rawn halfway between the wo, and center your whole tile ayout on it.

If you have a wall with a umber of features that must e tiled around, draw up a scale lan on tracing paper and lay his over a sheet of squared aper to represent the tiles. By noving the traced plan of the wall and its features around, you can determine the best starting point for the tiling.

The tiling technique is the same as that used for a backsplash: start at the cleated right-angled corner and spread just enough adhesive onto the wall to fix about a dozen tiles. Universal beveled-edge tiles will space themselves, but square-edge tiles need spacers at the corners. Work in level rows, using the cleat support, but checking at intervals with a spirit level, until the wall is covered with whole tiles. The adhesive must set for 24 hours before cleats are levered off and cut tiles placed in the gaps.

Ceramic tiles are ideal for creating a small decorative backsplash behind a handbasin in a bedroom or half-bathroom.

Cutting, completing, and finishing

Cutting tiles to fit is easy, but take care to measure each one accurately. Then either score, using a hand-held scriber, and snap over a couple of nails, or use a cutting machine just like the professionals. You can rent one from your specialist supplier very cheaply, and it makes the whole process simpler and speedier.

Cutting

Cutting tiles to fit into the gaps at the ends of whole rows, or to fit around door frames and other obstructions, can be done very simply, with a "pencil" scorer, tile cutting guide, and a couple of masonry nails. Hold the tile up to the wall, mark the area to be removed using a waterproof pen, and place the tile on a cutting surface. Score a line on the glazed face, with the scorer and guide. Then place a masonry nail under the scored mark at each end and snap the tile cleanly by applying downward pressure on each side. The guide is especially useful for the accurate cutting of narrow pieces, but where thicker ceramics are being cut to shape, a heavy-duty cutter with a tungsten carbide wheel is a better tool.

A cutting machine will save time on major jobs. Some heavy-duty versions have angled jigs as well as measuring guides, enabling you to cut tapers and angles by adjusting a side fence. Angled cut-outs and holes for fitting around pipes can be made by scoring the

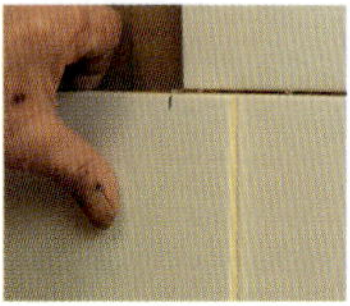

Mark tiles for cutting with a waterproof pen, holding them in place over the last whole tile.

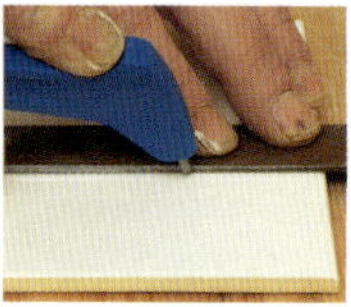

Hold a steel straightedge across the face of the tile and score the tile with a scriber.

Place a nail under each end of the line and press down with your thumbs to snap the tile in two.

Use a cutting machine if you have a lot of tiles to cut. Set the tile in place and score it.

Use the integral nipper to cut the tile to size. Angled cuts are possible using some machines.

For small cut-outs, use tile nippers to gradually nibble away the waste area of tile.

A tile saw is useful for cutting intricate shapes, as its rod blade will cut in any direction.

Tile nippers have angled jaws that make it easier to break a tile in two than using your thumbs.

ou can butt tiles together at an
nside corner or use a plastic corner
nolding for a neat finish.

At an outside corner apply adhesive and butt the tiles up to those on the adjacent wall.

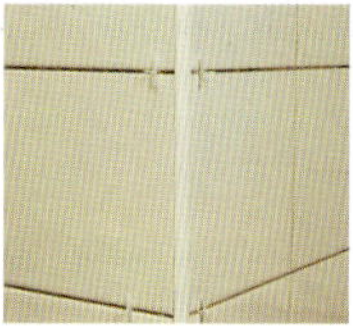

If your tiles don't have rounded edges, use corner trim to finish off an outside corner.

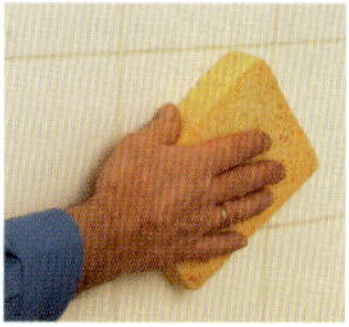

As you grout the tiles, wipe off excess grout with a damp sponge. Don't let it dry on the tile face.

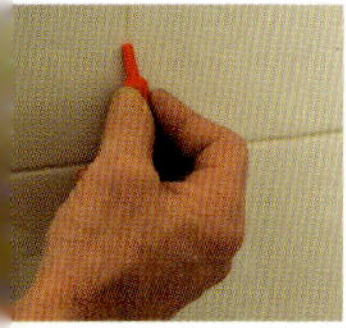

*ive the grouted joints a neat
rofile with a grout finisher.
hen polish the tiles clean.*

You can buy a variety of narrow ceramic border tiles to finish off the edges of tiled areas.

hape of the cut on the glazed surface, then breaking off or
nipping" the waste part of the tile using nippers or a small pair of
incers. Alternatively, make the cut-out with a tile saw fitted with
tungsten carbide tile saw blade that you can angle in any
irection. If the cut is not as smooth as you would like, jagged
dges can be removed with a tile file before the piece is held up
o the wall.

ompleting

ometimes space is very tight, such as in an inside corner, where
mall strips of tile must be placed to complete a row. In this
nstance, spread the adhesive directly onto the tile back, not the
vall surface, and push the tile into position. Unless you are using
lastic corner trim to finish off an inside corner, the tiles on one
vall should fit up to the adjacent wall, then the tiles on that wall
hould be cut to leave a grouting gap at the corner.

Some cutting machines incorporate a removable cutting gauge
hat can be used to measure the size of cut tile required and which
nakes an automatic allowance for the grouting gap. Since the tiling will always be centered on the wall, or some feature on it, it is extremely unlikely that you will ever finish a row at an inside or outside corner with a whole tile. If you have insert tiles as part of the layout, for example a toilet-roll holder, leave the correct space on the wall when tiling. Its extra weight means the insert tile must be fixed when the remainder of the wall has set. Use strips of painter's tape to hold it in position while the adhesive sets. Grout the tiled surface and continually wipe the surface with a damp cloth. If your tile kit does not include a suitable finisher, use a small off-cut of dowel with the end rounded by abrasive paper. Run it firmly along the grout channels for a uniform grooved finish.

Finishing

Tile trims, beads and rails, slimline borders, and chair rails are often available to add the finishing touch to your design. Workshops that make tiles by hand offer overall schemes with matching border and finishing tiles, and it is a good idea to investigate all the possibilities before making any calculations. You can also edge tiles with hardwood moldings that use the tile adhesive as a fixing. Try ramin quadrant or mahogany scotia as a top edging on a half wall, or use a hardwood angle molding pressed into an inside or outside corner.

TOP TIP

Most tile grouting is white, but sometimes a plain or very basic patterned tile can be given a new lease of life by using one of the colored grouts available. Existing white grout can also be transformed by treating with a colored dye, emphasizing the grid lines and linear structure.

Mosaics and mirrors

If small paneled areas of mosaic in a room are purely decorative, then mirror tiles can perform a useful function. Iridescent glass mosaic in pewter or cobalt can be bordered with waxed woodstrip in a small display; mirror tiles in a cleat grid can reflect much-needed light patterns along a dull corridor.

The use of wood strips to outline or emphasize specific tiled areas on a wall is particularly apposite when bordering mosaics. This usually decorative technique combines small pieces of ceramic, stone, or glass, called tesserae, to make up a larger picture or abstract image. Areas of similarly colored tesserae that are visually broken up by lines of grout benefit greatly from an external definition in the form of a natural wood border. This border can form any shape around any display; it does not have to be square or rectangular, although floor-to-ceiling strips of mosaic can be very effective on otherwise plain walls.

Using mosaic squares

The easiest way of making up a panel is to buy sheets of mosaic squares, consisting of equally spaced tesserae held in place by a mesh cloth backing or, in some instances, a paper facing. You will find a popular size is 12 x 12 in./30 x 30 cm, although other sizes are available. Specialist manufacturers offer many different color combinations, from strong greens and pinks to muted yellows, and with a suitable border these will add considerably to any scheme you choose. Being able to position complete sheets of ready spaced tesserae one after the other on the wall surface speeds up the whole process enormously.

Traditionally, the individual pieces would have been laid separately. All you need to do is stick and grout, as you would larger wall tiles. Mark out and prepare the wall as you would for any ceramic tiling job, then spread adhesive onto the surface. Some manufacturers recommend applying grout to the back of the mosaic sheet first, then bedding down on the wall with a homemade tamping block (a piece of plywood with a square of old carpet glued to it). Others ask you to follow tradition, which is to bed to the wall, leave it to set for 24 hours, remove any facing, and then apply the grout. The second method is faster, because you are able to grout the spaces between the tile sheets at the same time as the tesserae, as opposed to grouting twice.

Grids

The grid formed when strong grout lines make a visually distracting pattern can, of course, be used to advantage. Dark grouts

Use a tile to mark out a grid on the wall, allowing spaces for the horizontal and vertical cleats.

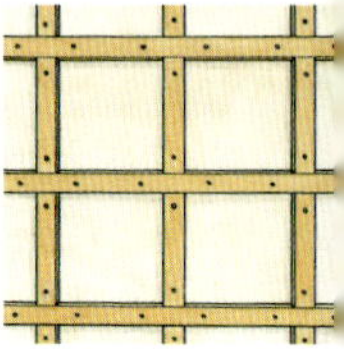

Screw the framework of softwood cleats to the wall and finish them as required.

Attach double-sided pads to the backs of the mirror tiles and press them firmly into place.

Pin lengths of hardwood molding to the centers of the cleats to conceal the fixing screws.

Use the mirror-tile grid idea to transform a narrow dark corridor. The tiles will reflect any available light onto the facing wall, giving the impression of greater space and airiness.

Mosaics are a natural for bathrooms. They are supplied in panels, letting you tile large areas quite quickly. What's more, individual tiles can be removed from the panels for fitting around obstacles. If any do need cutting, this can be done with nippers.

emphasizing pale mosaic squares make an interesting reverse image where the lines are almost more important than the squares. You can take the grid theme a stage further by using large tiles spaced by wooden cleats, the wood strips doing the same visual job as the grout lines, and forming a grid.

Mirror tiles

Using mirror tiles instead of ceramics inside the grid gives an interesting and practical result. When placed on a wall that receives direct sunlight, the reflected light patterns adjacent walls and increases overall light levels. A short corridor can be lengthened visually by using mirrored light in this way. Simply draw a grid of squares onto the appropriate wall using the mirror tiles and 2 x 1 in./5 cm x 2.5 cm planed wood as a dimensional guide. Fix the wood lengths to the wall following the grid. Screw 2 in./5 cm number 8 countersunk head screws into wall anchors, or use a contact adhesive. Position the mirror tiles in the squares formed by the cleats and stick them securely with the double-sided fixers. Pin a ¾ in./18 mm hardwood molding strip on top of the cleats as both a decorative finish and to hide the screwheads.

TOP TIP

Mosaic artists make up their own grout mix because they feel the grout emphasizes the spacing between tesserae, an important part of the design. Use soft sand (3 parts), cement (1 part), and a cement dye to color the mix before adding water. The color of the grout can contrast with or complement the tesserae. Current thinking is that white grout lines form a visually distracting grid pattern, as well as appearing to pull color away from such small pieces. If this is a problem on your wall, ready-mixed grouts are available, but color choice is limited. Any acrylic paint color can be added to a water-based mix. Adding color to the grout after it has set is also an option, although with a large area of mosaic this could be a tedious job. Similarly, attempting to shape the grout joints is not worthwhile, as the grout would dry before you had finished; simply sponge them flush.

Shelving: wood and tile effects

Building shelves into an alcove is easy—they sit on cleats screwed to the walls. You could also try something more adventurous like pinning TGV lengths to the cleats above and below the back and two sides of each shelf, thereby creating a stylish wood surround that also hides all the cleat fixings.

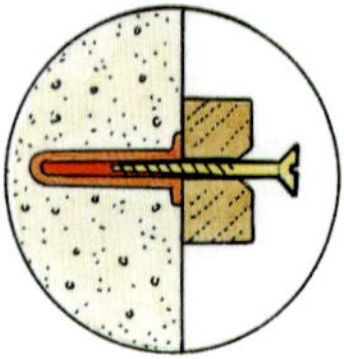

Shelves in alcoves can be supported by screwing cleats to the back and end walls. In a solid wall use wall anchors; in a hollow wall, screw to the studwork.

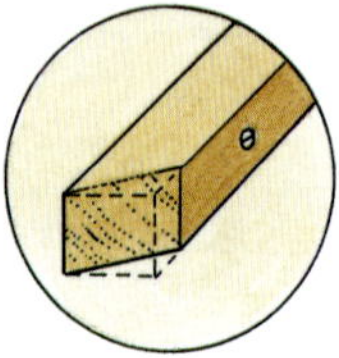

For neatness, miter the outer ends of the side cleats so that they become less obvious. Or hide them with a cleat beneath the front edge of the shelf.

Built-in shelving

The need for shelving to hold frequently used items is not confined to kitchens and bathrooms. The modern home has books, tapes, disks, and other paraphernalia that must be to hand. These items may still be kept in traditional free-standing bookcases, which were once essential items of room furniture. Their obvious advantage over built-in shelving is that they could be moved from room to room as needs altered. That advantage now seems outweighed by the amount of wall space needlessly taken up by such large pieces of furniture.

Built-in shelving solves storage problems while taking up previously unusable room space, such as small alcoves, chimney-breast recesses, and dead-end corridors. When shelving is placed at head height, the shelf fixings are fairly obvious, and support cleats

Cut the shelf support cleats to length, drill and plug the wall, and screw the cleats to the back and end walls of the alcove. Make sure that they are truly horizontal by checking with a spirit level.

Countersink the fixing screws, then conceal them by pinning on thinner strips of wood or decorative molding. Make sure this is flush with the top edges of the cleats.

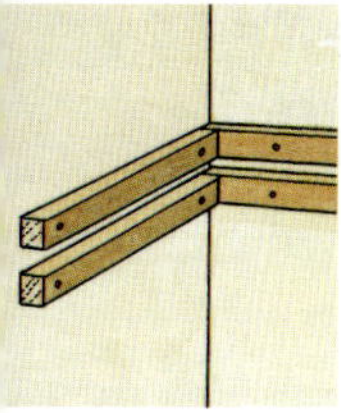

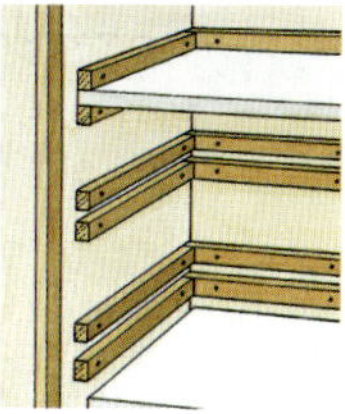

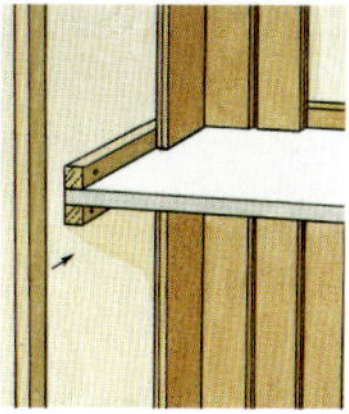

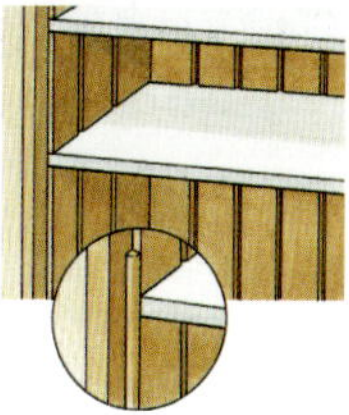

o line the alcove with paneling, it cleats to the walls above nd below each shelf position.

Slide the shelves into position and fit a vertical cleat to each side of the alcove.

Pin paneling to the cleats above and below the shelves, finishing flush with the vertical cleats.

Conceal the leading edges of the paneling where it sits on the vertical cleats with beading.

vith exposed screwheads will need a smaller woodstrip pinned on op to hide them. The cleat arrangement must then be painted to natch the wall. The shelves should be varnished or painted a ifferent color, so that the eye picks them out first, and the upports appear to be part of the background wall.

loor-to-ceiling shelving

deal for an alcove, this scheme maximizes the storage capacity of small area while taking up the minimum of floor space. If sited ext to a chimney breast, for example, the floor line should ontinue the line of the breast face for the neatest finish. On no ccount should a previously recessed area be brought out farther nto the room than the adjacent baseboard, because this will estroy the whole visual balance.

If you are considering a floor-to-ceiling scheme, support leats can be disguised slightly by painting them to match the vall, but a more attractive solution is available. Cleats supporting helving can perform an additional task: supporting wood aneling cut to fit between the shelves and giving the entire lcove a rich wood finish.

For this finish run two sets of cleats per shelf, instead of one, x one below the shelf in its usual position, and one above so nat the shelf slides in between the two. Position the shelves and x two vertical lumber lengths to the right front and left front, utting the ends of the horizontal side cleats. TGV or shiplap oards fit snugly between the shelves, pinned to the cleats. Cut ne sides level with the shelves, and finish off with a vertical ength of beading or molding pinned to the side uprights and the ront of the shelves.

This simple shelf is easy to install, but very effective and practical. When the support cleats are painted to match the walls, they become less obvious, as though part of the background wall.

Alternative shelving finishes

Combining different finishes in the same scheme always adds interest, both during the project and as a talking point when it is completed. Plain color wall tiles may look less than pleasing on a large wall area, but when added to a wood scheme they can act as a perfect partner for the complex grain structure in the lumber. Consider using 6 in./15 cm tiles as a shelf surface. You need to add 1⅛ in./29 mm to allow for the back cleat and panelling, plus ½ in./12 mm for a front beading, to the overall width. Allowing for grouting, you need to buy 8 x 1 in./20 x 2.5 cm PAR. Consider the colors with care; try a dark purple tile in a wood scheme where purple water-based dye has been run into the grain, sanded, and clear varnished. Contrasts work well too, such as royal blue with a yellow pine paneling, or a pale green colorwashed wood combined with dark red tiles. Smaller shelves can have mosaic tiles, visually complex areas that offset simple clear varnished woods.

Combination storage

Floor-to-ceiling shelving in any recessed area gives economic storage space, but you can take the principle a stage further. Instead of having open shelves from top to bottom, which only collect dust and partly protect the contents, you can enclose them. You can hang doors on all or some of the shelves, creating a customized unit. Although paired doors can cover the entire front, and obviously give the best protection, most rooms benefit from a combination of base cabinet and face-level shelves.

Bulky storage can be accommodated at floor level, and smaller items, such as books and tapes, can be stored on the shelves. Bein open, these shelves are also an ideal place for flowering and trailing plants.

Creating cabinet space at the base of your unit is not very different from the floor-to-ceiling shelving project, because the top of the cabinet becomes, in practice, another shelf about 37 in./940 mm off the floor. You can construct the top of the unit as before (see page 142), using wood paneling between the shelves, and screwing vertical wooden supports to right and left. The last shelf, now the cabinet top, needs a support under the front edge and at both sides, at right angles to the vertical side pieces. For these supports, 3 x 1 in./7.5 x 2.5 cm PAR is an ideal size. A final front piece level with the cabinet top edge acts as a joining length, as the sides and horizontal support can be fixed to it by screwing through from the back. Screw a base cleat to the floor to support the back of the side pieces, and consequently the hinges. You have now created the paired door opening. A parting bead, measuring ½ x 1 in./12 x 25 mm, pinned to the inside with the rounded side facing out is a good finishing touch and accepts flush hinge.

Cabinet doors

Probably the most intimidating part of the job, doors must be equal in size, square cornered, and fit the opening well. The simplest doors are cut from ¾ in./18 mm blockboard or plywood, and you can have them machined to size at the lumberyard. Measure the sizes needed to fit the opening, then deduct ⅛in/4mm from every side. This will let you pin a hardwooc edging strip around the outside. This protects the outer veneer, ar gives a professional finish. If you pin a 1 in./25 mm edging strip t a ¾ in./18 mm board door, flush with the back edge, overlapping the front, a lip is created. A ½ in./12 mm half-round molding, pinned on the board face abutting the lip and mitered at each corner, gives a simple, effective border, although many more decorative moldings are available.

If you have been tempted to tile the shelves used on the open part of the unit, you could try the same tile scheme on the door fronts, as a coordinating effect. The doors are cut as before, and

Floor-to-ceiling shelving can provide a lot of useful storage space. Putting doors in front of the shelves will not only conceal their contents but also protect them from dust and sunlight.

ged with 1 in./25 mm hardwood strip, overlapping at the front ge. Seal the door surface if needed, and clean off any dirt or ease. Apply tile adhesive and position the tiles centrally, so that y small pieces of tile cut to fit are equally spaced around the ge. Leave this to set for 24 hours, then grout in the usual way. ernatively, center complete tiles only, and pin a suitable lding around them to form an inner border. The door lip can be ed to form its own outer border with a half-round mitered lding as before.

Another way of constructing paired doors is to pin a simple mitered molding on a manufactured board cut to size, imitating a panelled door. The board needs to be edged with a hardwood strip, and looks better painted rather than varnished. The technique used to make wooden shutters (see page 198) can be easily adapted to make smaller cabinet doors. If necessary, the cleating can be fixed to both sides of the frame, making the door extremely strong. Finally, because the cabinet opening can be made any size you like, second-hand doors can be used.

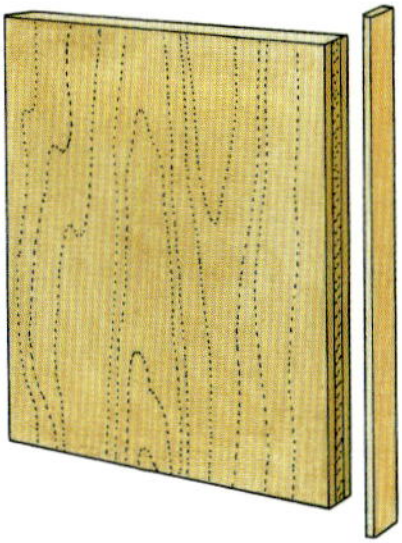

elves can be fitted with doors cut m plywood or blockboard sheets. ve them cut undersize and edge them with hardwood strips to provide a neat finish and protect the edge of the veneered face.

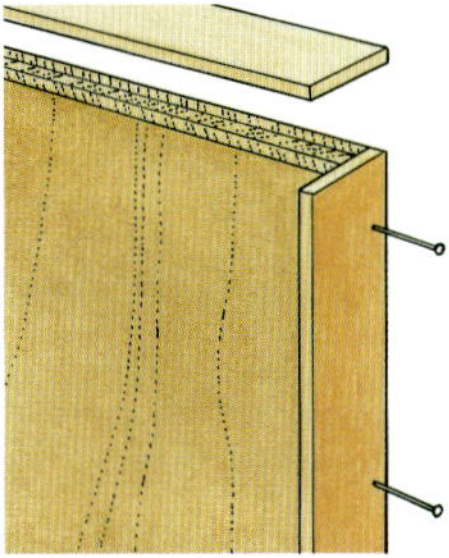

To make features of the doors, use edging strips that are wider than the doors' thickness. Pin these to the doors so that they are flush with the rear faces and project beyond the front faces.

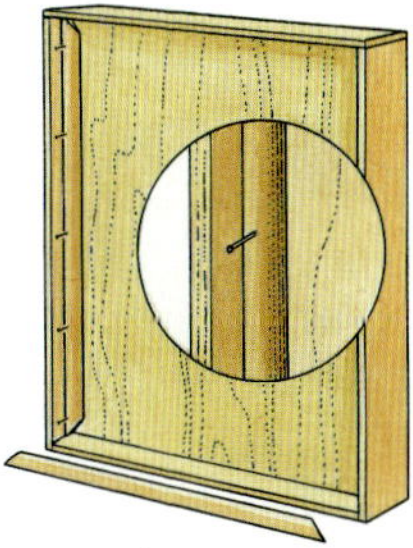

nish off the doors by pinning half-round molding around the side of the projecting edging strips. Miter the ends of the molding so that they fit together neatly in the corners.

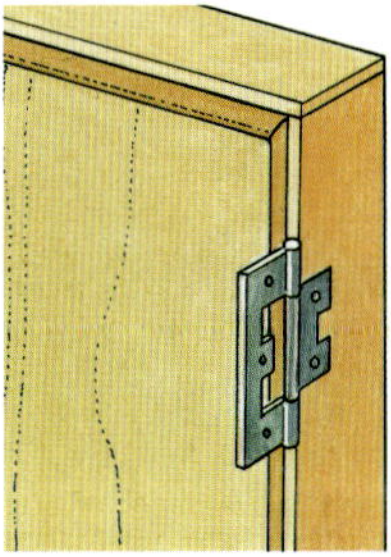

Fit the doors with flush hinges top and bottom (add a third if the doors are floor-to-ceiling height) and screw these to the framework surrounding the shelves. Finally, add suitable catches.

Customized fire surrounds

After a period of unpopularity following the advent of central heating, the fireplace as a decorative room feature is back in fashion. Whether you have a surround that you don't like, one that needs refurbishing or merely a boarded-up hole, the focal point that a fire surround provides can be custom-built to fit or custom-decorated to match your décor.

Take it out...

Although they had been a functional part of room design for centuries, the fireplace and surround really came into their own as a decorative feature in Victorian times. They were a piece of built-in room furniture, a multifaceted talking point that contributed much more to the living space than just its primary function, the supply of heat. With the introduction of central heating (a cleaner, more efficient way of heating the home) came a new style of living where the fireplace was no longer the center of attention. Designers had created a more modern environment, and the fireplace became part of history. Cast iron, tiled, marble, slate, and wood surrounds alike were thrown away.

...and put it back

Recent interior design principles do not entirely hark back to Victorian thinking, but they have resulted in a revival and reinstatement of the fireplace. Contemporary design and period fixtures are no longer considered to be mutually exclusive. Origina

Above: A fireplace often provides a focal point in a room. This period bedroom would be lost without its fireplace, which gives a feeling of warmth despite the high ceiling.

Right: Simple tiled fire surrounds are common to many prewar and postwar houses. Although basic, they can look good when teamed with sympathetic décor.

The dramatic pillars supporting the mantelshelf turn this plain modern fireplace into a dramatic statement. Always integrate the fireplace into the room's overall decorative scheme.

eatures can be updated with different color and paint finishes, iving them a new lease of life and ensuring they coexist happily longside modern schemes and furniture.

Replacing the fire surround is not a difficult task, but first you eed to establish the state of the chimney breast. The mantelpiece nd surround may have been removed, but the opening and reback left in place, cleated, covered with wallboard and skimmed vith plaster. If this is the case, there ought to be a ventilation rille, but if there isn't, you still need to investigate further by tripping back the wallcovering. Look for a join in the plasterwork, then chisel away to reveal the wood frame fixed inside the opening. Then remove the cleats, wallboard, and the resultant mess. If you are unlucky, however, and the opening has been professionally bricked up (the new brickwork will have been "toothed-in" to the original bond), then you need to consult a builder or fireplace specialist.

your fireplace has been boarded up, there hould be a ventilation grille in the closing panel o prevent condensation in the flue. Remove it.

Cut the plaster back from around the opening and lever the closing panel from its supporting framework in the fireplace.

Remove the wooden framework and clean up the opening ready for a new fire surround. Be prepared for a lot of mess.

Making a fire surround

Constructing your own fire surround is cheaper than buying one and it enables you to produce a unique decoration that will complement the style and décor of the room. The basic principles for creating a wooden fireplace surround are outlined here. You can paint and varnish the surround to your taste.

Fire surrounds

Second-hand fire surrounds are widely available, from specialist dealers and architectural salvage yards. If a period piece is your ideal, just make sure it fits before parting with your money. Buying a cast-iron fireplace full of character that doesn't fit the fire opening is an expensive mistake. Wood surrounds, on the other hand, merely need to be of the correct proportion to the breast; a separate fire basket fits the opening. Plenty of reproduction wood surrounds are available too.

The widespread popularity of central heating led to many fireplaces being closed off, especially in bedrooms. But a fireplace gives a bedroom a wonderfully cozy feel.

Making a wooden surround

An interesting project idea is to create a hand-made wood surround. All you need is a grid on the wall, and a firm fixing for the initial lengths of wood.

- Measure up and draw the template grid on the wall.
- Depending on the dimensions of the surround you are intending to build, you'll need about 10 ft./3 m of 1 x 2 in./2.5 x 5 cm, 1 x 4 in./2.5 x 10 cm, 1 x 6 in./2.5 x 15 cm and 1 x 8 in./2.5 x 20 cm.
- Fix the first lengths, 1 x 8 in./2.5 x 20 cm, to the wall with heavy-duty plugs and countersunk 2 in./50 mm number 8 screws.
- Butt the horizontal piece to the inside of the uprights, but don't miter the corners.

Begin the installation of this "stepped" design of fire surround by screwing a wide board to each side of the fire opening. Then screw a third board above the opening between the first two.

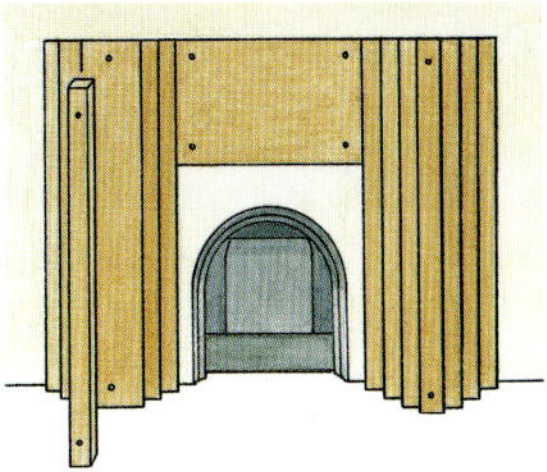

Add the vertical boards to each side, fitting progressively narrower pieces to hide the fixing screws of the previous boards fitted and to create "fluted" columns. You can color the boards as you add them.

Continue by adding the horizontal boards. Again, use progressively narrower boards to gain the stepped effect, but note that each is longer than its predecessor to fit between the side boards. Conceal remaining screwheads with pinned-on moldings.

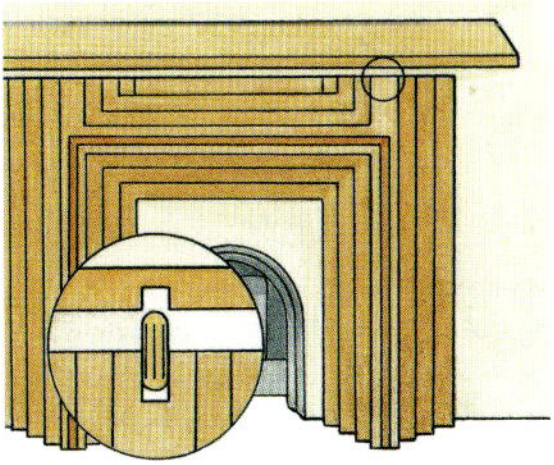

Cut the shelf to size and center it on the surround so that you can mark the positions of the fixing dowels. Drill holes for these in the underside of the shelf and the tops of the side columns. Apply glue to the dowels and fit them in place together with the shelf.

- The principle here is layering; each wood piece added to the surround hides the previous screwhead.
- Each completed layer can have its own color, as well. If you wish, simply apply an individual water-based mix as you proceed.
- Fix the largest size to the wall, then fix the remaining wood pieces to each other, centering the uprights in descending order of size, countersinking 1¼ in./30 mm number 8 screws.
- The horizontal wood pieces are fixed in the same order, and following the same principle, but you will note that each piece fitted is longer than the previous piece by the width of the step at each side.
- Screwheads in the final wood pieces can be covered by a centered molding or edging strip pinned into position. Alternatively, they can be hidden with filler.
- The two vertical sides act as supports for the mantelpiece, which can be cut from the 1 x 4 in./2.5 x 10 cm stock, or it can be wider if you prefer.
- Secure it with glued fluted dowels into the top of the side supports and the underside of the mantelpiece.
- If you have colored the wood pieces, several coats of varnish are needed to protect the finish. If not, any paint finish of your choice can be applied.

Tiled finishes in working areas

When you select tiles for decorative purposes, lining walls in living quarters or tiling surfaces that reflect light patterns, the choice is almost unlimited. Hand-made and decorated terra cotta, unglazed, iridescent glass, stoneware, three-dimensional, metallic, and retro are all available; the challenge is to match into your color scheme.

Tiles for use in a working area, in particular on preparation surfaces in a kitchen, need to be both decorative and functional, and not all tiles are suitable. Tiles that are intended to be part of a work surface must not stain easily, must be strong and not crack, must be suitable for wet areas, and be easily cleaned. In addition, crazed and cracked tiles that harbor dirt and germs must be avoided because they are a health hazard.

Tile selection

Tile makers—mass manufacturers and individual craftspeople alike—use many different clay types and glazes. The density of the clay and the glaze used affects the strength of the finished tile. For example, white and near-white glazes are much stronger than colored ones. For this reason most specialist suppliers have a "suitability chart," grading their tiles in terms of strength and color, to ensure that you make an appropriate selection. Before you make this selection, consider carefully the function the tile will have to perform. On working surfaces in a kitchen you will need the strongest tiles available in a color that will resist staining by food and its preparation. Special-effect tiles, such as iridescent glass or metallic, are not practical, however attractive they may look. Mosaic sheets need careful consideration, too. They are easy to install on a work surface because the backing sheet can be shaped to fit, but again, you will need the strongest tiles available. They require a lot of grouting, too, with a special epoxy grout recommended for kitchen surfaces.

Updating your kitchen

Refurbishing a kitchen or working area is not simply a matter of decorating walls. Storage areas and worktops must be upgraded as well, or they will detract from the finished scheme. Storage units can be fitted with new doors that are simple to make. Plywood cut to size and edged can be tiled to match a worktop style in the same way that the combination storage doors matched the tiled shelves (see page 144). TGV doors pinned to a softwood frame will help create the feel of a country kitchen. Even a partial paint job

When adding a tiled finish to an old worktop, work over the surface with coarse abrasive paper to provide a key for the adhesive.

Set out the tiles "dry" so that you can determine the best arrangement of colors and work out where you will have to cut tiles to fit.

Be prepared to revise your arrangement; change colors and patterns until you achieve the best layout before bedding the tiles down.

Mosaic panels can be used to good, colorful effect in a kitchen, although they do not provide the ideal surface for a worktop since they are unlikely to be thick enough.

…n the original doors can suffice, if it is combined with a new …vood stain or a simple stenciled motif. The really noticeable …ifference, though, will result from a new worktop surface, and …iling over the existing top will be the most effective economically.

…A new top

…elect your tiles carefully. A tough glazed stoneware tile with a …ood color range would be ideal, but, depending on your surface …ize, they ought not to be too large.

- To avoid unpleasant visual discrepancies when cutting strips to fill, 4 in./10 cm square would be small enough yet still allow for fairly simple grouting.
- Make sure the worktop is clean and dry.
- Abrade the surface with coarse aluminum oxide (40 grit) to provide a "key" if it is very smooth.
- Using a tile as a template, set out on the surface so that you achieve the best arrangement.
- Ensure cut tiles are at the back, where the wall meets the surface, not at the front.
- Allow space at the front edges for a wood edging strip if desired, although edging strips fixed at the sides of the worktop are best, protecting the top better and letting tiles be set flush against the edge.
- Spread the waterproof adhesive and bed down the tiles as you would on a wall, cutting to fit as needed.
- Leave to set for 24 hours.
- Before you grout the surface, make sure that your retailer has supplied the correct epoxy grout essential for these surfaces.

Finishing with wood

- Select a wood strip for the worktop edge. An astragal molding is ideal; it has no right-angled edge to knock against.
- Mark and miter to fit.
- Fix into position with 1¼ in./30 mm number 8 countersunk screws. Drive home the screws, setting them well below the surface of the wood.
- Fill the hole with a joint compound that can be sanded flush when dry.
- Alternatively, bore each pilot and shank hole in one go with a combination screwsink that leaves a counterbored hole, and drive the screw in.
- The hole is filled by a wooden plug, cut to the correct screw size from the same wood by a plug cutter, and glued in place.
- When set, cut the plug as flush as possible with a sharp chisel, and sand to leave a professional finish.

…Protect the perimeter of the worktop with wood …strips the same depth as the tiles. Cut to size, …mitering the ends and check the fit.

Pin the strips in place, overhanging the edge. Fix a reinforcing strip underneath the lip.

For reasons of hygiene, kitchen counter tiles must be grouted with a two-part epoxy grout. Use a small trowel to press it into the joints.

Storage box sections

Whether you need to reinforce sagging shelves with vertical supports or make up a self-supporting unit with stepped sides, the same simple wood joint can be used. Halving joints let the shelves slot together at right angles, forming a strong, unseen bond which can also be used as a decorative feature.

Weight for support

Shelving systems, constructed from 1 in./25 mm boards or ¾ in./18 mm plywood machined to size, are ideal for fixing in an alcove. The recess will generally be less than 6 ft./1.8 m wide and the shelf length, if supported on cleats to the side and rear, will be perfectly stable. Longer lengths, needed to span a gap where, say, two rooms have been knocked into one and the resultant distance between chimney breasts is over 10 ft./ 3 m, are liable to sag, particularly if they are 12 in./30 cm in width. Front support pieces glued and screwed under and flush with the front edge of each shelf, will help, but heavy weights will still cause problems.

A modular box-section storage system can provide a versatile means of containing and displaying a wide variety of domestic objects. Such systems can be tailored to meet your specific needs.

It is reasonable to assume that a long, wide shelf will be used to hold larger, heavier items than a small shelf, so it must be constructed with more support. Load-bearing shelves can have brackets screwed underneath, either as separate fixed items or as part of an adjustable shelving system, where removable brackets are slotted into steel uprights screwed to the wall. There are numerous adjustable systems on the market, all using the same principle, and the heavy-duty ones are very strong indeed. The wall fixings must involve no less than 2¼ in./56 mm number 10 countersunk screws driven into heavy-duty wall anchors. The uprights should be spaced 2½ ft./75 cm apart. Heavy-duty adjustable shelving is available in only very basic colors, however. Although you can paint it yourself, and it may look effective in a workroom, garage, or outbuilding, it isn't exactly subtle. There is a better, much more attractive, load-bearing support system for a living area, which you can construct yourself.

A self-supporting box system

This is a simple wooden unit that relies on horizontal and vertical boards meeting at a series of halving joints and providing mutual support. A halving joint is simple to cut and, when accurate, extremely strong and virtually invisible. The principle behind halving joints (also called half-and-half joints or half-laps) is that where the wood meets or overlaps at right-angles, one exact half of each piece is cut and removed to let the pieces slot together. The wood can be clamped securely, marked out with a knife, and cut together, so that the housings are the same width as the

Cut the first half of the joint in one board. You can subsequently use it as a template to mark the matching half with your marking knife.

Cut the joint by making a series of saw cuts through the waste to the bottom of each of the slots. Then remove the waste with a thin chisel.

Then check the fit of each of the joints. They should all be snug, and making saw cuts on the waste side of each marked line should ensure this.

Glue inside the housings of the corresponding joint halves and carefully assemble the boards.

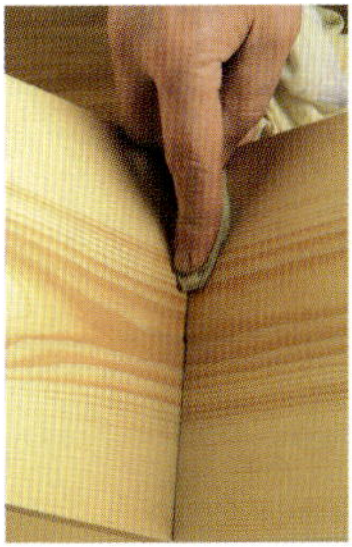

Clamp and wipe off excess glue. The unit can be strengthened by gluing and pinning on a plywood backing.

thickness of the wood, and cut back with a chisel to a shoulder half the width of the wood. Always saw on the waste side of the marked line when cutting halving joints. If you don't, the housings will be too wide by the width of the saw blade, and the joint will be loose.

Custom building

Any size of unit can be constructed in this way, depending on your storage requirements, and the space available. A drawing dividing the wall space into compartments is a good start. These can be any size, but square is easy and uniformly attractive. Consider using measurements that turn the unit into a series of cubes: if your chosen wood is 1 ft./30 cm wide, use the same figure for the inside dimensions of each box. A scaled-down model made of cardboard will give you a better idea of how it will look—slots cut in the cardboard will join together in exactly the same way as the wood.

The top of the unit need not reach the ceiling. A long top shelf for houseplants and ornaments is created by forming outside corners, which are simply one-sided halving joints.

Your unit is floor-standing, so you need to consider a plinth for the base, and this should be the height of the baseboard. Flush at the front and sides, the plinth can be set forward the width of the baseboard at the back of the base, so that the unit back is flush with the wall.

Securing and backing

If you are making a small unit, clamping it square as you glue the joints will ensure it is stable enough. Larger units can be glued in sections as you proceed, but any "play" in the halving joints will result in undue pressure being placed on the unit's square corners. A support cleat glued and screwed under the top back edge of each top corner box will hold that corner square, and let you drill through and fix the unit to the wall. If you prefer, you can attach a back panel, placing the unit face-down on the floor, and confirming that it is square.

Cut ¼ in./6 mm plywood to fit the outside back, and glue and pin into position with brads. Make sure that the best side of the plywood is visible from the front. The unit is now stable and free-standing. Screws driven through the backing into the wall can be used to provide extra security, if required (sensible if it is to hold heavy items).

FLOORS

The choice of a floor covering is usually a vote for practicality over style and fashion. Heavy traffic areas, potentially wet areas, outdoor access areas, and more intimate, friendly areas all have their own separate requirements which take precedence over decorative style. Expensive wall-to-wall carpeting is not compatible with large, muddy boots, while cold quarry tiling is not suitable for the children's playroom. Given today's lifestyles, versatility must be an important issue when deciding on your flooring; indeed, many modern flooring materials are described as multifunctional. In a modern living environment, choosing which floor covering to put where has never been more important.

Designer's notes

A floor serves a single purpose; it is there to be walked on. Therefore, the first principle of flooring and floor covering is practicality. There is a wide range of flooring materials to choose from. Depending on the purpose of the room, you may want warmth and softness underfoot, or a more hard-wearing surface suitable for heavy traffic.

Above: Fitted carpets provide a soft and comfortable floor covering that creates a harmonious link between one room and another.

Right: Vinyl flooring is very hard-wearing and ideal for use in areas of heavy traffic, such as a hallway. It is also easily cleaned.

To begin, decide on floor plans from a purely cosmetic viewpoint, and then look at the consequences. Stripped boards can allow drafts, especially if the house has a cellar. Light-colored or plain carpeting shows every mark. Scatter rugs can trip people up. Tiles can be cold in areas where people are likely to walk barefoot, as can lino and vinyl. Stockinged feet slide on polished floors, and thin woodstrip veneers wear out quickly in heavy human traffic. The way you choose to treat your floors has not only a decorative impact, but a noticeable effect on the quality of life around you. Don't overlook the effect a poor decision can have on your bank balance, either, should you be faced with the prospect of replacir expensive flooring that proved unsuitable.

Rugs can be used to provide colorful accents on a floor, but they can also be trip hazards.

Use special rug grippers to prevent them from moving and causing an accident.

Flagstones were often found in the kitchens of period houses. 'f you want to recreate the look of e past, they are ideal, and you can y modern imitations, but they will be cold underfoot.

/ork with what you have

:placing a floor is an arduous task, and one that should not : undertaken lightly. Quite apart from the floor surface, the iseboards will have to be removed and possibly replaced, imaging the wall surface and the decorative finish.

Unless you are renovating a property from scratch, or the :isting flooring is beyond redemption, try to work with what ›u have inherited. This need not mean covering up an area ith carpet or vinyl, relying on the "out-of-sight-out-of-mind" eory. Instead, identify the positive and workable characteristics the floor.

If you have original floorboards, check them for rot and damage. they are sound, you have an opportunity to sand, varnish, ›lorwash, stain, or simply leave them with a plain scrubbed finish. 'oken, damaged, or rotted boards need replacing. Note the width ıd depth of the wood and its type (pine, usually) and check out local architectural salvage yard.

Modern floors tend to be chipboard, an artificial board of no sual worth in itself, but which provides a sound base for painted :signs. A piece of woven matting placed centrally can be 'fectively emphasized by a painted border in contrasting colors. Chipboard is also a good base for vinyl floorcoverings, and for supporting interlocking boards of hardwood veneer on a backing of softwood or plywood, known as woodstrip flooring.

Period houses may have slate, marble, or flagstone floors, particularly in kitchen and washroom areas. Slabs are available from specialist suppliers, but they tend to be quite expensive. Imitation flagstones, made of concrete, can be bought at a fraction of the price.

Tiled floors can be refurbished, and encaustic tiles are available from specialist suppliers for repair purposes. Dull floors can be stripped and repolished. Quarry tiles were also popular throughout the ground floor and outhouses, and if you discover a damaged floor, you can easily replace individual tiles.

Start at the bottom

When you have identified the advantages inherent in your existing flooring, try to visualize the rest of the walls and ceiling in a finish that emphasizes these qualities. It may seem odd working up from the bottom, but if you can start from the point of a natural and practical asset, then you are much more likely to achieve a pleasing result that benefits the entire household design scheme.

Basic skills: identifying boards

Recognizing wooden floor types and sizes is not a particularly difficult skill to acquire, but dealing with defects and problems, sometimes caused by neglect or bad workmanship by previous owners, can be hard and time-consuming. Replacing floorboards may involve sourcing second-hand materials from salvage or reclamation yards.

Basic, traditional floorboards will be made from softwood—usually pine. You may find them as bare wood because scrubbed floors were preferred in many older properties, or they may have been varnished to imitate a darker, more expensive wood. Using cheap wood and varnishing it to deceive was a Victorian trick. This has found popularity again, although today's colors, stains, and varnishes give a much subtler finish. You may also find painted boards, either across the entire floor, or just at the edges where they would be visible if the room had a central carpet.

Boards were laid in a number of sizes, originally 1 in./25 mm thick timbers, in widths of 5 in./13 cm, 6 in./15 cm or 7 in./18 cm. Genuine old hardwood floors are rare, and the wood width will be significantly less than softwood. Be careful you don't mistake veneer strip flooring for the real thing.

Infestation

Check the condition of the floor carefully. If you have removed old carpets and underlays, or ripped up hardboard pinned or stapled in position, remember that this will have stopped the floor "breathing." Inadequate ventilation, combined with damp conditions, can lead to wood rot, so examine the entire area carefully, including baseboards. Dry rot can often be present in lumber with an apparently unaffected surface, although small splits may be visible close up. If you are suspicious, prod the wood with a blade—dry rot gives easily. Wet rot is found only in saturated conditions, and thus tends to be more obvious. Both cases are solved only by cutting out the infected wood, drying out the surrounding area and treating it with a wood preservative. You must remove the cause of the damp and ensure proper air circulation; otherwise, the problem may return. Woodworm is a constant concern in wood-framed properties. If you find tiny flight holes in the floor, inject them with woodworm fluid. If the problem is far-reaching, you must call in a professional.

Repairing and lifting boards

Repairs to basic floorboarding are straightforward, and they do not require many specialist tools. You will need a keyhole saw and electrician's bolster, but these should be part of your household kit

Far left: Wet rot is caused when wood is exposed to constant damp conditions. The wood begins to crumble and so loses its strength. The only solution is to cut out the damage and replace it with new wood, after having found and cured the cause of the original damp.

Left: Attack by woodworm can be identified by the small flight holes left when the insects bore their way out of the wood. Small areas of damage can be treated with fluid; large areas should be dealt with by cutting out and renewing the infected wood.

lentify the joist position (the fixing nails will elp) and drill a hole at the edge of the board ıst to one side of the joist.

Insert the blade of a jigsaw through the drilled hole and use it to cut across the floorboard alongside the joist.

Drive the blade of an electrician's bolster into the saw cut and use it to lever the cut end of the board upward.

ift the board sufficiently to wedge a length of leat beneath it so that it is held clear while you ut the other end over a joist.

Screw a short length of cleat to the side of the first joist, and flush with the top, to support one end of the new board.

Cut the new board to size and set it on the cleat and second joist. You can nail it down, but screws will allow easy removal in future.

nyway. A floorboard saw is useful if a lot of board cutting is eeded. The first task is always to identify the cause of any articular problem. More floor damage is caused by previous ttempts to access pipe systems and wiring runs than any amount f footwear. Access panels that are to be retained in the floor hould be screwed down, not nailed. Screwing down a wooden oard rather than nailing it should cure any annoying creaks nder carpeting that are caused by movement. If the board is ıanufactured (chipboard), it should ideally have been screwed own in the first place.

Check to see if the boards are anchored on all joists, and none is ıissed. Creaking, exposed floorboards that are to be varnished can lso be screwed down, but the screwheads need to be hidden. ither countersink the heads and fill with an appropriate colored lastic joint compound, or counterbore a hole and cover the head ith a chamfered wooden plug.

To remove a damaged section of board, or to gain new access, locate the nearest joist and mark a pencil line alongside it. The floorboard nails will be your best indicator. Drill a hole to the side of the joist, large enough to start the cut with a keyhold saw blade, then use a floorboard saw. Alternatively, use a jigsaw, cutting the board parallel with the joist.

Lever up the end with the electrician's bolster, lift it and slide a wood cleat under as support while you cut the other end, directly in the middle of a joist. Use a small backsaw for this cut; on no account try using a jigsaw, because you have a solid joist underneath and will snap the blade immediately.

Screw a cleat to the side of the first joist, to act as a support for the access panel or a new piece of board. It is important to bear in mind that if the boards are tongue-and-groove, you will have to saw down one length to cut through the tongue and release the board.

Preparing exposed floors

Old wooden floors that are recolored if necessary and varnished for protection look good in almost any situation. You don't always have to machine sand the boards, either; thorough cleaning is often all that is needed prior to the application of a decorative finish and a coat of varnish to seal them and make them hard-wearing.

The pros and cons of sanding

Sanding floors and varnishing them has become very popular, because the finished floor will look good with any room scheme, and is as versatile an asset as you could wish for. If some of the floorboards are damaged, they can be replaced by new ones. And, since the whole room is being sanded back, there will be no discernible difference in the surface color. However, one drawback to sanding is that it reduces the thickness of the wood: floorboards that were once ¾–⅞ in./18–20 mm, providing solid support and a fair insulation against sound, are reduced by ⅛–¼ in./3–4 mm, depending on the uneven nature of the floor. This may be no problem for you, but in houses with a cellar or exposed beams underneath, the noise level will be increased, as will the draft. If the boards are currently bare and in reasonable condition, consider washing them down and adding color instead of sanding them back. Replacement second-hand boards can be found at

'lean old boards thoroughly by scrubbing them with
ot water and household abrasive cleaner, working
vith the grain.*

When the boards have been left to dry, brush on the desired finish, again working with the grain and maintaining a wet edge.

rchitectural salvage yards, if needed; and even a new board or wo can be matched in.

Try experimenting with oil-based stains on a scrap of (new) oard, mixing them together, then diluting them with solvent. Vhen you have a reasonable match, brush it onto the new 'oorboard and sand it down. Oil-based stains penetrate deeper ıto the wood, so don't try this with water-based stains.

:leaning and preparing

'lain wooden boards in period properties were scrubbed vigorously vith a mix of sand and water, often resulting in a delicate-looking ray sheen. Elbow work is still required, but modern cleaners and brasives give every assistance and an impressive result. Start as ou would any dirty job, using hot water, abrasive cleaning cream, nd a stiff brush. Work the brush into and with the wood grain, ıot across it, and clean small areas of board at a time, washing lown immediately with clean water. Clean the entire floor, leave it o dry, and repeat the whole process if necessary.

You can now see if any problem areas remain, such as stains, laster lumps, or splashes of paint. Plaster, softened by the :leaning process, will lift off with a flexible-bladed knife. Stains nd old paint need brushing with a water washable paint remover. Vait until the paint blisters, and then scrape it off with a flexible blade. Repeat the brushing process if a paint residue is left, but use wire wool for the best finish and for getting into the grain beneath a stain. You may now be left with a fairly rough board surface. If so, this is because the water used in cleaning down has raised the woodgrain, and the board needs sanding slightly by hand. Wrap a fine grade of aluminum oxide abrasive (120 grit) around a sanding block and gently sand with the grain. It is imperative that the boards are completely dry when you start this job. If the floorboards are smooth after the cleaning process, which they will be if they have been varnished some time previously, they can be "keyed" to accept a new finish. Gently abrade the surface with a fine grade silicon carbide used wet, again working along the grain.

The next stage

Take time out to review your plans. Is the floor in good condition? If it is, all you need to do is decide on a wood finish. If it isn't, and the boards have shrunk slightly, leaving gaps, or boards have been carelessly lifted by tradespeople in a hurry, then you have to decide

Above: A blue colorwash can look good on washed floorboards, the blue blending with the grayish tint of the old pine. You can use thinned latex paint provided it is sealed with a varnish.

.eft: Removing a ceiling to expose he floor joists of the room above 'an be very effective.

Bear in mind, however, that sound and drafts can travel up through gaps between the floorboards.

whether or not to proceed. Entire board lengths can be replaced, but finding a lumber match for second-hand boards is becoming more and more difficult. Gaps between boards can be filled with chamfered wooden fillets glued, hammered into place and left to dry. In both these cases you would do well to consider sanding down the floor with a rented industrial sander, to achieve a level and color-matched surface.

You may find that the gaps do not bother you. As long as there is no cellar or basement with exposed joists beneath, electric light will not filter up through the gaps, which can ruin the effect of any stripped floor. If you have access to the joists from the cellar, however, it is a simple enough job to nail hardboard to the underside of the floor, between the joists. Cut the hardboard into long strips that fit neatly between the joists. Tack into position with ¾ in./18 mm tacks, at 6 in./150 mm centers. Don't be tempted into using longer tacks, unless you check first to make sure that the points won't break through the surface of the boards of the floor above.

Colors on washed boards

Old scrubbed boards will often have a gray appearance, and you can accentuate this with your color choice, using a gray-green or pale blue colorwash. Two teaspoonfuls of latex paint stirred into 1 quart (1 liter) of water will provide you with a wash that sinks into the grain, but can be wiped off the surface. This wash can be repeated until the color effect is satisfactory. Then, the board can be varnished or left unsealed. If you want to put color back into the bleached wood, try a wash of dark red, highlighting the grain, followed by an oil-based pine varnish. Dilute the varnish with mineral spirits so that it can be applied more easily, sinking into the wood surface. Finally, seal with a clear floor varnish.

Machine sanding

Rental centers will rent out two types of sander for your floor: a large machine that looks like an old-fashioned lawnmower with a dust bag attached, for the main floor area, and a small belt or disk sander for getting in close to baseboards. They will supply all the necessary abrasives, and, most importantly, face masks, and protective glasses. Make sure you understand how both machines work before you take them home.

Your first job is to hammer down all the nail heads, well below the surface of the floorboards, using a nail set or punch. If you don't take on this tiresome task, the nail heads will rip the abrasive

When sanding a floor, begin by making a series of diagonal passes with coarse abrasive across the boards. Then work diagonally in the other direction with a medium grade of abrasive.

A properly sanded and varnished boarded floor makes the most of the beauty of the wood grain.

sheets on the drum sander. Sanding a floor raises a lot of dust, and although the machine has a collecting bag, a lot gets into the air, so make sure you are wearing a protective mask and goggles when you start up the machine.

- Run the sander diagonally across the floor at 45 degrees to the boards, using coarse abrasive paper.
- Change to a medium-grade abrasive, and again sand across the floor, but this time at right angles to your first run.
- Then sand up and down, following the board direction.
- Change finally to a fine-grade abrasive, and finish off sanding with the grain.
- The small sander reaches into baseboard areas, doorways, and alcoves where the larger drum cannot reach. Here again, start with the coarser abrasive, finish with the fine.
- Clean dust from the boards before sealing and varnishing.

Sealing and varnishing

Clear varnishes are readily available, but they are expensive. Make sure you have the best quality, and that the varnish is recommended for flooring. Cheap polyurethane varnish intended for internal wood work will not put up with everyday wear and tear, and is false economy. It may crack under pressure of furniture castors, and you could be faced with the prospect of a repeat job.

'ext work up and down the boards sing medium-grade abrasive. hen fit a fine grade of paper to the machine and repeat the process, working in the direction of the grain.

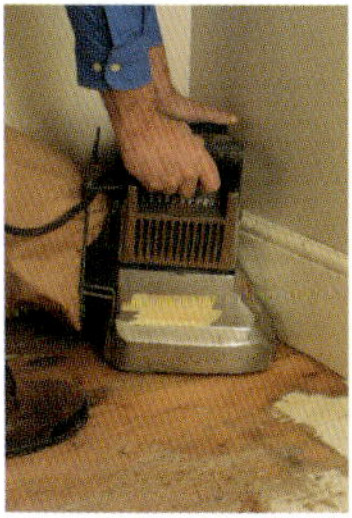

Use an edge sander to work up to the baseboards, using progressively finer grades of abrasive.

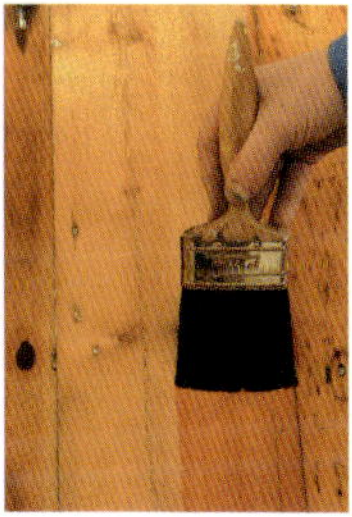

After removing all dust and debris, treat the boards with a sealer and apply u varnish.

Special effects on wood floors

Many of the paint and dye effects used on purpose-built joinery, items of furniture, and wooden frames can be used successfully on floorboards. The main consideration remains—that floors are there to be walked on—and therefore any scheme must be permanently sealed in order for it to be considered practical and hard-wearing.

isual effects can work well on both scrubbed and machine-sanded oors. The rule of thumb is that the darker colored schemes will end to suit the scrubbed, darker boards, while the pale-colored nishes are best on newly revealed surfaces on sanded floors. nless the reason for machine sanding was a very uneven surface, me and energy are wasted if the intention is to apply an overall ark finish.

uitable finishes

Vood stains and varnishes will alter the color of the wood surface, rain, or both, and decorate and protect the lumber. What they will ot do is alter the basic visual characteristics of the wood and its rain. A pine floor is still a pine floor, no matter what stain is on it. ust as the Victorians failed to disguise cheap pine doors by pplying a dark varnish resembling mahogany or dark oak, you will e unable to give the impression of expensive boards by brushing a an of rosewood stain onto a softwood floor. A basic rule of wood nishing is that cheap timber with an applied stain of oak does not ook like oak: it looks like cheap lumber with an oak stain on it. 'ou will achieve a satisfactory result only if you apply a finish that omplements the wood's natural colors and character. If you wish o obliterate it, you can simply paint it.

Vater- and oil-based stains

Vater-based stains are perhaps more suited to machine-sanded loors, their versatility emphasized by a lighter wood surface. They an be bought in convenient-sized cans, and are available in bright olors as well as natural wood shades. In a concentrated form they re not very subtle, but the addition of water makes for pleasing ints. They do not penetrate the wood as deeply, and, when used iluted, can be wiped or sanded off the surface leaving only the rain colored.

Oil-based stains are strong, penetrating deeper into the wood ibers. A dark stain applied to a surface needs much sanding to estore the surface to its natural state and leave the grain colored. Colored varnishes are available, combining color and sealer in one coat. However, one coat of sealer is not enough, so these types of varnish are best used to produce a decorative effect, with a clear varnish applied on the top as a hard-wearing finish.

A strong-colored stained wooden floor with a deep enamel finish greets visitors with a sense of opulence and warmth.

As with any wood, the natural color will alter the stain slightly and an experiment on scrap wood is always a good idea. Blues and greens diluted and washed onto scrubbed boards work well on the fairly gray surface. Different strengths of the same basic color, achieved by dilution ratios or repeat coats, can set up a floor of striped boards. Squares and checkered patterns can be achieved by simple measuring and masking with painter's tape. Test the wood first, however. If it is very absorbent, brush the stain up to, but not over, the tape or it will bleed underneath.

Any color you apply will require a protective varnish. Polyurethane will yellow slightly, so make sure your blues don't end up as greens by testing them first. Reds, though, improve when varnished because subtle shades of orange appear, so make sure you include the final seal in your color calculation. This is particularly important if you use a colored varnish decoratively before the finishing clear varnish, where, for example, a yellow pine finish is used over a diluted red. Red color is strong in the

Water- and oil-based wood treatments

woodgrain, but the surface is influenced by the pine and appears as a patchy yellow-orange. The yellow content will increase slightly with time since finishing coats of varnish react to the sun's rays in a well-lit room.

Paint and varnish combinations

Oil-based enamel paints are tough enough for floor finishes in some lesser used areas: in bedrooms, for example, where scatter rugs are the featured covering. Heavy traffic areas are different. Constant wear and tear, particularly from external entry points, will

Combining lumber treatments can produce some wonderful effects, such as this combination of a pale blue wash and pine stain. Don't be afraid to experiment, but try out your ideas on scrap wood first.

quickly damage the floor surface. These areas – hallways, corridors, and even "through routes" in living-rooms—need a very heavy-duty finish.

Special floor paints are on the market, but outlets are limited, as is the range of colors. However, if you are lucky and the color scheme is suitable, they are a good solution. Otherwise, choose your color from any paint source, and apply a flooring-quality clear varnish on top, building up a protective layer that needs to be at least two and possibly four coats thick, depending on the anticipated usage. Any design or color combination can be used because you are treating the paint finish in the same way as a colored stain. Remember, however, that the varnish will tend to add a yellowish cast to the colors, which may produce an effect that you had not intended or wanted. Recreate your intended scheme on scrap pine board and apply the required number of varnish coats. You may find that changing the base colors slightly will produce the effect you want. Many interesting marriages of stain and paint are thus open to you. Try painting the board with latex, and removing part of the surface when it is dry, revealing th woodgrain underneath. A sander can be used for this, but a more casual effect is achieved by hand, and you can use silicon carbide paper (used wet) instead of sandpaper.

Try experimenting with wax resists. This is an old technique relying on the principle that oil (the wax) and water (the latex paint) won't mix.

- Start by washing a diluted pale blue stain along the board, and leaving it to dry.

You can lighten scrubbed boards further by bleaching them with a proprietary, two-part wood bleach and neutralizer. Here, the bleached board has been treated with a simple varnish.

- Use steel wool to rub a clear wax, available from artists' suppliers and home centers, randomly along parts of the board, creating an abstract pattern.
- Before the wax is dry, overpaint the entire board with a mid-blue water-based latex paint, and this time let it dry out completely.
- Rub down the areas of the board that you waxed with coarse steel wool; they should appear slightly darker than the rest. The top paint will come off with the wax, leaving patches of pale blue stain showing through.
- The top paint can be blended in more subtly if it is still wet wher you rub it—the patches are less obvious since the paint tends to spread along the board.
- As with all combinations, the colors chosen give very different effects. Two-tone blues and greens are not as vivid as a mix of pine yellow and a dark red or brown, so test the scheme on scrap wood before you start.

Different wood colors

A rustic appearance can add to the appeal of bare wooden floors in smaller rooms, when the glazed look of expensive flooring found in town houses seems inappropriate.

Scrubbed floorboards can be further lightened by bleaching them. This technique should be used sparingly, however, perhaps one board in four across the floor area. Adding a pale gray wash and a pine stain at random to other boards, leaving the rest with a scrubbed finish, gives a pleasing range of tones. Proprietary wood bleaches are available from good hardware store, and are usually applied in two parts with a special brush available from the same source. When the bleach has dried out, the wood needs to be washed, first with a recommended neutralizer and then sparingly with warm water. A pine varnish on some of the other boards needs thinning slightly to sink into the surface. When it dries, sand back the top surface to remove any trace of a sheen.

The floor can be left as it is, varnished once to seal it and then sanded by hand gently to remove any surface sheen. Alternatively, to ensure maximum protection, the floor can be varnished in the conventional manner.

Using wax resists to create attractive colored finishes on wood is an old technique, but one worth investigating. Basically two colors are applied, but areas of wax prevent one color completely obliterating the other. Begin by brushing on a diluted stain, working along the grain. Leave it to dry completely.

Form a small pad from steel wool and use it to apply random areas of clear wax to the stained wood, creating an abstract pattern. Again work in the direction of the wood grain. You can buy the wax from home centers and artists' suppliers. Work quickly as you must apply the second color before the wax has a chance to dry.

Apply the second color, a water-based latex, which can be a darker or lighter tone of the base color or perhaps a contrast. Experiment on scrap wood first. Brush the color along the grain, making sure the entire board is covered. Then leave it to dry.

Use coarse steel wool to rub down the waxed areas of the wood, which will appear a different tone to the rest. The paint on top of the wax will come away with the wax, leaving areas of the base coat showing through. Finally, seal the finish in the usual way.

Fitting a floor, fitting baseboards

Renewing a boarded floor should not be undertaken lightly, as it involves a considerable amount of work and disruption. However, replacing a damaged baseboard is a job that can be undertaken as a weekend project. Care and accuracy are required as always, but normal household life can continue around the work.

Fitting a new softwood floor onto joists, replacing one that is too badly damaged to repair, keeping it square with the room sides, and finishing with a replacement baseboard in the house style, is a major undertaking. This task is best left to a specialist, unless you have some previous experience. Irrespective of whether you tackle the job yourself or not, it is helpful to know what is involved: the room will be out of commission for a considerable time. You must make allowances for time spent not only on the floor itself, but in making good the room. Wall damage is likely to occur when removing the baseboards, and this may involve plastering or papering. If you have two rooms knocked through into one, measure the size of the baseboard in each half of the new area—they may be two distinctly different styles. Period houses generally had a larger, more ornate baseboards in what was referred to as the Sunday room, than in the back or "living" room. If these rooms are now joined, the baseboards could differ in height by as much as 5 in./13 cm. A consistent baseboard size will be needed. If you fit the larger size to stay in period, you merely need to be as careful as possible during removal. If you are fitting a smaller size, a great deal of making good will be needed to tie in to the wall. Remember the finish, too. Quite apart from any paint effect, three coats of protective varnish will be needed, each requiring 24 hours' drying time.

Removal

- Hammer an electrician's bolster between the top edge of the baseboard and the wall, near the end of a length, opening up a gap.
- Pry the baseboard away from the wall. If excessive levering is required, protect the wall surface with a wood off-cut.
- The baseboard length may be nailed directly to the masonry, or nailed or screwed to sawn lumber blocks inset into the wall, or nailed to vertical studs if you have a stud wall.
- If the boards come away from the wall leaving well-secured nails still in place, it may be easier to hammer them in rather than risk more damage trying to get them out.
- Once the baseboard is out of the way, start at one end of the room and pry up the first few boards only.

In period houses baseboards can be of considerable depth, making a strong visual statement around the edge of the floor. However, they are vulnerable to knocks and may need replacing.

'rive an electrician's bolster behind the ·aseboard, near one end, to begin 'eeing it from the base of the wall.

Work along the baseboard, levering it from the wall and trying to minimise the damage to the plasterwork.

If any fixing nails pull through the board as it is removed, hammer them in rather than trying to pull them out.

Removing boards only as you replace them means that you always have a floor surface to kneel or stand on, lessening the risk of an accident.

Remove the floorboard or cut nails with the claw of the hammer during the process of removing the board; don't hammer them down.

Brush dirt and debris off the joist when it is revealed, and then you are ready to lay the new floorboards.

ift the first floorboard by driving an electrician's ·olster into the gap between the boards and ·evering upward.

Once you have the end lifted high enough, slip a cleat underneath and begin to drive it along below the board, which will be sprung free.

New for old

Unless you plan to fit a reclaimed wood floor, possibly utilizing some undamaged lengths from the old one, you will find the board widths will not be exactly the same as the ones that you have taken out. Actual metric sizes of finished timber have replaced the old imperial nominal sizes, so board widths will be close, but not exact. Because the entire floor is being replaced, this does not matter, and gives you the opportunity to select TGV boards, giving the floor overall additional strength and minimizing the risk of warping and lifting.

Measure the floor carefully, in the direction the boards run, and make sure when you order the wood that there will be enough boards of that length or longer to complete the job. This avoids cutting and shutting on the main part of the floor, and looks much neater because no break appears in the run of the woodgrain. If this seems overly fussy, remember that unmatched joins will be more noticeable if you intend to use a decorative paint or stain finish.

Alcoves or bay areas with shorter lengths can be cut from longer stock on site, but remember when making your calculations that bays may need miters. Begin at the end of the room; you may be able to use the old boards as templates for cutting the new, particularly if you have to start in a bay. Otherwise, transfer angles for cutting lines directly from a sliding bevel. Notice that the boards stop slightly short of the wall. This allows for any small expansion of the wood and helps air to circulate between the floor and ceiling. This small gap will be covered by the skirting.

Measure the floor carefully to calculate the number and length of new boards required. Try to keep joints in runs to a minimum.

If the ends of boards need to be cut at an angle, use a sliding bevel to transfer the angle accurately to the new boards.

Closing up the floorboards

Whether you use TGV or straight-sided boards, they need to be clamped together tightly. This will not only maximize the strength of the TGV join, but also minimizes the gaps that inevitably appear when using conventional boards, as the wood dries out fully even if it has been fitted after acclimatization. You must help this process by placing the lumber lengths in the room for a few days before installation. It still won't stop small gaps appearing over time, but it will tend to reduce the shrinkage.

As with all bought softwoods, the worst problems occur when cold, damp lumber is cut and joined, and the central heating is turned on. For this reason, really top-quality floors are relaid, closing up the boards, after six months or so.

- Lay half a dozen boards in position, leave a 2 in./5 cm gap, and place a wooden cleat across the joists, either nailed down or hel against the old boards yet to be taken up.
- Make up two identical wedges, about 1 ft./30 cm long. Place them in the gap and hammer together, tightening up the floor.
- Leave the wedges in place while you nail down the floor. In high quality TGV work, where the floor is to be left exposed, one board at a time must be laid and wedged tight, so that the invisible fixing (2 in./50 mm lost-head or finishing nail) can be made through the tongue and then hidden by the subsequent board. With TGV boards it is important not to damage the tongu when wedging, or subsequent grooves won't fit very easily. Cut a scrap piece of TGV in half, fit the grooved half over the tongue a protection, and hammer your wedges against that.

Lay six of the new boards in place, leaving a space between them and the old boards yet to be removed.

Nail a stout wooden cleat across the joists about 2 in./5 cm from the edge of the last new floorboard laid.

Cut two long, narrow wedges and drive them between the cleat and floorboard to clamp the boards tightly together for nailing to the joists.

Measure up for the new lengths of baseboard, beginning at the door opening and working toward the nearest corner.

Nail the board in place. At an inside corner, mark the profile of the baseboard on the adjoining board so that it fits over the first board.

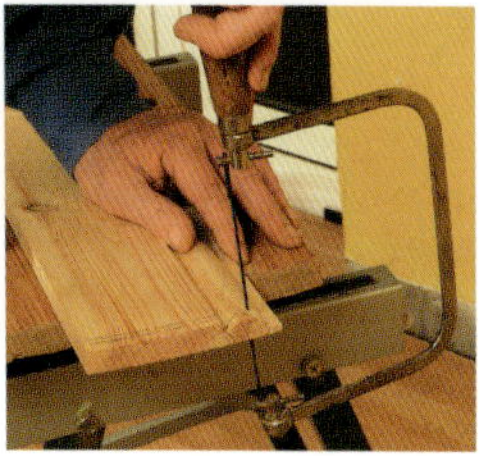

Use a coping saw to cut the profile in the end of the board. Its thin blade will be able to follow any intricate pattern with ease.

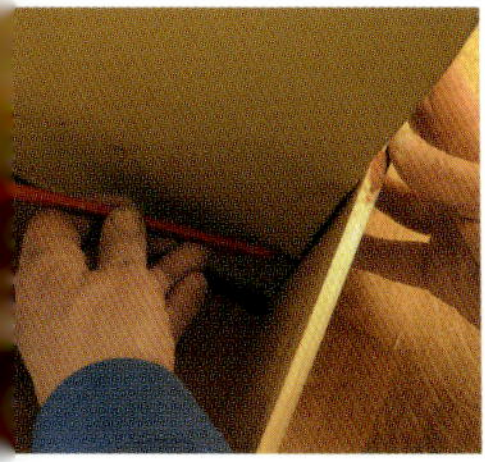

At an external corner, mark the board for length against the wall, then miter the end outward from this mark. Do the same with its neighbor.

Nail the boards to the wall on each side of an outside corner. Then pin through the end of one board into the other.

You can attach the baseboard by using the original method, nailing into the wall or wooden wedges, or screw it in place.

Putting back a baseboard

The size and form of a baseboard will often date a property, so make sure the one you pick is suitable, and not at odds with the rest of the décor. Larger, more ornate molded baseboards give a period feel to the room, and usually appear to be part of the wall, not the floor. Smaller, modern baseboards, often found with a two-sided profile so that they can be fixed either way around, tend to appear as part of the flooring, particularly if they have been treated with the same finish.

- When you have made your choice of molding, start from the door opening (a right-angled cut).
- Measure and cut right into the first corner, flush against the adjacent wall.
- Butt up the next board, mark the molding profile onto it and cut it to fit. All inside corners should be cut this way.
- Outside corner turns should be mitered—after fixing the first length, mark the inside of the next miter on the reverse side of the next board. Remember that the cutting line should run outward from the back face of the baseboard, as the 45-degree joint with the adjoining board runs out from the corner.
- Fix the baseboard in place either reusing the method that was used in fixing the old one, or screw into position, covering the counterbored heads with wooden plugs, cutting flush with a knife and sanding. This fixing method is recommended if you intend a stain and varnish finish.

Staircases

Staircases come in a range of shapes and styles from the purely functional to the elaborate and ornate. Get to know your staircase type and its functional parts; for example, whether it is a straight, sweeping, half-turn, quarter-turn, or dog-leg style staircase, and whether it has a closed or open string, or open tread.

Types of stairs

Modern staircases tend toward one style, the closed-string stair, which takes up the minimum of space, usually against a wall, and is the most economic to construct. Other styles in timber staircases include the open-string, where the strings are sawn to the profile of the steps, and the stair treads sit on the cut-outs, or the open-tread, where the risers are omitted altogether. Other staircases, such as spirals, are often functional space savers installed to gain access to loft rooms or basements.

If you own a period property, you will already know that, historically, the staircase was much more than a functional way of changing floors—it was a status symbol. The Victorians, in particular, favored elaborate, decorative stairs and their house design emphasized ornate hallways, where the stairs could be admired by a visitor to the front door. By the time the stairs reached the servants' floors, however, best-quality joinery lumber was replaced by cheap pine, painted or varnished a darker color as an attempted disguise. Whatever the age of your staircase, it contains the same functional parts, all of which are replaceable.

Basic staircase repairs

Creaking stairs are usually caused by loose-fitting treads or risers. Under foot pressure the loose part moves against an adjacent fixed piece. The repairs are fairly simple, however:

- Locate the source of the creak, and check the wedges that should hold the tread and riser firmly in position.
- If one is loose, remove it, checking that it is not broken or split. If it is, use it as a template to make up a new one. Replace the wedge, hammering it into position with a wooden mallet.
- Check the glue blocks, regluing if necessary.
- On troublesome treads, you could try screwing and gluing a cleat of 1 x 1 in./25 x 25 mm underneath the complete width, joining the tread and riser together.
- Countersink 1¼ in./30 mm number 8 screws—don't use longer ones or you risk them coming through on the other side.
- Still underneath, drive the same screw size up into the bottom edge of the riser through the back edge of the tread.
- If you cannot gain access to the underside (if the soffit is plastered, for example), approach the problem from the front.

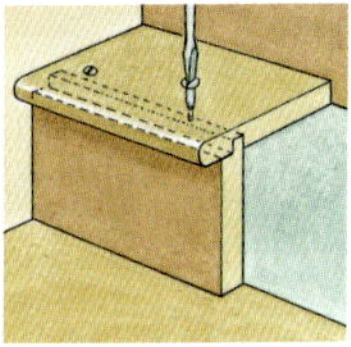

Screws can be driven down through the tread and into the riser below to reinforce the joint.

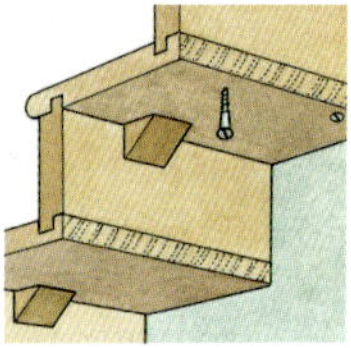

From beneath the stairs, drive more screws through the tread into the riser above.

Return nosings can be pried off and replaced. They also give access to the baluster base.

If access to the underside of the stairs is impossible, reinforce the treads and risers with L-brackets.

Staircase terminology

1 **Tread:** the part you stand on as you ascend or descend, usually overlapping the riser with a rounded or semirounded front.
2 **Nosing:** separate molding on the tread front, or the rounded tread front itself. (Return nosing is the same as the nosing, but hiding the end grain of the tread and side base of the baluster on staircases built with open strings.)
3 **Riser:** the vertical lumber joining the back of one tread to the front of the next.
4 **Strings:** the sides of the staircase. Against the wall side, the inner string forms part of the continuous baseboard. The outer string, which can be open or closed, holds the balusters in place.
5 **Balusters:** usually decorative turned sections of wood acting as banister supports. (Balustrade is the collective of balusters.)
6 **Banister:** hand rail, running on top of the balusters.
7 **Newel:** anchored support post, at the stair foot, and where the stairs turn.
8 **Glue blocks:** positioned at the back of the joint between riser and tread, as reinforcement.
9 **Wedges:** positioned underneath, securing both tread and riser to the string.

- Your only choice at the back of the tread is a right-angled metal support bracket to hold it to the riser.
- Mark the position with a pencil and carefully chisel the depth of the metal out of the wood.
- Screw into position with ½ in./12 mm number 6 screws.
- At the front of the tread, countersink 1¼ in./30 mm number 8 screws down through the tread, into the riser edge, at 4 in./10 cm intervals along the length.

Finishes on wooden staircases

If you have been forced to repair a tread from the front, using visible brackets and screws, you have little choice but to fit a carpet or runner. Functional and conventional, coverings reduce the noise of feet on the stairs. Closed string cases suit a fitted carpet, but open strings encourage the use of a centrally positioned stair runner, allowing both exposed sides to be varnished or painted.

There is no reason why stairs in good constructional condition should not have a paint and varnish finish. Try a combination of royal blue or dark green with a clear varnished natural wood, where the balusters and the risers are painted and the banister, tread, and nosings varnished. The different woods of banister and stair contrast well with each other and the painted parts.

Use a top quality floor or yacht varnish on the treads, applying four coats as a minimum and sanding gently between coats. Don't reverse the stair scheme, though. Paint on the treads won't last long unless it is over-varnished, which rather defeats the object.

Wood floors

A wood floor in good condition can be the center of attention in any house. Its good looks ensure that a wood floor fits well with almost any architectural style. Wood flooring makes a statement about your lifestyle and evokes memories of an age when floors were part of the decorative scheme in houses.

A popular choice

Current market research indicates that real wood strip and veneer flooring will remain a popular choice for the foreseeable future; it is hard-wearing, stylish, and relatively low maintenance. Real wood floors are warm and inviting in cold weather and have a cool feel on hot summer days. Health is an issue, too, because carpeting of any kind harbors dust mites, and asthma and hay fever sufferers can benefit from the low dust-retention qualities of wood flooring. Strip wood manufacturers have been quick to publicize their good environmental policies, claiming they do not cut any endangered tropical species, and take supplies of hardwood only from controlled areas where the rate of replanting equals the rate of harvesting.

The beauty of a real wood floor will set off any room's décor to perfection. The richness of the color and grain pattern will provide a feeling of warmth in winter and coolness in summer.

Strips and tiles of real wood

Real hardwood floors can still be laid, using solid boards of oak, yellow pine and ash, among others. Flooring specialists will supply and install a new wood floor, and often take on restoration projects. The cost can be prohibitive, though, and the rise in popularity of laminated wood flooring is testament to this fact. While solid hardwood strips will always be the top of the line, expensive and time-consuming to install, the newer laminated types of wood flooring offers a good-looking alternative at a price closer to the average budget. Real wood veneer forms the top layer of a composite construction, which includes a shock-absorbing middle layer and a stabilizing base. The three different layers consist of wood strips laid at right angles to each other, not unlike plywood, to minimize expansion and shrinkage of the floor panel as it experiences changes in temperature and humidity. The veneered panels are finished with up to five coats of varnish offering ultraviolet protection and offer almost the same visual qualities as solid floors. The tongue-and-groove planks of laminated flooring are priced per square foot and are often sold in bundles covering 10 ft. (3 m) or more. They can be fairly simply installed as "floating floors." The veneer thickness, about ¼ in. (4 to 5 mm), allows the laid floor to be sanded down and finished in the same way as a solid floor, and as the years pass, it will age and color in the same way. The same sanding and varnishing technique

Laminate flooring provides an inexpensive alternative to real wood flooring and can be very effective. The panels snap together and have a synthetic finish representing various woods.

needed for most wood-tile floors, although a few manufacturers ıpply prefinished units. Wood tiles consist of five or more strips of 'ood joined along their longest edge into a square, then bound ɔgether at right angles to similar units on a cloth backing to form square tile. The small strips may be solid hardwood, but usually ıey are veneer on a softwood or manufactured backing board. ⁄ood tiles offer a wide choice in wood types and are sold in undles, again priced per square foot. The main difference between ıese tiles and the laminated :rip flooring is that the tiles 'e glued into position ɔnventionally, while the strips re joined to each other and ot to the subfloor.

aminate flooring

' real wood veneer laminated ooring is the economic lternative to a traditional ardwood strip floor, then laminate "wood effect" floor panels are the cheap alternative to real wood veneers. The top layer is a photograhic effect, a fairly good plastic representation of a hardwood finish, either in colors pertaining to real woods such as cherry, chestnut, and ash, or in plain blues and greens.

These easy-to-fit tongue-and-groove panels are sometimes glued and sometimes snapped together, but they always need a flooring underlay and an installation kit. Be aware that the top "wood effect" layer is very thin and will not tolerate heavy traffic. Again priced per square foot, laminate flooring is available in bundles usually covering about 2.4 square yards (2 square meters). A fair indication of its quality is the price tag—about 20 percent of the price of a real wood veneer floor; and it would be more realistic to offer this product as an alternative to linoleum or vinyl than as an alternative to real wood.

Whatever type of flooring you choose, bear in mind that looking at small samples will not necessarily give you a good idea of the effect produced by the finished floor; some types of wood and some wood tile patterns may become overpowering when they are used over a large area.

⁄ood mosaic flooring comprises ʒuare panels of wood strips on a 'oth backing, which are laid like les. The strips may be cut from ɔlid lumber, softwood, or board ɪced with veneer, and offer a ɪnge of hardwood finishes.

Plastic laminate flooring boards offer a cheaper alternative to real wood.

These real oak laminate boards are tongued-and-grooved for jointing.

Locating the right floor

Always consult with your supplier to ensure the flooring panels of your choice are suitable for the domestic location you have in mind. Depending on the manufacturer's recommendations, certain panels may be deemed unsuitable for bathrooms (wet areas) or kitchens (high-humidity areas), or be classified as suitable for entrance halls or bedrooms (high- or low-traffic areas). Some boards are unsuitable for heated floors, such as beech, whereas some woods are ideal for humid areas where high dimensional stability is required. Bamboo, for example, has a low moisture content and works well in bathrooms.

Preparing to lay a floating floor

As usual, the hard work in laying a floor is unseen, being underneath. Preparation is the key to a good floor, while the actual laying of the panels should proceed reasonably quickly, permitting an ever increasing view of the final result. The preparation must include leveling of the existing floor, if necessary. A basement with a solid floor may need screeding with a concrete mix, or sealing to prevent damp problems. Slightly uneven or pitted concrete floors can be made good by pouring on a self-leveling compound;

Parquet flooring strips are traditionally laid in a herringbone or basketweave pattern. The latter lends itself to mosaic panels.

hardboard can be pinned over floorboards. Cleating and fitting a TGV chipboard under-floor is a good idea in a basement; howev headroom is often a priority in these areas, and if height does not permit cleating, then you must work on the concrete floor. If your room has a skirting, consider whether or not you wish to remove i for laying, or replace it altogether with a matching wood finish. Floor panels must have a ⅜ in./10 mm expansion gap all around the perimeter of the room, to facilitate absorption and loss of moisture, either covered by the new baseboard or a strip of beading pinned to the old one. Finally, prepare to lay your hardwood panels on a dry, level surface called a sub-floor, which i an underlay on a roll that can be supplied with the boards. The cushioning effect of this underlay disguises any (small) defects in the old floor surface, and lets the new floor "float" on top.

Floating the floor

When you are happy with the sub-floor, set out the hardwood panels. Lay the panels with the tongues facing into the room, following the direction of the longest wall, unless the room is square, when you should set out in the direction of the incoming light. Don't lay the panels in a strict grid; offset to make sure the butt joins do not line up across the floor. Make sure your first row of boards is straight—remember that the wall may not be—and us ⅜ in./10 mm blocks to create the expansion gap. Saw the last panel in the row to fit, using its offcut to begin row two. Glue the panels to each other, at the sides and end, by running glue into th upper side of the groove and gently tapping with a mallet and protective block. Panels will probably need cutting to fit lengthwis when you reach the final row: mark the cutting line with a pencil by placing them on top of the previous row. Remember to include he expansion gap, and that your calculation must include the ongue-and-groove joint. Glue the final row of panels to each ther, position the expansion blocks, and leave to dry. Finally fit he baseboard to cover the expansion gap after removing the ⅜ in./10 mm blocks or, if the baseboard has been left in place, it a decorative quarter-round molding or similar.

You may find that you have to fit the flooring around central eating pipes, in which case take careful measurements of each ipe's position and transfer these to the appropriate board. Bore hole in the board, making it large enough to clear the pipe, then nake cuts from the hole to the board edge. Retain the off-cut. it the board in place around the pipe and glue the off-cut back ehind it. If the flooring is to stop at a doorway, fit a hardwood hreshold across the bottom of the frame and lay the boards up o it. Use a profile gauge to copy the shape of the frame, or make paper template, and transfer this to the flooring, cutting around he shape with a coping saw.

Lay out the wood panels, working away from one wall with the tongues facing into the room.

Maintain a ⅜ in./10 mm expansion gap y inserting slivers of wood between he wall and boards.

As you work, glue the panels together by applying a bead of glue into each panel groove.

Tap the panels together, using a hammer and protective block to avoid damaging the edges.

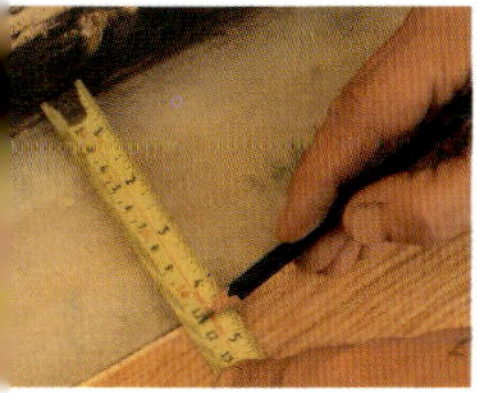

When you reach the far wall, measure or the cut board, allowing for the xpansion gap.

Transfer the dimension to a board, making allowance for the tongue-and-groove joint; cut it to width.

Use an angled metal strip to tap the cut boards into place. Then cover the gaps with beading.

Basic skills: Tiled floors

Tiles are more popular than ever before as a decorative floor covering. This is due in part to the array of options now available, from basic ceramics from a discount warehouse to diamond-sawn slate from a specialist supplier. They can be easy to clean, hard-wearing and, of course, very good-looking.

Tiles used for a decorative flooring effect in period houses were well made and extremely hard-wearing, surviving decades of abuse from working boots with nailed soles and heels that tramped in street dirt. Encaustic tiles in basic colors were used to make patterned floors in hallways and corridors; older houses sometimes had flagstones or slate tiles in kitchens and laundry rooms downstairs, but quarry tiles were more common in these areas. If you uncover a tiled floor in an older property that is basically sound, consider using it as a room feature rather than replacing it. Old cleaning principles and techniques can restore the look of a tiled floor simply and cheaply soda crystals in hot water will take off grime and grease, and traditional polishes are still available

from specialist suppliers. Encaustic (where colored clays are burned in) and geometric tiles (natural clay fired into simple shapes and inserts) are available again, and it may be possible to match a tile design if floor damage has occurred. An independent tile workshop or supplier can advise you, or consult a restoration specialist.

Types of tile

If you intend to lay a new floor, several tile options are open to you. Specialist shops offer diamond-sawn slate, marble, and many types of natural stone slabs, and reclaimed terra cotta in tile form polishes up beautifully. Quarry tiles are functional, good-looking, and easy to keep clean, if rather cold to the touch, and ceramic

Flagstone tiles make for a practical, hard-wearing yet attractive floor in a kitchen or hallway. They are easily cleaned, retain their color and pattern well, and require no maintenance.

Encaustic tiles with simple patterns were commonly used in the hallways of period houses. Modern versions are available, making the restoration of this kind of flooring a viable proposition for those seeking to recreate an original look for their homes.

floor tiles are as easy to lay on a floor as a wall. Other options are presanded cork tiles, laid with adhesive but requiring a sealer, or presealed cork that is easy to maintain. Vinyl floor tiles are usually self-adhesive, and come in a wide variety of color schemes, but if vinyl is your choice, consider loose-laid sheet vinyl, available in many designs and colors but often found as imitation wood or tiling complete with three-dimensional effect and colored grouting. Similar to sheet vinyl is linoleum, sold the same way by linear meter off a wide roll. A wide range of decorative patterning is available, to suit any room area, but particularly a children's play area because it is tough and easy to keep clean. Its drawback is that it is more difficult to fit, being stiffer and less easy to manipulate, and more awkward to cut.

Repairing and leveling solid floors

No matter what type of tile you plan to install on a solid floor, the floor itself must be level. Quarry tile, stone, or any ceramic tile bedded in mortar must sit on a level surface. If the floor is slightly uneven, you can use a homemade strike-off board to level the mortar bed or you can use a self-leveling mortar compound. This special mortar, available from any good building supply outlet, comes dry, usually in 55 lb. (25 kg) bags. Mix the contents in a bucket, following the manufacturer's directions, so that the fairly liquid, lump-free compound can be poured onto the floor. The principle is that it finds its own level, but you need to assist it by troweling it out with a plasterer's trowel to form a thin layer. The compound dries hard and smooth, and although you can walk on it in a couple of hours, you must leave it for a day before attempting to lay a floor on it.

Concrete that has cracked or has deeper surface damage can be patched. Use a strong mortar mix (3 parts sand to 1 part cement), wetting the cracked area first and then filling and leveling it off with a trowel. Slightly damp floors can be treated by brushing on two or three coats of a commercial waterproofing liquid, but if the floor is really wet—probably because the waterproof membrane under the surface has failed—this will not solve the problem. You can stretch a new membrane over the concrete and then cover it with flooring-grade tongue-and-groove chipboard, creating a dry "floating" floor. Ideally, the new waterproof membrane should be continued up the walls to meet the sill.

Using a mixing attachment in an electric drill will speed the mixing of self-leveling compound.

Trowel the compound into small shallow depressions, making sure you fill them completely.

Pour the self-leveling compound directly from the bucket into large depressions.

Feather the edges of the compound with the trowel and leave to dry completely.

Heavy tiles

These need to be bedded in mortar, and a concrete (solid) floor is ideal. Floorboards or chipboard over joists (a suspended floor) may not take the extra weight and is not really suitable for this type of tiling. Vinyl, cork, or a veneered floating floor would be more sensible, but if you really must have heavy quarry tiles or similar on a suspended floor, check with a professional builder first.

Laying ceramic tiles in adhesive

First set out a dry run: simply place the tiles on the floor to find the best arrangement or sequence before any permanent positioning is done (remember to leave a gap for the grout). Setting out corridor shapes, long and thin, can often be done by eye, following the longer dimension, but regular room shapes should be started at the center. The room center can be determined by using lengths of string to join the central points of opposing walls, forming a cross where the strings meet. To confirm that the grout pattern is square when you open the door, run a third string from the door frame to the opposite wall, forming a 90-degree angle. A right angle should occur where all the strings cross; if it does not, then the room is out of square. If this is the case, use the string from the door frame as the starting guide, and adjust the center point strings to form the required right angles. When you are happy with the setting out, either chalk the strings and snap them to the floor surface, leaving a guideline, or if you are confident that they are fixed securely, use the strings themselves as guides. Spread the adhesive to the required depth, using a notched spreader. The notch size is designed to spread different thicknesses. Your specialist tile supplier will advise you, and ensure you have the correct adhesive: flexible on a suspended floor, water-resistant in potentially wet areas. Don't spread too much adhesive at one time; start with a square yard or square meter or so, until you are confident that you can work more quickly. Line up the first tile with the guides, press firmly into the adhesive bed, and place tile spacers (or wooden match sticks) to ensure correct positioning and spacing of the next tiles.

As you proceed across the floor, check that the work is level, using a straight edge. When the floor is covered with complete tiles, leaving only the borders to cut to fit, clean the joints and remove excess adhesive.

Set out the tiles dry first to establish a starting point for the rows and determine where cut tiles will be necessary. You may have to rearrange them several times until you are happy.

As when tiling a wall, use a notched trowel to spread a layer of adhesive on the floor. The notches ensure a uniform amount is applied.

Only cover a manageable section of floor at a time with the adhesive; otherwise, it will begin to set before you can lay all the tiles.

Bed the tiles in the adhesive, working away from your guide strings.

Remove excess adhesive from between the tiles. Grout the joints when the adhesive has set.

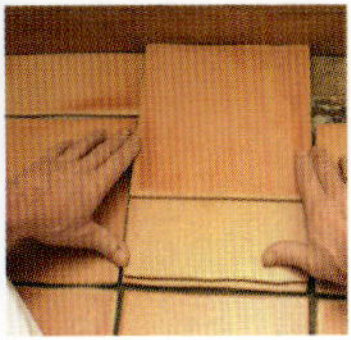

Lay a tile on the last whole tile laid and butt another against the wall to mark the cutting line.

Score along the line and snap the tile in two in the same manner as ceramic wall tiles.

Tile nippers are ideal for making small cut-outs in tiles to fit around pipes and other obstructions.

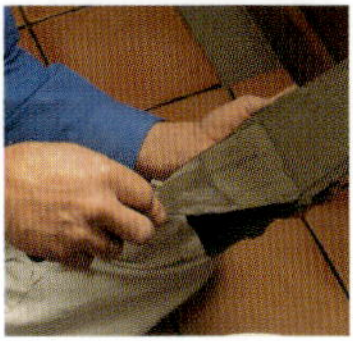

Spread adhesive on the back of a cut tile and press it into place. This protects adjacent tiles.

When the adhesive has dried, mix up the grout and spread it into the joints.

At the edges of the floor, work the grout into the joint between tiles and wall.

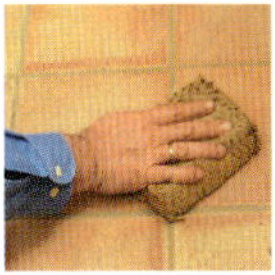

Use a damp sponge to wash off all traces of excess grout before it has a chance to dry.

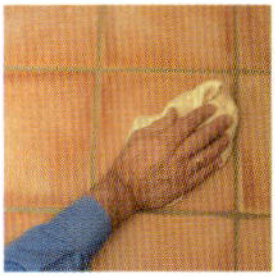

When all the excess grout has been removed, polish the floor with a soft cloth.

Make sure you remove any powdery deposits left in corners by the sponging.

To measure the border tiles for cutting, lay a complete tile directly on top of the last one laid in that row, place a tile on top, butted to the wall or baseboard and mark the gap with a line on the tile underneath. Cut the tile by scoring and snapping, or by using a tile cutting machine which you can hire by the day. Fix the cut tile in place, and follow the same sequence in the next row. When the entire floor is completed, clean down and leave for 24 hours.

Grouting and finishing

Spread the grout on the tiled surface, and force it down between the tile edges into the joint lines using a squeegee. Use a damp cloth to wipe the tile surface clean, rinsing the cloth regularly. The lines of grout now need to be smoothed out, you can use a grout finisher, available from your specialist supplier, or a short length of dowel will do just as well. When you are happy, and all tiles are free of excess grout, polish the surface with a clean, dry cloth.

The finished floor will give many years' service and will maintain its good looks throughout.

Laying vinyl and cork tiles

Good setting out and a level surface are the keys to successful laying of cork or vinyl tiles on a suspended wooden floor. Gaps between floorboards will show through the tile, even if level; covering the boards with hardboard is the only way to achieve the flat surface needed. TGV chipboard floors that are not uneven need sanding at the joins to ensure a smooth surface.

A hardboard subfloor

Before you lay hardboard sheets onto conventional floorboards, you need to punch the existing nail heads below the surface; otherwise, the overlaid sheets will not lie flat.

Use a nail set and hammer, just as you would if you were sanding down the floor. Use the largest size of sheet that you can conveniently handle, to cut down the number of joints, and fit each shiny side down onto the floor. The textured face provides a good key for the tile adhesive.

You will need to stagger the joints from row to row, so that you do not create a line across the room, but as hardboard cuts easily, either with a saw or knife, this is a fairly simple job. Secure the sheets with hardboard pins, punched in at 4 in./100 mm centers and 4 in./100 mm intervals along all the edges, or use an industrial staple gun.

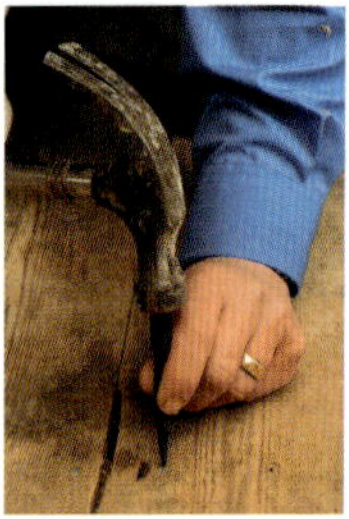

Before covering a floor with hardboard sheets, drive all the nail heads below the surface.

Use a panel saw to cut sheets to size as necessary and stagger the panels from one row to the next.

Setting out and laying the tiles

Set out the tiles following the guide for solid floors, finding the room center and drawing a cross on the floor. This centers the arrangement in the room, but, if this leaves a narrow border that does not suit the decorative design on the tile, you can adjust it. This is easier if you use string to make the initial centered cross, dividing the area into quarters. The string can be tied to pins driven into the floor, or secured with tape. If the tiles are patterned, ensure the design matches up as you place a dry run of two rows of tiles from the center to the baseboard, butting the tiles to the stringline. If there is a narrow gap at odds with your tile design, adjust the strings so that complete tiles butt to the wall in two directions. When the arrangement is satisfactory, rub chalk onto the strings and snap them against the floor to leave accurate marks or leave them in place and use them as guides. Peel off the backing of the tiles (if they have one). Position, working along the guidelines to the wall. Some cork tiles use adhesive, which is spread on the hardboard (not the tile) with a notched spatula. Lay one tile at a time, pressing it down firmly. Cutting tiles to fit is a matter of overlaying on the gap and marking the waste, then cutting the tile with a sharp snap-blade knife held against a steel straightedge. Use a tile offcut as a cutting mat. Unusually shaped objects such

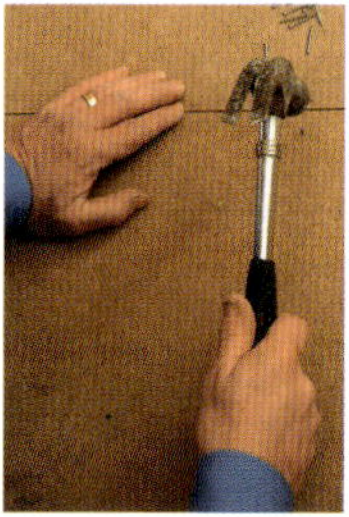

Staple or nail the hardboard sheets to the floor, spacing the fixings at 4 in./100 mm centres.

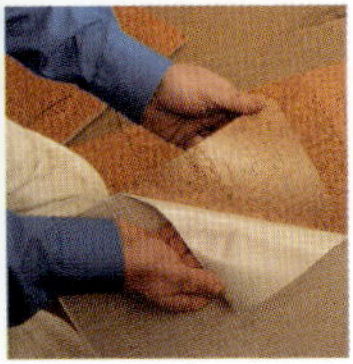

Some cork tiles are self-adhesive, so all that is necessary is to peel off the back and press them down.

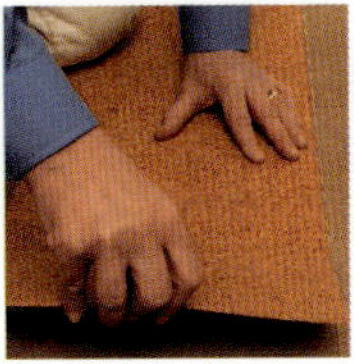

Press the tiles into place on the floor, aligning the first rows carefully with strings.

Center the arrangement of tiles on the floor, using two strings at right-angles to maintain the alignment.

To fit a tile around a bathroom fitting, make a paper template and transfer the shape to the tile.

Mark tiles for cutting by laying one over the last tile laid and butting another against the wall.

Using a steel rule or straightedge as a guide, cut the tiles to size with a sharp knife.

Press the cut tiles into place around the edge of the floor to finish the job.

as pedestals may need a template of paper to aid fitting. Tape scrap paper to the floor and cut a series of slits into the pedestal shape from the edge. Press a fold line around the shape with scissor points, remove it from the floor, and cut out around the fold. Tape the template onto the tile and follow the outline with a snap-blade knife.

Sealing the floor

Plain cork tiles are easy to fit. They need sealing after laying, but vinyl-coated cork does not. When the plain cork floor is finished and the adhesive has set, lightly sand rough areas at the edges of the tiles with fine-grade sandpaper wrapped around a cork block. Brush away dust, and wipe the floor with a rag damped with mineral spirits. Use two or three coats of cork sealer or clear polyurethane varnish to finish the job.

Cork tiles can provide a stylish, attractive, and warm floor covering for almost any part of the house, including the kitchen.

Woodwork

Wood surfaces about the home need a sympathetic treatment if they are to look their best. Fashionable finishes are beneficial if they add to the character of the original wood, but if they disguise it, they are merely doing the same job as a lick of paint, commonly used by builders to cover new wood with well-marked growth rings and carrying defects. Traditional treatments like color waxing, intended for the best quality stock, and combinations of paint and stain washes will have a different visual effect depending on the wood surface. They can be used to emphasize and exaggerate lumber defects, resulting in a unique, abstract patterning.

Designer's notes

The decorative scheme you apply to the woodwork in your property should be viewed as an important finishing touch – if not exactly reflecting the period of construction, then certainly not being at odds with it. There are so many different finishes to choose from, whether you want to let the natural grain pattern show through or disguise it with solid colour.

Older-style houses have more elaborate moldings and door frames than modern properties, and the use of bright, glossy, modern paint schemes can detract alarmingly from their intended elegance. Enamel paints of any color can reflect both natural and controllable artificial light startlingly, causing flare and highlight in moldings and recesses where none was intended, often appearing to change the shape of the wood and certainly destroy any of the joiner's intended subtlety. Original period moldings were painted with "flat" oil colors and varnishes, the lack of any sheen on the finish emphasizing the decorative qualities of the joinery. Today, "dead flat oil" is again available as a paint finish from specialist suppliers, but attractive alternatives include water-based effects and finishes which can be sealed with a mat varnish, or oil-based low luster paint that can be partially rubbed down and "distressed" before a sealer is applied. In this way, bright colors can be used together without causing light to flare across molded surfaces, and the original integrity of the joinery can be maintained as well as updated. Whatever the period, always seek to enhance the natural characteristics of your property, rather than work against them. Modern housing, often having smaller, plain, or chamfered wood surrounds, is more suited to simple enamel treatments; often the narrow, minimalist frames match the glossy, plastic feel of PVCu window systems. These styles are based around advanced technologies, where expensive woods have been replaced with metals, plastics, laminates, and manufactured boards. The increased use of metals, and a new awareness of customer interest and demands, have led to innovations like hot baseboards, where metal snap-on sections carry electric heating next to the floor. Standard panel radiators, so often a room design problem, can now be replaced with a variety of space-saving linear sculptures like multicolumns, and heating art designs such as continuous coils. As with period properties, work with the technology, not against it: powerful primary colors on narrow, plain surrounds complement minimalist room sets and provide defining borders for large wall areas.

Intricate mouldings and panels must be treated with sympathy.

Paneled doors can be painted with solid colors, which let the shapes of the panelwork show through.

Too fussy an effect would produce a confusion of shapes and patterns.

Shutters make an interesting addition to any window. In period houses the original shutter boxes may remain, needing only new shutters to be made. However, they can also be added to more modern homes.

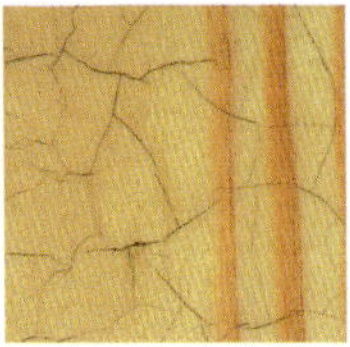

Crackleglaze is a two-part varnish that can be applied to wood to produce an aged look.

Doors offer all sorts of possibilities for decorative finishes, whether they be stains or paint.

ealing with doors

lodern technology has changed the look and installation of many oom features, and paint and decorative systems have adapted ong with it. The basic principle behind room entry doors, storage oors, and shutters still remains the same, however, and this is an ea worth exploiting decoratively.

Entry doors, either new or reclaimed, that are made from solid ood can be color stained and varnished to emphasize the grain ructure. Cheaper modern doors that have plywood panels or ther manufactured inserts benefit from a combination scheme: nsert panels can be painted a solid color, and the real wood frame vashed with a tint of the same color. Seal or varnish to protect the nish. Try matching up cabinet or storage doors in the same color ystem as the main door, or consider commissioning or building hutter doors to replace drapes. They can be constructed to the same basic door style fairly simply, and the same combination paint scheme will result in a coordinated wood finish. Bear in mind, too, the other woodwork in the room, such as baseboards, chair and picture rails, valances, and wall paneling.

hoose from a variety of paint ffects to cheer up old cabinets hroughout the home.

A rubbed, oil-based wax-resisting red latex paint and an abraded green colorwash.

Same technique, different area

Using the same paint effect on different door types and sizes, irrespective of the wood grain or board surface, is fairly logical because it achieves an overall pattern in the room. What isn't quite so obvious is that the majority of effects can be made to work on any wood surface, irrespective of where you may have seen them used, and the only limit is your imagination.

Techniques based on the principle of oil and water not mixing together, for example, as in wax resists used to distress floorboards, can be equally effective on moldings. Soft solvent-based wax can be rubbed onto the top relief surface of a molding, and the entire crown molding painted with water-based paint. Rubbing down with steel wool takes the paint off the surface molding, but leaves it in the recesses. Wax resist techniques, often used to distress furniture, can look good on baseboards, especially when an underlying color is revealed. Likewise crackleglazing, normally associated with small areas such as picture frames, can be used on inset door panels with a matching tint varnish on the frame of the door. Always remember that paint effects on wood can be applied to more than just one area, and, as long as the finishes are practical in the areas that you intend to use them, are versatile and interchangeable.

Basic skills: wood

In any decorating job in the house you must decide what finish you desire before you prepare the surface. Paint on woodwork must cover defects such as holes and knots, therefore they must be filled and sealed; or stains and varnishes can be used creatively to emphasize them, if this is appropriate for your chosen décor.

Preparation of surfaces

The surface preparation for the envisaged job will obviously depend on how you have visualized the finish. Wood only offers two basic choices, putting paint on, or taking it off. If you intend to repaint, and the existing paint surface is sound, you do not need to strip it off, only to remove the sheen completely using a medium-grade silicon carbide paper soaked in a hot solution of sugar soap and water. Abrade the surface using plenty of liquid until the area is of a dull mat appearance. Switch to a fine grade of paper to achieve a smooth finish if necessary. It is important, after using wet abrasives and washing down, to let all surfaces dry out thoroughly.

Wood may be stripped in two ways: with a chemical paint stripper (left) or a blow torch (above). Both methods need care as they are potentially dangerous.

You can now overpaint directly with an oil-based enamel if the color is similar, but a totally different scheme, such as dark blue replacing a pale yellow, will need the paint maker's recommended undercoat. If the existing paint surface is unsound, however, showing obvious visual defects like cracking, flaking, blistering, peeling, or chipping, then the paint must be stripped back to reveal the bare wood.

Stripping wood

Stripping paints and varnishes off wood surfaces is a time-consuming, dirty job. Unless you are stripping a door, which can be

Old paintwork should be rubbed down with abrasive paper to provide a key for the new paint.

Wash down the paintwork with a sugar soap solution and let it dry completely.

Areas of bare wood should be primed, and the surface sanded back where they join.

After undercoating, apply one or two top coats, keeping a wet edge to ensure no obvious joins.

Paneled walls offer a range of decorative possibilities, whether you stain and varnish them or apply a solid paint scheme.

ken off its hinges, the job must be taken on in situ. Paneling, ames, and baseboards are best tackled with a burner and gas ɔttle; a flexible blade or shavehook follows the flame through ›ftened paint and scrapes it off the surface. Heat guns are also ›itable, but they are heavy, and as they must be held in the vrong" hand (the "right" hand is holding the scraper for greater :curacy) are tiring to use. Paint strippers are another option, the ıemical action causing the paint to blister and bubble, so that it ın be scraped off easily. They are recommended for crown oldings where delicate moldings can be stripped by the use of eel wool, rather than damaged by a clumsy blade. If paint :ripper is your choice, use the water-washable kind, and keep a ıcket of warm water beside you. Liquid chemical strippers are ɔrrosive and must be handled wearing gloves and protective othing; any splashes must be washed off immediately. Another ption for removable doors is dipping in a caustic tank. Small firms ffering this service will frequently collect and deliver, solving any ansport problems, but the drawback is that caustic solutions tend ɔ eat into the glued joints as well as stripping the paint. When ɔur door is returned, be prepared to reglue the joints and clamp

ny holes can be concealed with ɔint compound, which should be left roud and rubbed down when dry.

Treat knots with stain blocking primer to prevent them from bleeding resin through your finish.

ıe door with sash locks overnight. The door will need sanding own as the grain will have been raised by the stripping process, nd the wood will appear dry and dull. If a natural wood finish is equired, use danish oil applied with a soft cloth to replace the atural oils taken out in the caustic tank.

Filling

Wood preparation includes filling or sanding irregularities, old fixing holes, dead knot holes, splits, or cracks. If the wood is to be varnished, that is the grain and color will be part of the finish, the filler applied must match the wood color. Plastic wood filler can be bought to fill different woods, labeled pine, oak, mahogany and so on. Slightly overfill the hole with a small flexible blade, to allow for some shrinkage and for sanding flush when hard. If the wood is to be painted, joint compound can be used, which is easy to sand when dry. When filling window frames and other occasionally exposed wood areas, an oil-based stopper or putty should be used, and this should be applied after the primer coat, not before. Otherwise, you risk the unsealed wood surface drawing out the oil, the filler shrinking and consequently falling out.

Knots in painted wood surfaces

The treatment of resinous knots must not be ignored if you are to achieve a first-class finish. Brush the knot with a stain- and knot-blocking primer, and leave to dry before applying the next coat. Knots literally weeping resin must be scraped clean, and dried out as much as possible with a burner flame before sealing. Resin stains already covered by paint will eventually show through a fresh paint film. To remove the problem you must scrape the paint off back to the bare wood, apply stain-blocking primer, and repaint. Simply painting over resin stains is no good.

Painting doors and windows

Interior doors that are to be painted or varnished do not need a weatherproof finish. You can use oil-based finishes for protection against knocks, or the water-based variety. Windows, though, are exposed to wet conditions, cold in winter with condensation on the inside, and humid in summer, and they should be given a tough finish.

Door sequence

Paneled doors

Remove the door furniture and paint the door edges first. If you are only painting one side of the door, wedge it open. If the door opens toward you, paint the leading edge only; if it opens away from you, paint the hanging (hinged) edge. Wipe off any paint that has fouled the other face of the door. Now paint the panel moldings and then the panels, taking care that any excess paint in the molding channels does not "run" onto the panels or rails. The horizontal rails are next, followed by the vertical center rails or muntins, and then the outer stiles.

Flush doors

Remove the door furniture and paint the edges as before, but then the similarity ends. You need to treat flush doors more as you would a small wall area, dividing the area into thirds and painting one third at a time. Lay the paint off toward the edges as you finish each section, and work quickly enough to maintain a wet or "live" edge so that the sections join together easily without leaving an obvious join. Leave the door wedged open until the paint is dry, and do not raise any dust in the room, as this is liable to stick to the paint film and ruin the finish. When the paint has dried, replace the door furniture.

Paneled door: for the best results, follow this sequence when painting a paneled door.

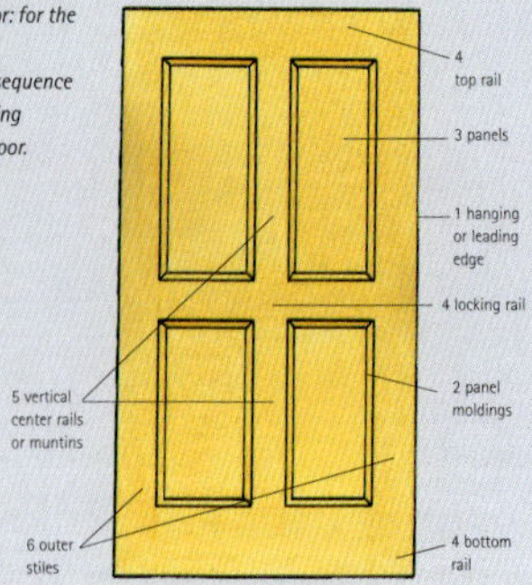

Flush door: paint a flush door a third at a time, keeping a wet edge.

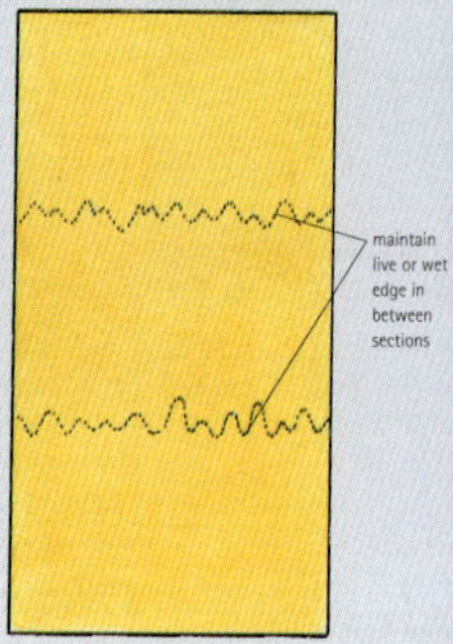

Sequence for painting windows

Vindow sequence

ouble-lung windows

ift the lower sash and pull down the top sash so that the meeting ail can be painted first, ensuring that it has the longest drying me. Paint the top sash, then use a stepladder to reach and paint ıside the top of the framing and trim, making sure no paint gets n the sash cords. Reverse the sash positions, and paint the casing, ompleting the stepladder work. Now paint the lower sash, apron or kirt and stool. Be careful when painting up to the glass in the two ashes: the paint should be cut in to overlap the putty slightly, ɔrming a seal and preventing condensation from entering any gap etween putty and glass.

'asement windows

emove the window furniture, and paint the opening window first. tart with the glazing bars and edge moldings, then the face and anging edge of the casement. Follow the same sequence for the ixed casement, then paint the external frame and center frame ıembers, and the rabbet for the opening window. Lastly, paint the tool. If you have used painter's tape to get a clean edge up to the lass, remove it as soon as the paint is touch dry.

Though functional, like doors, windows can contribute positively to the décor of a room.

Crackleglazing and surface resists

Cracked and crazed finishes are frequently used for special effects, paints and varnishes being specifically applied so that the film tears or breaks during drying. This crazed effect can be used to give an antique-style finish to varnished woods, or, if combined with paints, a rustic appearance that might be found in a country kitchen.

As with all distressed finishes, as they are sometimes called, the aim is to prematurely age timbers, in this case imitating cracked, well worn, and weathered surfaces. In the main, distressing techniques rely on the incompatibility of consecutively applied coats. Surface resists also have as their origins a mistake in application, or paint defect, where a second coat will not adhere to the previous layer. Waxes are a prime example—oil-based wax rubbed indiscriminately onto a molding and then painted with a water-based latex paint will give a patchy torn-up finish that can be further emphasized with wire wool. In this case the oil base has rejected the subsequent coat of water-based paint.

Crackleglazing or cracklefinishing

This is the result of the difference in drying time, elasticity, and flexibility between an oil-based varnish and a water-based varnish brushed over it. Artists working usually in either oils or water-based paints found that mixing the two caused problems if they were applied in the wrong order; oil could be brushed over acrylic and water bases but not vice versa. Historically, in the paint-finishing trade, the rule was that consecutive paint films should be of a similar elasticity: a hard-drying top coat, such as low luster or enamel, should not be brushed over a softer, more elastic base coat, or cracking would result. The top coat or finish needed preferably to be slightly more elastic than the preceding coats, unless a crazed finish was specifically required by the client. This generally applied to paints mixed by hand on site.

The introduction of proprietary paint systems where paint-makers supply primers, undercoats, and finishing coats ready-mixed has all but eliminated this problem. As a consequence, crackle finishes are rare as mistakes, but commonly employed as special effects, often using oil- and water-based varnishes supplied in kits, complete with all directions. In today's decorating marketplace, what concerned yesterday's paint finishers is a practiced art form.

Using a cracked finish on wood

Cabinet doors or shutters are a good surface for a cracked finish. They are not too large an area to appear as an overpowering effec and they provide a choice of cracked color or wood surface. The surface must be sealed, either by varnish or paint, depending on your scheme. Brush on a coat of oil-based varnish and leave it until it is just touch dry and therefore slightly tacky. Now brush or the water-based varnish, thinly for subtle crazing, more thickly for obvious cracks, and leave the surface near a source of heat, such as a radiator. Some manufacturers recommend the use of a hairdryer at this stage, but care is required not to wrinkle the entire surface accidentally as the cracks start to appear. The cracks can be left as they appear on a painted base, or have a contrasting

Brush on oil-based varnish. While it is tacky, add a water-based varnish. A hairdryer will speed drying.

To make the cracks more obvious, rub a contrasting coloured oil paint into them with a soft cloth.

color rubbed into them, using an artists' oil paint applied with a soft cloth. If the scheme has cracks formed on a natural wood surface, they can be emphasized in the same way, using black oil paint, or alternatively a coat of contrasting latex paint can be applied over the top. Use a wide brush or roller, and make one pass only; otherwise, the top coat will sink into the cracks, ruining the effect. Whichever of these versions you choose, when the surface is dry, seal with a clear coat of varnish.

Wax resist on wood

Most effectively used on moldings and crown moldings, solvent-based wax is rubbed onto the molding top surfaces, but not into the recesses. Paint the entire surface with water-based paint, and let it dry out. Rubbing the waxed areas with steel wool takes the paint off, leaving the top surface moldings looking as if the paint had worn off during the passage of time. Thinner surface streaks can be removed by substituting a candle for the solvent-based wax.

Small projects

Smaller areas, such as built-in cabinet doors that already have a varnish applied, can be given a period feel without a base coat. Simply "key" the surface using a fine abrasive paper. Otherwise, seal bare wood with two coats of clear oil-based varnish and leave it to dry. Apply a coat of oil-based crackleglaze, brushing it out well over the surface to give a thin, even coat, and let it dry out until the surface has a "tacky" feel. This usually takes about two to three hours, depending on conditions. Now brush on the water-based crackleglaze. A thick layer will take longer to dry out than a thin one, and the resultant cracks will be more obvious. You can speed the process of drying and crackling by gently warming the surface with a hairdryer if necessary. Don't hold the dryer too close and stop as soon as the cracks start appearing. Rub an oil-based artists' color into the cracks with a soft cloth to aid definition, selecting a contrast to your original wood color. Oil- and water-based varnishes and the oil colors used in this technique are available from artists' suppliers.

Leave the oils to dry for 24 hours, and seal the finish with oil-based varnish to protect it.

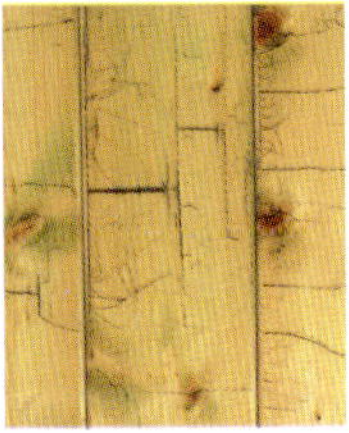

A close look reveals very obvious cracking. Thinner varnish coats can produce more subtle effects.

Wooden furniture can be given an attractive period feel by the use of 'distressing' techniques such as crackleglazing.

Basic principle

Crackleglazing is intended as a wood finish, suitable for paneled doors and frames. The basic principle involved, which is the different drying times of water- and oil-based varnishes, can also be applied to large wall areas.

Large projects

For larger areas you will need to substitute color latex paint for water-based varnish. The oil-based crackleglaze lets the base color show through the cracks in the top latex coat. This effect works best with contrasting colors, so try brushing on a dark base color, and leave it to dry. Apply the crackleglaze, followed by a top coat of contrasting pale latex paint, which should be watered down.

The effects in this technique vary from the subtle to the obvious. Some experimentation on scrap board will help you decide how far you want to go with your ideas.

Crackleglazing effects on timber with contrasting color cracks.

Waxing and french polishing

Waxing and french polishing, once common practice, are restricted in their use today to small craft studios and homeworkers. Sourcing of materials for traditional practices is more difficult, but still possible, and using the techniques on simple projects is a welcome and challenging alternative to mass-produced finishes.

Completing any joinery project about the house will cause you to consider a choice of decorative and protective finishes, although experienced craftspeople may well have preselected a finish, and therefore sourced a wood accordingly. Wood finishes on simple shelving and paneling jobs can vary from straightforward clear varnishes, taking a minimum of effort, to more time-consuming decorative effects. A great number of these can be produced using modern paints and varnishes in a variety of combinations, and all materials can be found in neighbourhood stores. While this has the advantage of convenience, it gives no historical perspective to colors and finishes painstakingly crafted by hand in days gone by.

Sand the item to be french polished with fine abrasive paper to ensure a smooth surface.

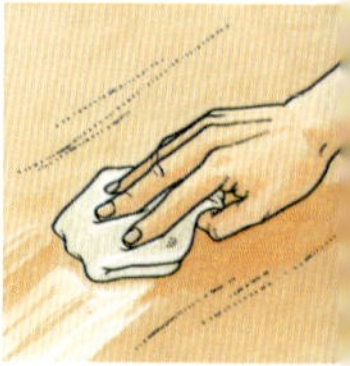

Prepare the surface by fadding, applying a thin continuous film of polish to seal it.

Waxing

This was once a very popular finish. As well as protecting, it slightly darkened the surface of the wood, and the oils in the wax stopped the wood from becoming dry. A rise in popularity of french polishing sent waxing into decline, but today the versatility of this finish is recognized, and clear, neutral, white, and colored waxes can be found in artists' suppliers and hardware stores. Original waxes were easy to apply and gave a luster finish not dissimilar to low luster; today's waxes should contain a color that can be worked carefully into the woodgrain and slowly polished off the relief surface. White wax, for example, worked into the raised grain of a rich colored wood with steel wool and polished, gives a limed finish.

French polishing

This is a considerably more difficult application than waxing, and although it is a finish popular among traditional craftspeople, particularly on bespoke furniture, it is rarely seen elsewhere. Second-hand furniture pieces inherited or sourced from antique shops may be finished in this way, and it may be of interest to know a little about the basic technique, for restoration purposes or even as a matching finish for a bookshelf or bookcase project. French polishing will seal and fill in the woodgrain, stabilizing the surface, resulting in an easy-to-clean, hard-wearing finish. Kits are available from specialist suppliers.

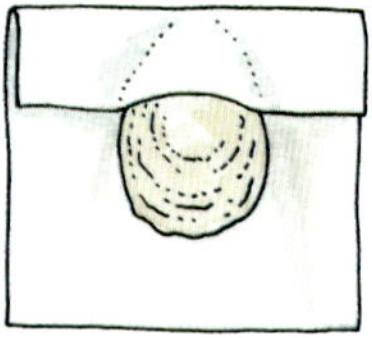

To make a rubber, you need a ball of wadding and a square of clean, lint-free cotton cloth.

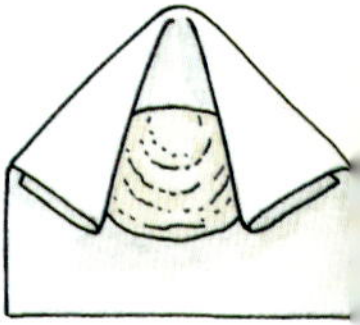

Place the wadding in the centre of the square and fold over the top two corners to form a point.

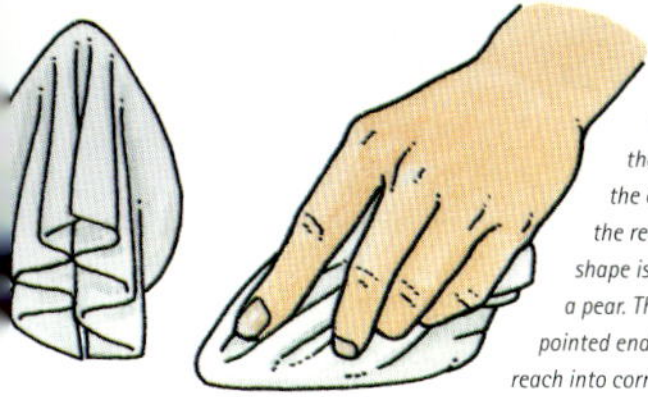

Gather the rest of the cloth so the reverse shape is that of a pear. The pointed end will reach into corners.

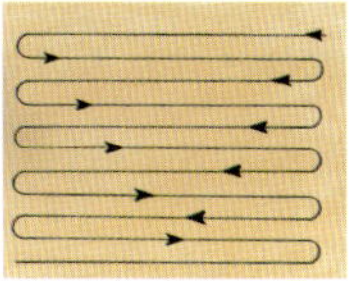

Apply polish with the rubber by working with the grain.

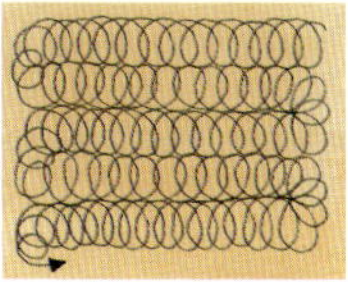

Finish off by bodying-up, applying polish with small circular motions.

Polishing a surface

French polishing involves layering thin films of shellac onto a wood surface. It is a difficult process to master, and you should first select a suitable piece of hardwood to practice on.

Sand the surface flat and smooth with fine sandpaper, and remove any dust. Form a key between wood surface and polish by "fadding" (the fad is a folded piece of lint-free wadding dipped in polish) covering the surface with a thin, continuous film of polish. Let the surface dry completely, then sand down with fine sandpaper, again removing all traces of dust. The next stage, called "bodying up," is to apply polish with a rubber over the surface, working with the grain. The "rubber" is used instead of a brush to keep the surface as flat as possible, and is made up of the same lint-free wadding as the fad, wrapped in a square of cotton rag.

French polish is a common finish on quality period furniture. It produces a hard glossy finish to wood that lets the beauty of the grain shine through, but it needs skill to apply properly.

Place the wadding in the center of the rag and fold over the two top corners, forming a point. Fold over the rest of the rag into a ball shape, and shape the top point so that the reverse side of the rubber looks like a pear, the shaped point letting rabbets and moldings be polished.

Open the rag, and pour french polish onto the wadding until it is fully "charged," refold and gather up the rag, squeezing polish through to the rag face in the process.

Now apply polish by passing the rubber over the wood surface, from end to end, with the grain, squeezing the rag ends so that polish comes through in a continuous moist film. Slide the rubber on and off the surface, making sure the runs of polish all join, forming a continuous film. Wait until the polish is dry before applying a second coat; never try to go over a damp surface, or it will tear up. After three coats, leave to dry, and then lightly sand down.

Finish bodying-up by polishing in small circles over the surface. If the rubber starts to stick on the polished surface as you work, use a little linseed oil to lubricate the rubber face. As the shine begins to appear, the bodying is over and the surface needs to dry overnight. Lightly sand the surface, and again remove any dust.

Finish by applying polish in the same way, using long gliding strokes with the grain, exerting less pressure each time, and leave the surface to dry for about an hour. Now add a little methylated spirit to the rubber, diluting the polish that is left, and pass lightly and quickly over the finished surface, removing any traces of linseed oil that may remain.

Make sure the finishing rubber is not too wet, glide on and off the surface as before, and don't stop the stroke on the surface, as this will ruin the finish.

Simple wooden shutters

Internal wooden shutters were an integral part of window design in Georgian and Victorian period houses. The shutters were paneled, often had moldings that matched the panelwork in and around the bay recess, and folded neatly away into shutter boxes at the sides of the window. They provided security, privacy, and noise reduction.

YOU WILL NEED
- 2 x 1 in./50 x 25 mm Softwood TGV paneling boards
- 1½ x ⅜ in./38 x 10 mm Softwood
- Decorative molding
- 2 in./50 mm Number 8 screws
- 1 in./25 mm Number 6 screws
- 1 in./25 mm Molding pins
- Wood glue
- Spackling compound

If you have a period property that has had the shutters removed, but still retains the side boxes, seek the advice of a local joiner, for pine shutters can be made up to fit and match, restoring the window area to its former glory. Period shutters are usually associated with double-hung windows, either full-length and covering the glazed area from floor to ceiling, or more usually covering the lower part of the window only. They look at their best in recessed bays, but were and still can be stylish and functional at any window, and there is no reason why you cannot fit them to modern double-hung and casement windows. Sashes can still be fitted with any height of shutter, but casement window styles look better with full-length screens, having no meeting bar to form a visual parallel to a half- or three-quarter-length shutter.

Made to measure

To install simple shutters to a window, first measure the opening carefully, and look to see if you need to fit wood cleats vertically inside the recess to hinge onto. If so, remember to subtract this measurement from the calculation. Small windows can accommodate two shutters easily, which gives you a nicely balanced scheme, but if the window is too large, or you prefer smaller shutters, then measure up for two hinged together on each side, or a total of three with one side doubling up. In this scheme, three shutters span the gap, with one side having two shutters hinged to neatly fold back to back. Check all your measurements twice, then cut to size 2 x 1 in./50 x 25 mm lumber for the inner support frame, TGV cladding for the shutter body, an external frame that overlaps the front edge from 1½ x ⅜ in./38 x 10 mm wood, and a decorative molding.

Glue and screw the inner support frame first, using right-angled butt joints, driving home 2 in./50 mm number 8 screws. Use a combination screwsink to counterbore a hole enabling you to drive the head into the middle of the woodpiece at right angles. Fix a centered cross-piece for extra strength, and then screw the TGV lengths to the front of the frame, using 1 in./25 mm number 6 screws. Countersink the heads just flush with the surface, and

Begin by assembling the inner support frame, using right-angled butt joints. Glue and screw the joints for maximum strength.

Mark the position of the centered cross-piece on the uprights and drill to accept the reinforcing screws. Glue and screw the piece in place.

Cut lengths of TGV boards to size and screw them to the front of the frame, countersinking the fixing screwheads, flush with the surface.

Attach the outer frame so it projects at the front, using glue and molding pins, which should be punched below the surface of the wood.

Cut lengths of panel molding to fit inside the projecting lip of the outer frame, mitering their ends for neat corners. Pin them in place.

Fill any defects and pin-heads, using a matching spackling compound if a clear varnish will be employed, and sand down to a smooth finish.

make sure their position will be covered by the molding that you will add later. Glue and pin the outer frame in position, counterpunching 1 in./25 mm molding pins below the surface, flush at the back and overlapping at the front. Finally, measure and corner-miter the molding to fit neatly into the rebate created at the front, pinning it with the same molding pins.

Fill all pin holes prior to sanding down the surfaces. If you choose to paint the frame and molding, a joint compound is good enough here; if you intend to varnish the work, use a spackling compound because the wood and grain will show through even if it is colored. A painted frame and molding with a similar color varnished TGV inside makes a good combination effect. Attach the shutters to each other and to the frame with 3 in./75 mm flush hinges in a brass finish, using brass screws.

You could adapt the basic framework of these shutters to make louver shutters that will allow cooling air into the room in summer while shading it from the sun. You would need to rout a series of slots into the inside of the frame at an angle to accept the slats.

Louvered shutters are very practical in the heat of summer, shading the interior from the sun. Here they are used to divide a room.

A customized valance

It is possible to completely transform a window and drapes arrangement by simply fitting a valance. A decorative front and customized wall brackets are easy to make from lumber stock. Using solid lumber may mean that more support is needed, but you can then pin to the front interchangeable seasonal arrangements, such as dried lavender.

Measuring and cutting

Measure the width of your window, and the drawn drape positions, then check to see if you have enough space to let you fix into the frame surround or whether you need to drill into the wall. In either case, the made-up brackets should be positioned to allow an overhang at each end of 1 in./25 mm. The principle is that two fixed brackets support, but are not permanently attached to, a valance that is designed to be fixed to the wall itself in a hidden position at top dead center. This allows for easy valance removal, for frame painting for example, by taking out one screw and lifting down, rather than removing bracket screws neatly but inconveniently hidden inside the valance, a difficult job calling for small hands and a stubby screwdriver. The cut bracket must be made up to fit exactly inside the inside right-angle of the valance. For example, if the valance is cut from 4 x 1 in./100 x 25 mm nominal size wood, planed to a finished size of 3¾ x ¾ in./95 x18 mm, the inside dimension is 3 in./75 mm. Cut the

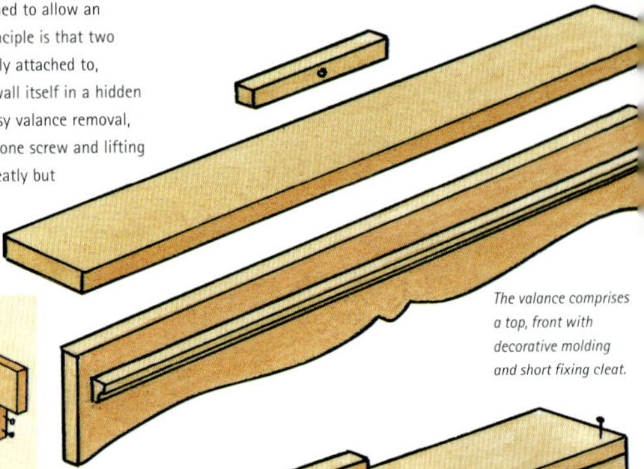

The valance comprises a top, front with decorative molding and short fixing cleat.

The upside-down L-shaped brackets take the weight of the valance and are screwed to the wall on each side of the window opening.

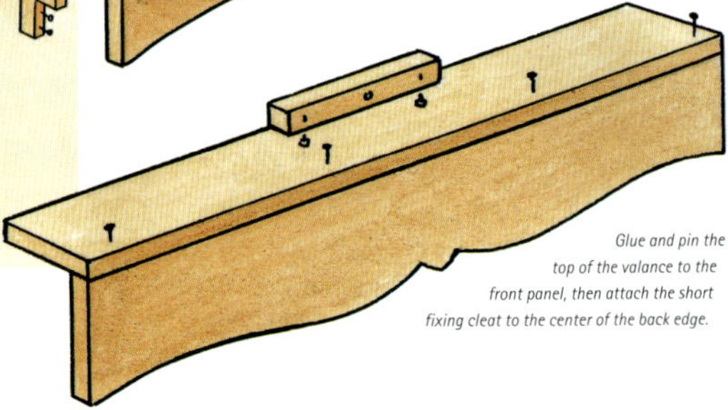

Glue and pin the top of the valance to the front panel, then attach the short fixing cleat to the center of the back edge.

bracket to this size at the top and part of one side, forming the support, then cut back to form a rabbet. A section of wood ¾ in./18 mm wide and deep, and 4¾ in./120 mm long should be left, and this takes the wall screws, as shown in the diagram. Shape the bottom edge of the valance into a design of your choice with a jigsaw. Glue and screw a lumber support, 1 x 1 x 4 in./25 x 25 x 100 mm with a centered fixing hole onto the top center of the valance so that you can screw through into the wall.

Using seasonal flowers and foliage to decorate a window opening provides a means of extending the garden into the house, blurring the distinction between the two areas.

Joining together and fixing

Make up the valance by gluing the top to the front, and pinning with 1½ in./38 mm brads. On the front face, directly butting the join of top and front, pin a decorative strip molding, using ¾ in./18 mm molding pins, which disguises the butt join. Now attach the wall brackets, using a suitable length number 8 such as 1¼ in./32 mm if you are fixing to the wood surround, or a countersunk 2¼ in./57 mm number 8 screw into a wall anchor if you are driving into the wall. Position the valance, and equalize the side overhangs, then fix the top center support to the wall, again countersinking a 2¼ in./57 mm number 8 screw into a wall anchor.

Position the valance on its brackets, screw to the wall through the top cleat and varnish.

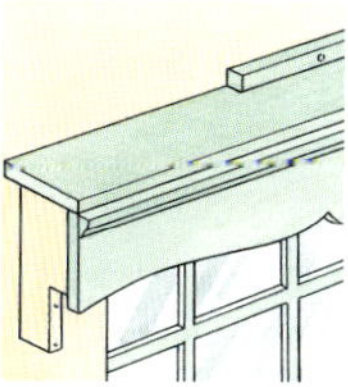

The finished valance is designed to accept seasonal floral decoration pinned to the front.

Finishing

Fill the screw holes and sand the surfaces smooth. Again, select a filler that is suitable; decorator's fillers are fine if the surface is to be painted, but a matching wood-colored spackling compound is needed if the wood grain is going to be visible under a varnish, as this will tend to "disappear."

Clear or colored varnishes will certainly look good on the valance, but you could also consider painting the brackets to complement the wall color, blend in with the wall decoration or to match exactly the wood surround. In this way the brackets are disguised slightly and full prominence is given to the wood finish on the valance that will support your choice of seasonal floral decoration.

Lower wall paneling

Protecting the lower portion of a wall, in an area of heavy human traffic, by easily cleaned wood panels finished with tough exterior varnish, is both visually attractive and practical. Utility rooms, hallways, and landings are all suitable areas, although this finish, particularly if it is stained wood, will look good as a decorative scheme anywhere.

Home centers sell paneling kits, with all necessary parts including chair rail and baseboard, primed and ready to fix. If you intend a painted finish, or a paint effect that uses a flat color as a base, then this is an option worth considering. Real wood finishes, however, are worth constructing yourself, and two basic schemes are described here.

Tongue-and-groove paneling

Mark out your wall area, using a spirit level to ensure verticals and horizontals are true. Fix two horizontal cleats to the wall, parallel with the baseboard, out of 2 x 1 in./50 x 25 mm woodstock, countersinking 2 in./50 mm number 8 screws into wall anchors. Cut TGV boards to fit, measuring from the floor to the top of the upper cleat, and pin it to the baseboard and the top and middle cleat lengths. Start in the corner with the groove to the wall, and pin the first piece through the face; thereafter invisibly pin each piece through the tongue, covering the pin heads with the next groove. Use ¾ in./18 mm molding pins driven in at an angle. You

TGV paneling boards are suitable for a wide range of decorative jobs around the house. Use them in a bathroom to give a period feel to the room. However, make sure they are treated with yacht varnish to protect them from the steamy atmosphere.

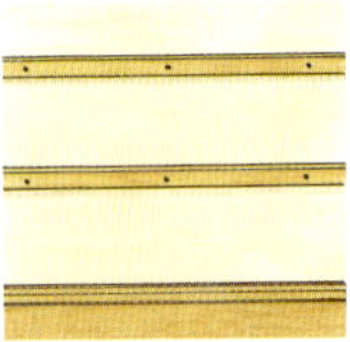

For vertical boards, attach horizontal support cleats to the wall above the baseboard.

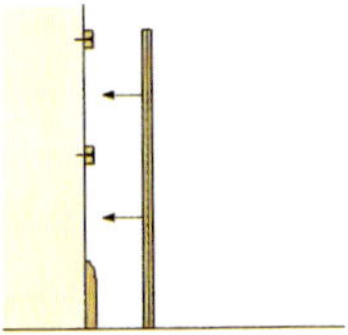

Invisibly pin the boards to the cleats, using the existing baseboard as the lower support.

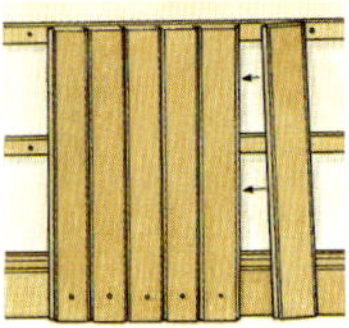

Work along the wall, slotting the tongues and grooves of the boards together.

Finish off the top edge of the boards with a decorative molding and pin on a new baseboard.

can face pin the bottom fixing if preferred, because this will be concealed by a new baseboard, itself nailed in place with 1½ in./38 mm lost-head nails, with the heads counterpunched below the surface and filled. Cut a straight top piece from 2 x ½ in./50 x 12 mm woodstock, and pin it on top, using 1 in./25 mm molding pins, covering the end grain of the TGV lengths. The top overlaps slightly, and a final piece of decorative molding is pinned in position directly underneath, again with 1 in./25 mm molding pins, the heads being counterpunched and filled in the same manner as before.

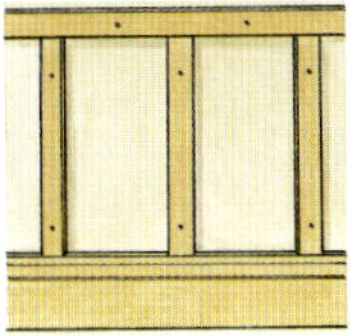

Plywood paneling needs a grid of upright and horizontal support cleats screwed to the wall.

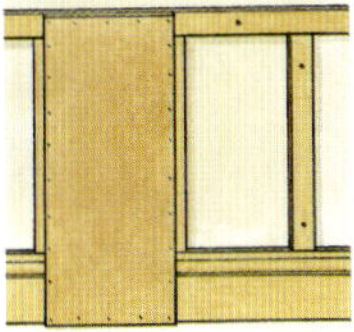

The uprights must be placed so that each supports the edges of neighboring panels.

Wood panels

More difficult and time-consuming to construct, this paneling uses a top cleat and the existing baseboard as before, but has additional vertical cleats equally spaced along the wall. These cleats are wider, being 3 x 1 in./75 x 25 mm, but are fixed in the same way.

Plywood panels are pinned to the cleats with ¾ in./18 mm panel pins, butting together on the vertical cleat center line. Plywood panels ¼ in./6 mm thick can be bought from home centers with a hardwood veneer facing, 2 ft./607 mm wide, requiring the cleat centers to be this same distance apart. If this is too wide for your scheme, cut the panels to your preferred size, and adjust the distances between the cleats.

The panel height is from the bottom of the baseboard to the top of the upper cleat. Fix the baseboard piece into position as before, but use a straight length of 4 x 1 in./100 x 25 mm lumber, because a top molding is not needed.

Using 2 x ½ in./50 x 12 mm woodstock, frame each panel on the remaining three sides, using the center line of the wall cleats as your guide at the sides and sitting flush with the panel edge at the top. Pin with 1 in./25 mm molding pins, countersink the heads and fill. To finish, measure and corner-miter a molding of your choice to fit inside the panel frame on all sides, and add a top piece from 2 x ½ in./50 x 12 mm woodstock. Pin in position and counterpunch the heads as before, and fill all holes with a wood filler.

Stain the softwood so that a match is achieved with the veneered panels, and seal the surfaces, or apply any decorative paint finish that suits the remainder of the area.

Decorative moldings are pinned in place to conceal the joints between neighboring panels.

Add a decorative molding to each panel, mitering the ends for neat corners.

Wooden wall paneling adds a touch of elegance to a dining-room, especially when teamed with ornamental moldings framing panels of hand-blocked wallpaper.

Furniture Facelifts

Many special decorative finishes are considered unsuitable for large wall surfaces, either because they are messy and difficult to control given the size, or because the result is simply too overpowering. They can be ideal for small projects, though, like table tops, cabinets, and chairs, irrespective of age. Bare wood knock-down, self-assembly pieces are suitable, as are traditional auction and flea market finds, but best of all, and the most economical, are those long forgotten items from the past stored in lofts and cellars. So, before you hunt for that expensive new piece to take pride of place in a new environment, consider what a makeover will do for an old friend. You may be surprised at the transformation.

Kitchen shelves

YOU WILL NEED

- Various abrasive papers
- Sanding block
- Screwdriver • White liming wax • Clear wax • Colored pigments • Fine steel wool
- Polishing cloth • Wood glue

An old self-assembly pine unit that had fallen apart and was about to be thrown away provided a perfect set of surfaces for subtle waxed finishes, each one looking as if it were reflecting a different colored light into the room —a great improvement on the original polyester finish.

Step 1 The unit was loosely reassembled, and the original surface removed using medium grade, followed by fine grade, wet silicon carbide abrasive paper.

Step 2 The finish residue was removed from the dowel holes using an old screwdriver, and the surface sanded using 240 grit aluminum oxide around a sanding block.

Step 3 Clear wax mixed with color pigment was rubbed into the grain with fine steel wool.

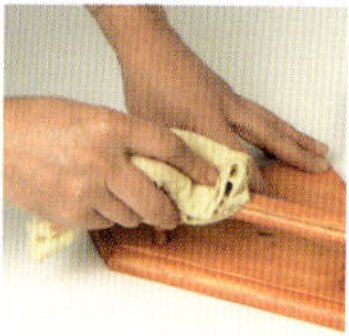

Step 4 The waxed surfaces were polished to a fine sheen using a soft, lint-free cloth.

Step 5 Wood glue was run into the dowel holes, prior to re-insertion of the fluted dowels.

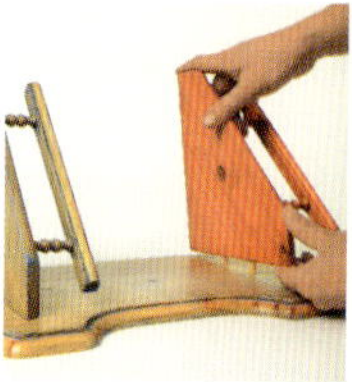

Step 6 Reassembly—the different color-waxed shelves were glued to the other half of the dowels.

Wooden cabinet

YOU WILL NEED

• Paint stripper • Steel wool • Stripping knife • Paint brush • Sandpaper 240 grit aluminum oxide • Screwdriver • Latex paint • Colorwash • Varnish • Liming wax • Clear wax • Brass fittings • Patterned glass • Putty • Quarter-round molding

Several different finishes—paint, colorwash, stain, varnish, and wax—are used, together with replacement glass and simple brass furniture, to give this well-made but badly neglected cabinet and drawer combination unit a new lease of life.

Step 1 The old multilayered paint finish is removed using a scraper to take off blistered paint after applying water-washable paint stripper. Remember to wear gloves!

Step 2 When all the paint is removed, steel wool dipped in sugar soap is used to clean the surface thoroughly. Always rub in the direction of the woodgrain.

Step 3 The door is removed and cleaned, and old glass, molding and putty discarded. A coat of white latex is "distressed."

Step 4 The inside of the cabinet needs to reflect a warm, friendly glow; orange latex paint from a sample pot is ideal.

Step 5 Diluted woodwash (available in small cans) is painted onto the base and top of the unit. Turquoise was the chosen color here.

Step 6 The multi-finish theme continues—diluted ultramarine water-based dye is brushed into the side grain, avoiding the front edge.

tep 7 The front will remain as are wood, cleaned up with 40 grit aluminum oxide round a sanding block.

tep 8 The waxed drawer is tested ɔ ensure it slides well. Blue and /hite waxes have been applied nd polished.

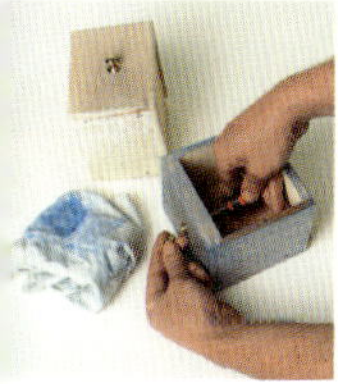

tep 9 New brass drawer and abinet door furniture is fitted to eplace the old plastic knobs. Small ands and a stubby screwdriver are eeded to gain access to the inside f the drawers.

Table mosaic decoration

YOU WILL NEED

- Aluminum oxide
- Sanding block • T-square
- Pencil • Tiles • Hammer
- Rags and cloths • Ruler
- Wood glue • Molding pins
- Counterpunch • Spackling compound • Tile adhesive • Grout spreader • Woodwash
- Clear varnish • Latex paint

This table has an interesting top surface; its octagonal shape is emphasized by softwood angles that form corner triangles. The resultant cross is tiled with different shades of blue mosaic, the dark blue pieces matching the triangles, and contrasting with the pale blue colorwash on the softwood.

Step 1 The top is abraded to remove all traces of sheen and to provide a 'key'. Aluminum oxide is used around a cork block.

Step 2 Guidelines are drawn for the wood pieces, using a soft yellow pencil so that they can be clearly seen.

Step 3 A cloth is wrapped around a tile. The tile is broken into small pieces with a hammer.

Step 4 The design is checked to see whether there are enough pieces of the right colors.

Step 5 After mitering the wood pieces, they are glued and pinned following the yellow guideline

Step 6 Spread the adhesive ⅛ in./ 3 mm deep with a ribbed spreader.

Step 7 The tile pieces are positioned in the adhesive.

Step 8 The spaces are grouted, after the adhesive has set.

Step 9 The mosaic is polished; the table is painted and varnished.

Revamping a wooden chair

YOU WILL NEED
• Sugar soap • Rag
• Sandpaper • Latex paint
• 1 in./25 mm brush • Pencil
• Tracing paper • Artists' brushes • Artists' acrylic colors

A small chair found in the loft, dirty from its travels, could be considered ideal for a child's nursery. A distressed paint scheme is envisaged for the chair. The scheme will match the room décor and a hand-painted design on the seat and back support will give the chair its own individual character.

Step 1 The wood surface is sanded down using medium followed by fine sandpaper, to give a smooth finish prior to painting.

The chair was cleaned with sugar soap first, so that dirt and grease wouldn't clog the abrasive and the paint would then go on evenly.

Step 2 The entire chair was painted with a first coat of red latex.

Step 3 A second coat (pale blue latex) was overpainted.

Step 4 The surface was abraded so the red paint showed through.

Step 5 The seat design (a colorful tree) was traced.

Step 6 The tree design is painted using artists' acrylic paints and a number 5 artists' brush.

Step 7 Flowers and leaves are added using a finer brush and bright acrylic colors.

Step 8 Finally a protective coat of clear satin varnish was brushed on.

Stylish Space Savers

The modern living environment and time-specific lifestyles require the best use to be made of limited available space. Traditional lofts and cellars are often converted to form part of the living quarters where once they were dark, cold, long-term storage areas rarely visited. The clamor for personal space in a smaller world is thus one of the contradictions of our time, and householders face a difficult task attempting to maximize potential space while retaining a personal decorative style and concealing everyday items that are unattractive but necessary.

Hanging racks and containers

Hanging racks and wall boxes save space around the home because the floor or worktop space below them can be utilized for another storage purpose. Often cookware was hung on butcher's hooks from ceiling-mounted racks, but modern low ceilings and the dangers of falling pots have relegated even kitchen racks to a wall mounting.

Storage in a hallway should be both practical and look good. In a small space a simple hat stand and shelf unit provides places for guests to hang their coats; in larger spaces closets can be built-in for all the family's needs.

Extra storage space is always useful in the kitchen. Open shelving is easy to fit into small corners and can be used to add an informal country feel. It's also a good way to show off attractive pots and implements, as well as having things close to hand for the cook.

Open shelves in a bathroom give you a chance to show off expensive and beautifully packaged items.

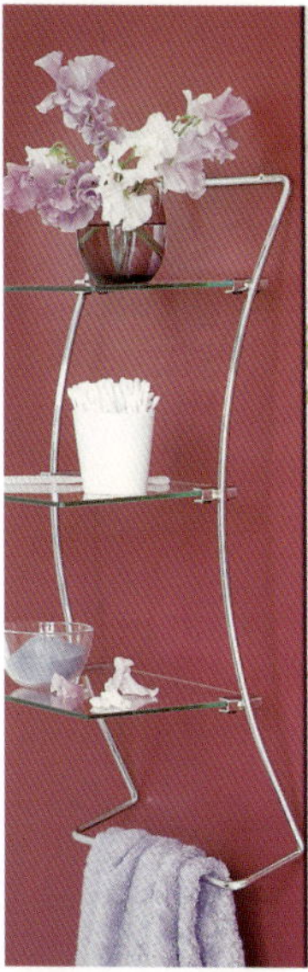

Bathroom shelving comes in a variety of styles and materials so you can easily find storage to suit your bathroom décor. Wicker storage boxes give a natural feel, as well as hiding away the clutter of personal items. Displaying towels on open shelves adds a touch of warmth and softness to metallic modern design.

Shelving systems

The fittings of the modern home have advanced, none more so than the humble shelf, which has evolved from a rectangular unit holding books and ornaments to a multi-purpose linear structure. Today's systems support all manner of audio and visual electronics, and must display designer qualities themselves, as well as showing off decorative accessories.

Shelf units today are so beautifully designed that they can be used as a feature of the room, not just for practicality. These small shelves let you display mementoes in a stylish and imaginative way.

Book shelves can be far more than an easy way to store books; they can also act as an attractive means of displaying them and a range of other items.

Modern style shelving can be made out of lighter, less obtrusive material than wood. Lightweight shelving such as this gives the room a modern feel.

Window sills can be used as an alternative to more traditional shelving, but don't think practical, think beautiful. Sills can be used not only to display the occasional objet d'art but are a great place to grow things. Let seedlings thrive by placing them on a warm sun-filled window ledge, and reap the benefits of bringing your yard indoors at the same time.

Long, narrow corridors may feel like a waste of valuable space, but with some thought and imagination you can utilize even the narrowest hallway both for storage and to add interest. A clever mix of stored items will provide a talking point in any hallway.

Storage screens: fabric

Fabric screens can be simple lengths under a sink, hiding the household necessities, or complex, three-way, self-standing frames used as changing screens or simply to indicate an area of privacy. The free-standing, folded fabric screen is both stable and lightweight; its portability and decorative qualities make it functional, fashionable, and very versatile.

Fabric screens do so much more than hide ugly clutter, they are also attractive additions to any room. Screens are widely available, but also easy to personalize to suit individual taste and décor. The true versatility in fabric screens, however, lies in the fact that you can position them wherever you want.

Even hard furnishings like closets need no longer be "hard." Use lengths of fabric draped over a frame, or hung like drapes round a small space, to add an exotic feel to your bedroom. Choose silks and velvets in bright and luxurious colors to create a spice trail feel, or white cheesecloth to bring a touch of softly flowing colonial days.

Under-the-sink drapes bring a special charm to any kitchen or bathroom, making a sink a feature not just a fixture. An ideal way to add color to a room, they hide necessities and add a finishing touch to soft furnishings. Choose your fabric carefully and make sure that you allow enough not just to cover but to drape attractively. Reminiscent of early twentieth-century homes, with the right fabric under-the-sink drapes can be brought up-to-date while retaining that country feel.

Storage screens: wood

Much heavier and less portable than fabric screens, wood screens are often used as room dividers to cordon off large areas into more user-friendly spaces. Traditionally, screens with solid, jointed frames made by craftsmen were inlaid with veneers of exotic and rarely seen woods, and some were exercises in grain pattern mirror-imaging and picture marquetry.

Wood always adds warmth and texture to a room. Wooden screens bring character but also have a highly practical function as room dividers. With an amazing variety in design and wood types to choose from, they can really bring your room alive.

Lighter screens can add an attractive feature to a bedroom. Choose a type of wood and style to complement your existing furniture.

You can even stain the wood to match your decor. Wooden screens are a great way to hide clutter, to divide rooms, or simply to add a feature.

To give an exotic feel to a room, choose a darker wood. Filigree work in the wood turns a room divider into a piece with character and interest. Screens are an ideal way to change the function of a room, turning an everyday kitchen-cum-diner into a sophisticated and romantic dining-room.

Boxes and containers

Storage chests are traditional favorites, a fashionable way to store items in a piece of wooden furniture that looks good in any room. Fabric-covered boxes, the lid doubling as a seat, can match room décor in a coordinated scheme, and wicker laundry baskets will assume a new identity if they are stained in bright colors and sealed with sprayed varnish.

Storage boxes are more than a place to store unsorted clutter. From coffee tables to seating, strong wooden boxes have become a fashionable feature in many modern homes.

Wicker boxes are highly fashionable nowadays and are a distinctive way to store anything from dirty laundry to letters, newspapers, and magazines.

The ottoman is the traditional place to keep bedding. Still placed at the bottom of the bed, this ancient piece of furniture has been given a modern make-over through the use of new materials and modern colors.

A collection of wicker baskets provides storage for knick-knacks and larger items and makes an attractive feature. They can also offer a handsome hideaway for your dirty laundry if you don't favor the more modern canvas laundry bins (right) that can be equally fetching.

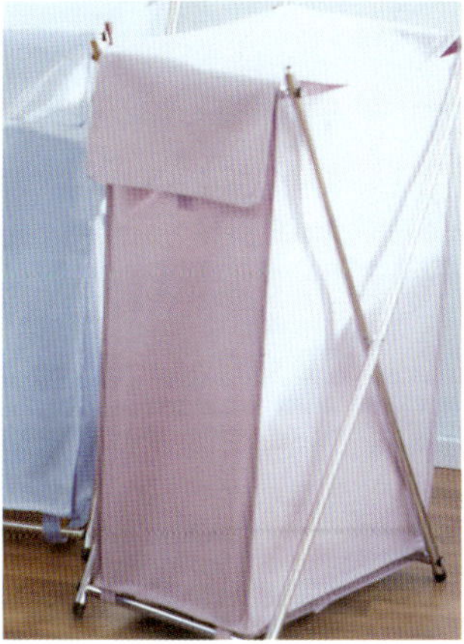

ACCENT ACCESSORIES

If the decorative style of a room is largely dependent upon the characteristics of the building, seeking to emphasize original features and disguise less attractive areas, then the accessories around the room depend on and reflect the character and interests of the occupants. Vases, containers, lamps, boxes, and frames can all underline a particular personal curiosity, be it historical or geographical, classical or modern. Accessorizing can vary from subtle frame distressing, reflecting an interest in traditional woods, to hand-painted floor coverings that pay homage to other cultures.

Vases

Enliven a plain vase by decorating it with ceramic paints, available from arts and crafts suppliers. Decant the paint into a small kettle or pot and sponge on tint combinations of the same color, or be more adventurous and mask out an area for hand-painting a foreground design.

YOU WILL NEED

• Transparent self-adhesive plastic film • Pencil • Scissors or craft knife • Natural sponge • Range of colors of ceramic paints • Artists' brushes

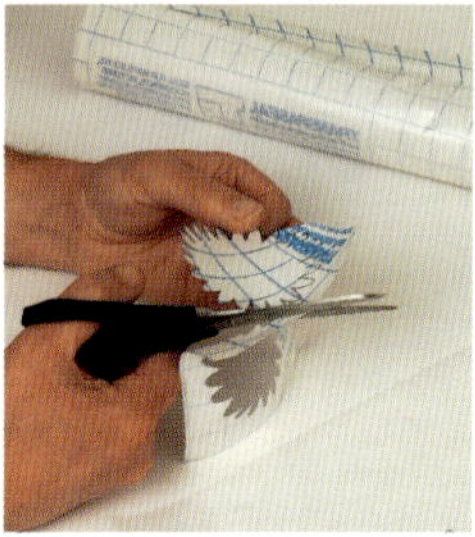

Step 1 Draw a sunflower head on self-adhesive plastic film and carefully cut out as a mask.

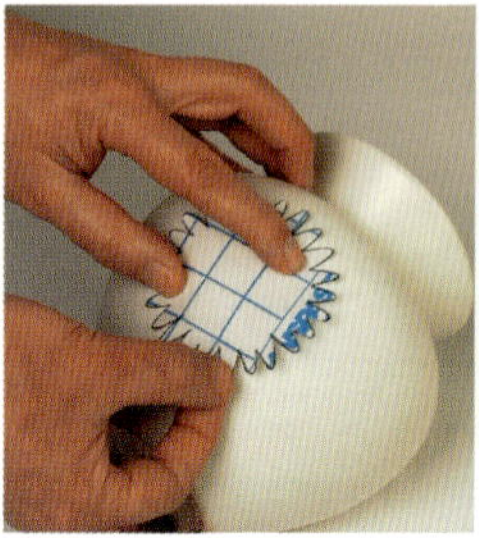

Step 2 Hold the mask up to the vase to check the size and position.

Step 3 Using a natural sea sponge, put on the first tint of the color.

Step 4 Sponge on the second tint, to start the build-up of the broken color effect.

Step 5 Now add the third, darker shade; this gives a three-dimensional feel to the design.

Step 6 Peel off the sunflower head mask and the vase is ready for hand-painting.

Step 7 Paint in bright yellow petals using a number 5 artists' brush. The shadow detail in orange will require a thinner brush.

Step 8 On a mid-brown base, touch in the minute black detail in the sunflower center with a number 4 brush.

Revamping a lamp

YOU WILL NEED

• Electrician's screwdriver • Silicon carbide paper • 1in./25 mm brush • Latex paint • Painter's tape • String • Marker pen • Flat artists' brush • Round artists' brush • Stencil • Artists' acrylic paint • Clear gloss varnish

An old lamp base that was spray-finished in black, hiding the woodgrain, and sporting a plain cream basic shade, was worthy of a stylish makeover designed to emphasize, not disguise its character. The shade was vignetted, creating colored stripes, and a simple symbol designed to complement the wood grain exposed on the base was added.

Step 1 Separate all the parts to allow access to the base. Disconnect the electrical components, remove and store carefully.

Step 2 Remove the original finish with medium and fine abrasives.

Step 3 Emphasize the grain pattern on the base stem with a pale orange wash.

Step 4 Sand down the outer base and give a first coat of latex, in bright orange.

Step 5 Distress the entire base using moistened fine grade silicon carbide paper.

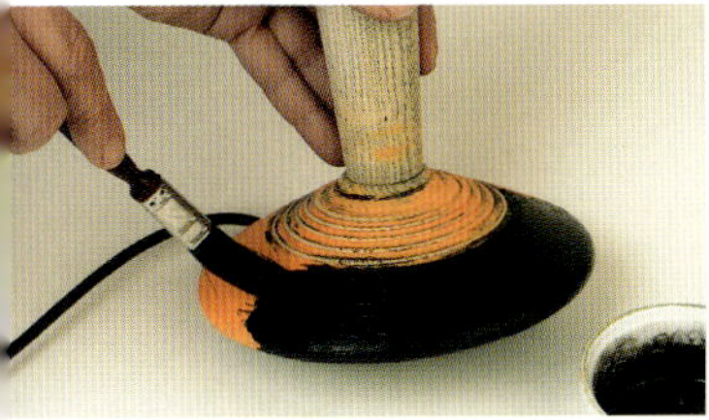

Step 6 Apply black latex paint to the outside of the distressed orange base, matching the original finish left in the grooves.

Step 7 Remove the black top coat with fine abrasive when dry. It remains in the grain structure, and the orange shows through.

Step 8 When the distressed finish is satisfactorily completed, protect the entire base by brushing on a clear gloss varnish.

Step 9 Divide the shade into equal segments, using string as a measure, and mask off.

Step 10 Apply a diluted pale yellow wash to alternate segments. This will bleed at the edges.

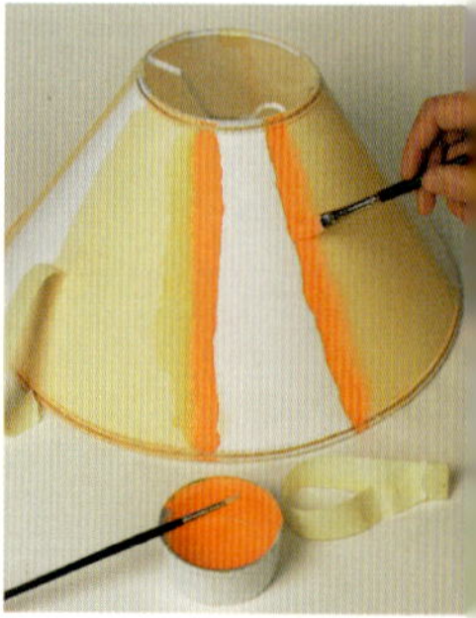

Step 11 Add an orange stripe, and use a number 6 flat brush dipped in water to vignette.

Step 12 Wash the color to achieve a smooth gradation.

Step 13 Test the tree symbol stamp and green color on scrap paper.

Step 14 Press the stamp firmly onto the (supported) shade, in the center bottom of alternate segments.

Step 15 The symbol in position. If the pressure applied is insufficient, you will need to retouch with a small brush.

Two-tint distressing

YOU WILL NEED

• Fine sandpaper • Silicon carbide paper • Water-based wood dye • Latex paint • 1 in./25 mm brush • Clear satin varnish

A clear-varnished wooden picture frame with rounded molding creates shadows from sidelighting on its surfaces. In this simple project, two tints of the same color form half the frame each, and are distressed with white and abraded to emphasize these side shadows.

Step 1 Remove the original finish using sandpaper. Fold it over to sand inside the molding.

Step 2 Brush over two sides of the frame with a strong red water-based dye.

Step 3 Using a more dilute mix of the same color, complete the other two sides.

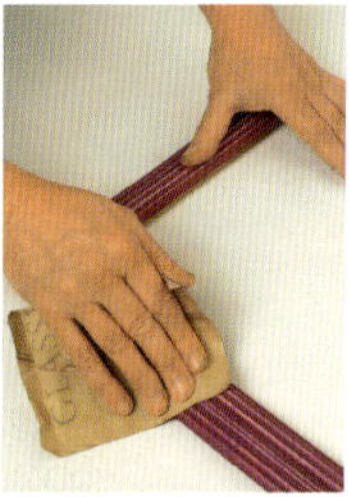

Step 4 Distress the frame with fine sandpaper until bare wood appears on the surface of the molding.

Step 5 Brush on white latex paint diluted half and half with water and leave to dry.

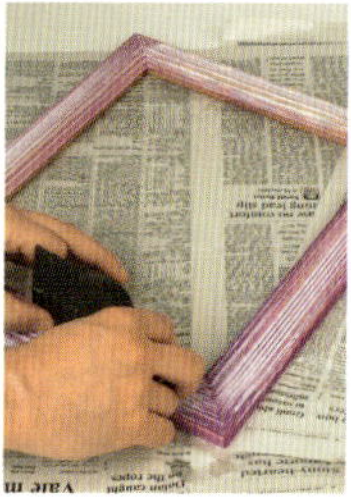

Step 6 Using wet silicon carbide, abrade the surface and inside molding detail.

Step 7 Apply a coat of satin varnish to darken the distressed wood areas for a subtle finish.

Floor cloth: painting canvas

YOU WILL NEED

• Artists' canvas to size • Design reference • Ruler • Pencil • Scissors • Set square • Combination square • Straightedge • Iron • Double-sided carpet tape • Painter's tape • Acrylic prime • Colored emulsions in sample pots • 2 in./55 mm brush • Number 6 flat brush • Round artists' brushes • Mat varnish

Hand-painted, individually designed canvas floor coverings owe their origins to the early New World pioneers, who reputedly reused their boat sails as the raw material. The design on this canvas continues on an historical American theme, using colors and shapes used by native peoples of the Southwest desert states.

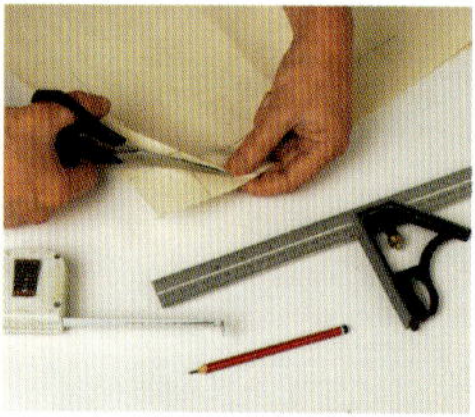

Step 1 "Square up" the raw canvas, leaving a 2 in./50 mm border to be folded over, and cut the corners diagonally.

Step 2 Fold the border to conceal the rough edges, and iron in the crease after damping down the canvas.

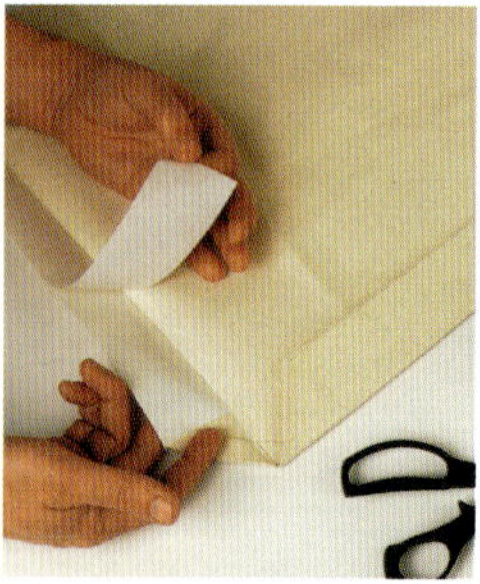

Step 3 Use double-sided carpet tape (available from hardware stores) to secure the folded border permanently in position.

Step 4 Some canvas is sold preprimed, some raw. If you buy yours raw, give it a coat of white acrylic primer.

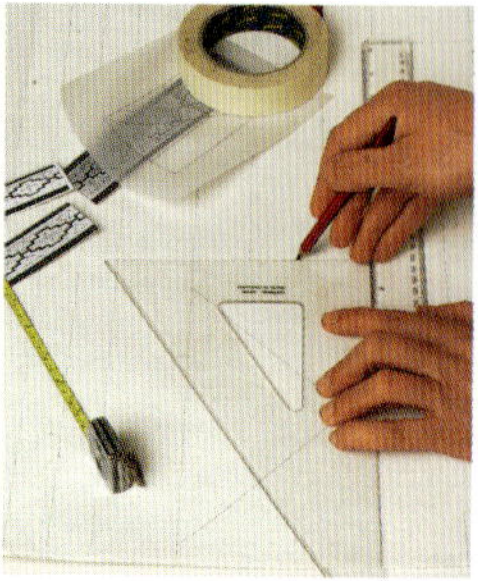

Step 5 Pencil your geometric design onto the canvas, using set square, measure, and straightedge to keep it symmetrical.

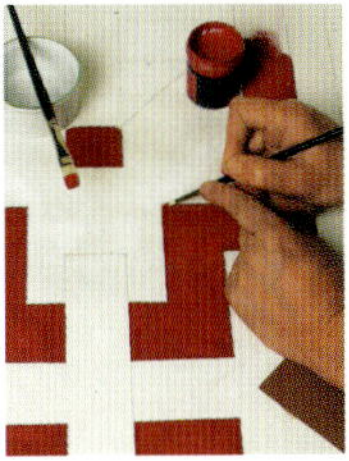

Step 6 Painting: use a number 0 artists' brush to fill in the corners.

Step 7 Use painter's tape to achieve an accurate, straight side stripe.

Step 8 Use brown paper to protect the finished areas as you work.

APPENDICES

Don't skip this section just because it's the last bit at the back of the book before the glossary, because these appendices cover important general safety aspects of decorating work. Many readers will rightly regard the advice as no more than common sense, which it is, but it also contains more specialized tips for protecting people and machines from accidental damage. The acquisition of a basic tool kit, always open to question, and the age-old problem of materials sourcing, particularly in the second-hand marketplace, are discussed at some length, as are the fundamentals and practicalities of artificial lighting.

Safety

Whatever your style or type of property, living and working in it with the minimum of risk to yourself and others is always a priority. Safety issues in the home can vary enormously, from keeping sharp kitchen knives out of the reach of small children, to making sure that your power tools have a circuit breaker fitted between you and the main power supply.

Accidents in the home account for a vast number of hospital admissions, particularly in the springtime, when there is a rush to take on DIY "improvements." To avoid accidents, however, all you need to do is to take sensible precautions and follow some simple guidelines, many of which are little more than common sense.

Working safely in the home

Whatever the task about the house, here are some useful guidelines:

- Move obstructions such as furniture, decorative items, and toys—don't "work around" them. If you were "on site" elsewhere, you would ask for a clear working space, for fear of damage to the contents of the room, so do the same in your own house. Working in an area that is cluttered and not easily accessible leads to over-reaching and losing control of the tool, and on a stepladder can result in overbalancing.
- Position your stepladder safely, so that you can reach the job height and width without stretching. DIY jobs are not always conveniently sited for a person standing on the floor. The requirement is likely to be a variety of heights for differing tasks.
- Position the tools for the job on a temporary table surface, never on the floor.
- Route cables from power tools around the sides of the room, not across the middle.
- Clear up as you go.
- Work in a tidy area so that you can easily see and check all aspects of the job in progress.

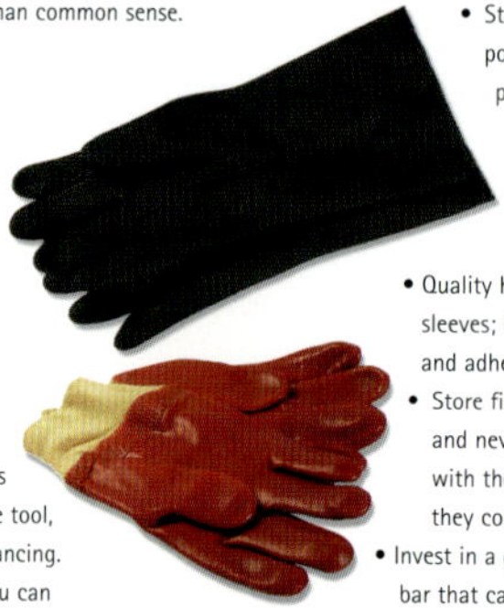

Different types of glove will help protect your hands from chemicals, paints, stains, splinters, and other sharp objects.

Safety in the workshop

- Make sure that small children do not have access to your tools, whether your equipment is left in a cabinet when not in use or is stored in a dedicated workshop in a garage or basement area.
- Store cutting tools and potentially dangerous power equipment sensibly, that is to say, with protective sleeves and guards in place.
- Never leave power tools "live"; disconnect the supply or remove the battery, and if possible keep them in carrying cases or secure boxes.
- Quality handsaws and chisels come with protective sleeves; if you lose one, make up another from card and adhesive tape.
- Store files on their sides with the blades retracted, and never leave snap-blade and marking knives with the blades exposed loose in a drawer where they could cut rummaging hands.
- Invest in a good-quality, solid tool box, or a tool bar that can be fixed to a wall to store your valuable equipment.
- Keep the workshop area clean and tidy.
- If you use a bench to cut, plane, shape, and drill wood pieces, make sure that a fire extinguisher is within easy reach, as wood shavings burn easily.
- Keep the workshop floor free from obstruction.
- Store bolts, screws, nails, and pins by type and size in marked containers so that they can be easily found. Don't leave them lying on the bench. Many a piece of fine woodwork has been accidentally scarred by nails or screws that have been left carelessly in the way.

Power tools

- If the tool has a lead, fit a circuit breaker, and always isolate from the power supply when changing the bits in a drill or blades in a saw.
- Always make sure you know where the cable is, and keep it behind you if you can.
- If you prefer battery power, remember that the tool is continuously "live." Disconnect the battery when changing bits and blades.
- Use the correct bit for drilling, and make sure that the saw blade is suitable for the material you intend to cut, and that both are sharp.
- It is dangerous practice to force bits and blades, and there should be no need.
- When drilling, back off the hole and stop the drill before removing it; likewise with a power saw, back off or stop the cut, and let the blade stop completely.
- Always read the direction manual carefully before using any tool, and familiarize yourself with its operation.
- Do not switch on any piece of power equipment unless you know how to turn it off.

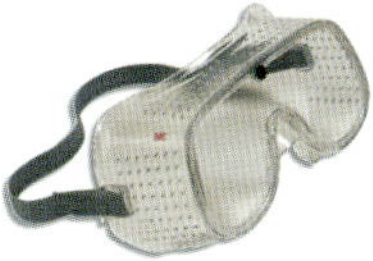

Safety goggles are essential for some jobs to protect your eyes from flying debris and dust. Some fit over regular spectacles.

Protective clothing

- Site workers always wear safety clothing: protective shoes, coveralls, and helmets all the time; safety glasses, ear defenders, and dust masks when required. As you are doing the same type of work, you should wear the same types of clothing, most of which have obvious functions.
- Shoes need to be strong with reinforced toe caps; trainers may be comfortable but they offer no protection if you drop something heavy on your foot.
- Gloves will protect your hands from chemicals and corrosive liquids as well as from paint and oil stains.
- A helmet may not be needed in the house, but consider wearing one in the loft where the roof clearance is minimal.
- Coveralls are better than old clothes, because they are designed in one piece so nothing gets caught up in machinery, and all the pockets are in the right place and can hold useful items.
- Try wearing a tool belt: all the heavier hand tools can be supported around your waist, so they are instantly accessible, and this is very useful on a stepladder.
- Dust masks are recommended in do-it-yourself stores as a matter of course when you buy materials and equipment for a dirty, dusty job, but wear one even when sweeping out the work area.
- Use ear defenders for heavy-duty masonry drilling and other noisy jobs, but always ensure that you can still hear warning noises.
- Protect your eyes when working; if you find that goggles tend to mist up, impairing your vision, try safety glasses (which can be worn over eyeglasses), but make sure they have side protectors. Slivers of wood, particles of rust, and lumps of masonry can fly from any angle, not just straight at you.

Take a break

- Plan a sensible working schedule, with breaks for drinks (nonalcoholic) and food.
- Don't start early and finish late in the hope of completing the job quickly; working long hours leads to mistakes and sometimes accidents as the attention wanders. At best, standards drop and the job is put at risk. Pace yourself and take breaks.

Always wear clothing that is appropriate for the job. Coveralls will protect your clothes, gloves will save your hands from damage, while a cap will keep dirt and dust out of your hair.

Basic tool kit

This is a somewhat misleading title, as anyone who has attempted to assemble a basic tool kit will testify. It is perfectly possible to put together an impressive array of expensive tools, and still find that your door handle undoes with a hex key that you do not possess, instead of the screwdriver bit that you have in the basic toolbox.

This is an unfortunate fact of life, and you will have to add items to your kit every time you take on a job around the house. Don't be tempted to "make do" with what is in the tool kit, either, because disaster is just around the corner. Using the wrong tool for the job can result in an accident; at best it can make the problem you are trying to solve considerably worse. Buying the correct tool for the job lets your basic tool kit grow with your experience and become a comprehensive tool kit, and before too long you will have a kit that you are confident of using.

For starters

A few basic items will be found in all domestic tool kits: measuring and marking tools, cutting tools, a drill and set of screwdrivers, a hammer, pincers or pliers, tools for making good, and basic painting equipment.

Measuring and marking

- **A retractable steel tape** that measures to 16 ft./5 m is a real asset; measuring shorter distances is simple with smaller tapes, but they won't run the length of a room. This forces you to add dimensions together, which can lead to miscalculations.

- **A small spirit level** can fit comfortably in an overall pocket.

- **An engineer's square** is essential for checking right-angles.

- **A soft pencil** should be included in your basic toolkit for use on lumber surfaces.

- **A waterproof pen** offers a very useful way of marking enamel-painted surfaces.

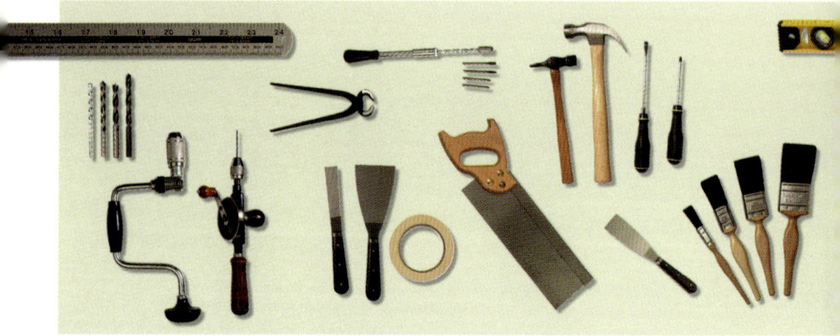

Cutting tools

- **A snap-blade or utility knife.**

- **A small saw**: pick a medium-sized small backsaw to start with; it can be identified by a heavy-duty brass or steel strip on the top edge of the blade, keeping it straight. It is a simple saw to use, and can cut across large lumbers as well as make smaller, more intricate cuts for joints. Always use the protective teeth guard.

Drills and drivers

These are needed for plugging walls and driving screws.

- **Drills**: Whether your choice is **mains supply powered** or **cordless** is entirely personal, but in either case, don't buy cheap. DIY superstores are full of "bargains," but don't be tempted. Cheap, badly made, noisy, inaccurate equipment is no investment; it will not last and will prevent you from doing a good job. Try to find a tool that will satisfy all requirements—wood, masonry, and screwdriving—and which has variable speed control.

- **Bits**: An extensive range of bits is available for power driving, but consider a quality manual tool as well, such as a small **spiral ratchet driver with interchangeable blades.**

- **An electrician's screwdriver.**

- **Hammer**: its role is self-explanatory, but there are several types. A **curved claw hammer** would be the most useful starter, the claw able to extract nails and pins. In confined spaces, a **pair of pincers** will do the job of the claw.

Gripping work

- A pair of **combination pliers** and an **adjustable wrench** are called for in gripping work, but it is worth including **long-nose pliers** because they can sometimes reach where conventional pliers cannot, and are useful when undertaking electrical work.

Tools for making good

Decorating tasks inevitably need tools for making good such as:

- **a scraper**
- **a putty knife**
- **a roller and tray combination**
- **a selection of quality small and medium size brushes.**

Boxing clever

Whereas some consumer items are replaceable because they simply wear out, the majority of your tools will be with you a long time, particularly if you buy quality ones.

Invest in a toolbox that will protect your equipment, and secure it with a padlock. There is no worse start to any job than a search party attempting to locate lost, borrowed, or broken tools. If you store them in a protected, secure environment, you will minimize the risk of damage.

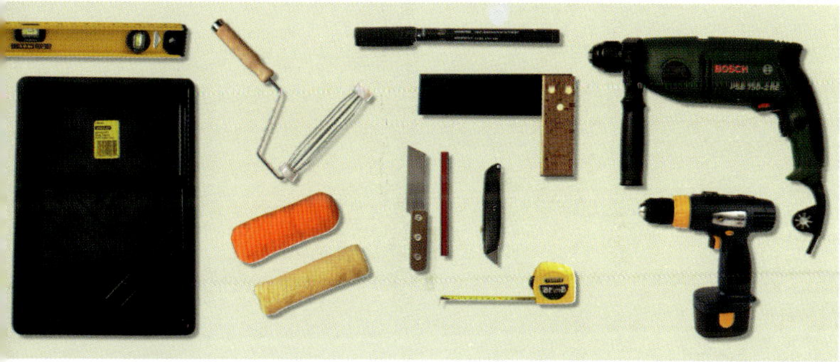

Lighting principles

Buildings of every type experience a series of different visual moods as the sun describes an arc from sunrise to sundown. They may be cool and aloof in the morning shade, and warm and friendly in the afternoon sun. Nothing is quite as dramatic, however, as the difference between day and night. Here we discuss how to make the best of the light your room receives.

Lighting-up time

How you see an object, how you define its visual balance and shape, whether or not the angle of the light has caused distortion, or whether the color is enhanced at all by the light, depend on the position of the source. During daylight hours this is the sun, its movement causing long shadows and distortions early and late in the day, and a flattening effect when it is high in the sky. Colors that can seem washed-out at midday intensify at the end of the day as the sun sets, and contrasts temporarily increase before darkness descends. Artificial lighting assumes the same role: that of the source, flattening or emphasizing areas, objects and decorations depending on its position in the room.

Add or subtract

As a result of the sun's movement, a house will experience more or differing visual moods in its south-facing rooms than in its north-facing accommodation. The lighting designer can work with the natural elements, enhancing the effect, or seek to rebalance, adding artificial light to darker, colder areas and throwing highlights onto angles and edges. Just as the afternoon sun casts a warm glow onto a wall, the designer can carefully position wall washers of differing power to throw graduated light onto the area in the same way. Conversely, in rooms where the sun makes only fleeting contact, the designer can employ hidden lighting techniques combined with light-sensitive switching, warming up what was once a cold, unfriendly environment.

Create the right mood

Try to select lighting that enhances the feel of the room and creates the type of environment that suits the family members that use it. Lighting is not merely functional; it is, or should be,

Lighting should set the mood in a room. Using strategically placed table and standing lamps will produce soft pools of light and create an intimate, relaxing atmosphere.

atmospheric. Centrally sited lighting can be used to great advantage in rooms with dark or rich colored walls, as they absorb a lot of light rather than reflecting it, and the low-key mood can be added to by low-level lamps, up- and downlighters or flicker lamps. Conversely, centrally placed lighting in areas with white or pale colored walls and ceiling can look austere to the point of unfriendliness; wall lights would throw light and shadow onto each surface simultaneously. Lights recessed in an alcove would create more interest still, adding to the wall's shape. If your decoration has involved a special finish, emphasize it by throwing light on the wall. If it is a textured finish, use the lighting to cast long shadows, increasing the three-dimensional effect.

Practicalities

Each member of the household will remind you of individual needs, be it lighting suitable for working on a computer, or reading by the fire. Your lighting arrangements should allow for all necessities, but at no detriment to anyone else. For example, reading lights positioned behind a bed should let one partner read without disturbing the other. Two separately switched directional lamps are needed here.

Areas used by everyone must be well and continuously lit, especially stairwells. Sudden changes in light levels can be hazardous, and for this reason lighting for a stairwell and lights along a corridor should be operated by the same switch. These areas will benefit from a nightlight, too, if you have children or elderly relatives who need to visit a bathroom in the early hours.

Kitchen areas pose a particular problem, in that food preparation and dishwashing tasks are usually performed at perimeter units. Consequently a central light will force kitchen users to work in their own shadow. A series of downlighters is a good solution, each positioned over a work area—sink, stove, work counter, and any appliance in regular use, such as a washing machine. Two separately switched parallel tracks of interchangeable, directional spotlights offer another alternative.

The bathroom needs to have a central enclosed light for background illumination. The basin area needs a separate light for shaving or the application of make-up; arrange it so that the user is illuminated, not the mirror.

Remember that no one in the house will be particularly appreciative if you install lighting that has an abrasive and inaccurate fluorescent effect when they are using the bathroom early in the morning.

Lights with a purpose

Always make sure your lights perform the function they should, and review the situation as your needs change. Good planning will ensure that your system is versatile enough to be multifunctional, providing ambient light for background, directional light for atmosphere and decorative highlights, working light for specific jobs around the home, safety light in heavy traffic areas, and security light as a deterrent to crime.

Stairways should always be well lit to prevent anyone from missing their footing in the dark. Placing downlighters beneath a handrail (above) provides the answer without having to resort to harsh overhead lighting. Wall lights (right) create warming pools of light that emphasize décor.

Materials

Quality specialist materials are best sourced from an outlet that trades specifically and knowledgeably in that area of supply, and is therefore in a position to offer help and advice on requirements, amounts, techniques, and tools needed, based on experience gained in the field.

Buying materials

The rise of DIY superstores in recent years has led the home improvement enthusiast to believe that all the materials for any job can be found under one roof. However, many of the materials for special projects around the home can be sourced from smaller suppliers who have specialist knowledge in particular areas.

Lumber and joinery materials

Superstores and larger hardware or decorating stores often offer "packs" of shrink-wrapped lumber, but the packaging can make it difficult to check the quality. The alternative is to buy from a lumberyard. Pick a yard that offers a machining service, and that lets you select and cut your own lengths from properly stored woods. This will let you select lengths that are not warped or twisted, and do not suffer from sap or wet stain, or have shakes and splits. Lumber should be racked horizontally, and be kept under cover. If you find a cheap yard with wood open to the elements or stacked upright on its end grain, walk away. Finally, as price is always a consideration, remember that cheap lumber can become very expensive if you have to throw half of it away because of defects or substandard machining.

Specialist suppliers

Basic paints and varnishes can be found in your local decorating store, but these shops cater for all tastes, and space is limited. As a result, particular effect paints and glazes are not usually a priority, and you must source from a specialist outlet. Many of these suppliers can be found in the classified pages of consumer magazines and trade journals. The supplier may be nowhere near you, but will offer a telephone or internet buying service, and a delivery service, except, of course, where the product is a fire risk.

Many small specialist suppliers have the time and the knowledge to advise you, both on the products they sell and the technique you are about to use. They are usually able to supply materials needed for any project—for example, french polishing—in the form of a kit.

Buying economically

Don't automatically assume that you can save money by buying in bulk. True, it costs little more for a 55 lb. (25 kg) bag of cement than for a small sand/cement mortar mix, but what exactly are you going to do with what's left over? If you store it in even a mildly damp place, it will be useless, and you will end up throwing it away a few weeks later.

Larger quantities of paints, varnishes, plasters, cartridge sealants, and adhesives must be sealed and stored correctly to be of any use at a later date. A cellar will be cold and damp, an outside shed prone to frost, and the garage (if it's big enough) may have no heating. Lumber lengths must be racked level, and at room temperatures, too; if you take wood from a cold shed into a warm room, you will have no straight lengths to build anything with. So, unless you have the luxury of good storage facilities, think twice before chancing the often false economy of bulk buying.

Reclamation yards

Probably associated more with restoration projects than small home improvement tasks, the reclamation yard is nonetheless a good bet for stripped doors, old fire surrounds, old floorboards, and all sizes of second-hand lumber. Old lumber sourced here will be of better seasoned stock than new woods, and if you have access to a machine saw, can be resized to live a new life.

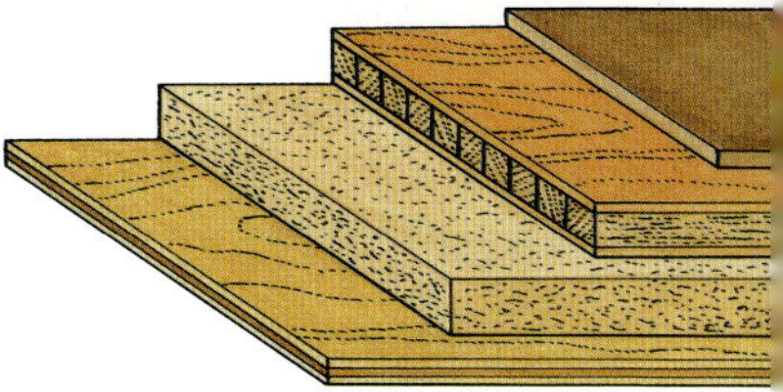

Measurement conversion tables

The lumber supply industry is a worldwide industry and you might find you have to convert from metric to imperial measurements or vice versa when you are sourcing materials to redecorate or revamp your home.

Here are two tables that might be useful to you:

- "Wood: Metric and Imperial Lengths" shows the metric sizes that wood comes in, with the equivalent imperial measure and the nearest traditional lengths.
- "Conversions: Feet/Meters" is a general conversion table. The figure in the central column refers to meters if you are converting to feet and feet if you are converting to meters. For example, in the first row of figures the number of units is 1. If you look in the left-hand column, you will see that this means 1 meter converts as 3.2808 feet. If you look in the right-hand column, you will see that this means that 1 foot converts as 0.3048 meters.

WOOD: METRIC AND IMPERIAL LENGTHS

Metric	Equivalent Imperial	Nearest Traditional Length
1.8 m	5ft. 10⅞in.	6ft.
2.1 m	6ft. 10⅝in.	7ft.
2.4 m	7ft. 10½in.	8ft.
2.7 m	8ft. 10¼in.	9ft.
3.0 m	9ft. 10⅛in.	10ft.
3.3 m	10ft. 9⅞in.	11ft.
3.6 m	11ft. 9¾in.	12ft.
3.9 m	12ft. 9½in.	13ft.
4.2 m	13ft. 9⅜in.	14ft.
4.5 m	14ft. 9⅛in.	15ft.
4.8 m	15ft. 9in.	16ft.
5.1 m	16ft. 8¾in.	17ft.
5.4 m	17ft. 8⅝in.	18ft.
5.7 m	18ft. 8⅜in.	19ft.
6.0 m	19ft. 8⅛in.	20ft.
6.3 m	20ft. 8in.	21ft.

CONVERSIONS: FEET/METERS

Feet	Number of Units	Meters
3.2808	1	0.3048
6.5617	2	0.6096
9.8425	3	0.9144
13.123	4	1.2192
16.404	5	1.5240
19.685	6	1.8288
22.966	7	2.1336
26.247	8	2.4384
29.528	9	2.7432
32.808	10	3.0480
36.089	11	3.3528
39.370	12	3.6576
42.651	13	3.9624
45.932	14	4.2672
49.213	15	4.5720
52.493	16	4.8768
55.774	17	5.18163
59.055	18	5.48644
62.336	19	5.79125
65.617	20	6.0960
68.898	21	6.4008
72.178	22	6.7056
75.459	23	7.0104
78.740	24	7.3152
82.021	25	7.6200
85.302	26	7.9248
88.583	27	8.2296
91.86	28	8.5344
95.14	29	8.8392
98.42	30	9.1440

Paint and paper charts

Use the chart on the right to work out how many rolls of wallpaper you'll need and the chart below to find out what sort of paint(s) will be required for your redecoration plans.

PAINT: TYPES AND USES

Primers/Undercoats	Base	Thinner (Cleaner)	Surfaces
Stain-blocking primer	Oil	Mineral spirits	Wood knots, resin channels, and resin stains
Wood primer	Oil	Mineral spirits	All softwoods; softwood veneered boards
Aluminum wood primer	Oil	Mineral spirits	Hardwoods, oily timbers, resinous woods, powdery surfaces (old plaster)
Alkali-resisting primer	Oil	Mineral spirits	New plaster, fire-resistant boards
Penetrating stabilizing primer	Oil	Mineral spirits	Crumbling, powdery surfaces of brick or plaster
Red oxide primer	Oil	Mineral spirits	All ferrous metal surfaces
Acrylic primer/undercoat	Water	Water	Interior softwoods; softwood veneered boards
Oil/resin undercoat	Oil	Mineral spirits	All softwoods, hardwoods, and boards
Finishes/Top Coats			
Vinyl mat latex	Water	Water	Walls and ceilings
Vinyl silk latex	Water	Water	Walls and ceilings
Enamel latex	Water	Water	Interior wood finishes, small walls
Enamel	Oil	Mineral spirits	All types of wood, metal finishes
Low luster	Oil	Mineral spirits	Woodwork, walls, and all smooth surfaces
Low luster latex	Water	Water	Woodwork, walls, and all smooth surfaces
Smooth masonry paint	Water	Water	Brick and mortar finishes
Floor/Tile paint	Oil	Mineral spirits	Concrete, brick, tile, cement, mortar

ESTIMATION OF NUMBER OF ROLLS OF WALLPAPER NEEDED

Height from skirting to coving/ceiling (feet)	Total measurement around walls (feet)							
	28	36	44	52	60	68	76	84
7–7½	4	5	6	7	8	9	9	11
7½–8	4	5	6	7	8	9	10	11
8–8½	4	5	6	7	8	9	10	12
8½–9	4	5	6	8	9	10	11	13
9–9½	4	6	7	8	9	10	12	13
9½–10	5	6	7	9	10	11	12	14
10–10½	5	6	8	9	10	12	13	15
10½–11	5	7	8	9	11	12	13	15

KEY

- *Match height of wall (right-hand column) with total horizontal measurement (top row) to identify number of rolls needed. For example, a 10 feet high room 76 feet around would require 12 rolls.*
- *Each roll is assumed to be 10.05m/33ft long, and 520mm/20½in wide.*
- *Measurement listing includes average window and wall recess (door) areas. Increase/decrease as needed.*
- *Large (wasteful) patterns will need an increase of 1 roll in 5.*

1 quart will cover	Recoatable in	Notes
N/A	N/A	If wood is very resinous, combine with aluminum wood primer.
36–39 sq. ft.	16–24 hrs	Use oil with oil-based undercoat and finish. Clean surface with mineral spirits before application.
46–52 sq. ft.	24 hrs	Leave for 24 hours before recoating.
30–33 sq. ft.*	Overnight	* Figure quoted for hard plaster surfaces; more porous surfaces will use more primer.
20–26 sq. ft.	16–24 hrs	Sticky and splashable: wear eye protection and gloves at all times.
30–33 sq. ft.	16–24 hrs	Clean off rust stains with steel wool; best base for oil-based finishes.
39–43 sq. ft.	1–2 hrs	Inside use only; suitable for water-based enamel finishes. Not as durable as oil-based paints.
52–60 sq. ft.	16–24 hrs	All purpose undercoat, use with oil-based enamel. Manufacturers color matches undercoat with enamel.
39–46 sq. ft.	2–4 hrs	Cannot be wiped clean—unsuitable for kitchens
33–39 sq. ft.	2–4 hrs	Washable/wipeable finish.
30–33 sq. ft.	3–6 hrs	"No undercoat" versions available; not as hard-wearing or as glossy a surface finish as oil-based enamel.
52–60 sq. ft.	16–24 hrs	The ultimate paint finish for wood/metal. Smooth, shiny, tough, and permanent. Use inside and out.
63–66 sq. ft.	16–24 hrs	Low luster finish. Also found as silk, luster or satin finish. Good base for paint effects on walls. Needs no undercoat.
33–39 sq. ft.	2–4 hrs	Not as hard-wearing as oil-based low luster.
30–33 sq. ft.	6 hrs	Limited colors; intended for external walls, but ideal for cellar walls.
33–39 sq. ft.	16–24 hrs	Limited colors. Ideal for red ceramic tile floors, conservatories and utility rooms.

Glossary

Abrasives
Sheet materials with differing grit sizes used for taking back a surface, removing a finish or sheen. Available in grades from coarse to very fine.

Admixtures
Additives to a mortar mix; for example, liquid plasticizer, mixed in to provide a supply of minute air bubbles. This makes the mix easier to work and improves resistance to frost when set.

Anchor bolt
A fixing bolt securing a wood or metal frame to a masonry wall or solid floor, also called shield anchors, or sleeve anchors for a low stress fix.

Aspect
The direction that a house or room faces, its fronting; for example, southerly aspect faces directly south.

Auger bit
Large-channeled, self-starting spiral drill piece for wood boring.

Backsaw
A small to medium size handsaw for accurate cross-cutting, especially wood joints, so called because it has a stabilizing steel or brass strip folded along the top of the blade.

Blistered work
This is a defect, a finish in paint or varnish where small air bubbles have appeared on the surface.

Bond
In brickwork, this is a decorative system used to mortar bricks together to form a strong and cohesive wall arrangement.

Bowing
Wood lengths bent out of true by uneven shrinkage or supporting heavy weights.

Butt
As in butt joint: items meeting but not overlapping.

Casement
Hinged, opening window frame, in metal, plastic, or wood, forming part of a larger frame.

Chalk line
A taught, straight string, fixed at each end and dusted with chalk, which, when "snapped" against a surface, leaves an accurate guideline.

Chamfer
A 45-degree symmetrical bevel, removing the right angle of a board.

Chuck
Lockable, adjustable jaws allowing insertion of differing diameters of bit, for rotary drilling applications.

Circuit breaker
Protective device disconnecting the mains supply to a power tool in the case of fault or overload.

Cleat
A length of softwood, often used as an invisible support.

Contact adhesive
A glue that is applied to two surfaces that bond instantly on meeting, without the use of clamps or support fixings.

Countersink
To drill a cone-shaped recess in wood, letting a similarly shaped screwhead sit flush with, or slightly below, the surface.

Counterbore
To drill a straight-sided hole, to be filled later with a plug, letting a screwhead be hidden below a wood surface.

Counterpunch
To set a nail below the wood surface, filling the entry hole with a matching colored filler.

Crown molding
Traditionally a molding for doors and windows, covering the gap between frame and wall.

Dry rot
Lumber decay, caused by damp and poor ventilation, appearing as right-angled splits with a powdery appearance.

Distemper
Traditional water-based colored paint with a mat finish that dries to a powdery bloom. Lighter in color when dry than when applied.

End grain
The exposed wood fibers at the ends of cut lengths, prone to splitting and very absorbent.

Epoxy grout
A two-part, epoxide-resin-based, ceramic-tile grout, with a tough, hygienic waterproof finish needed in food preparation areas, which has to be mixed on site.

Face
The front surface of a wall.

Feather edge
Using abrasives to sand back the rough, chipped edges of a previous finish, to provide a smooth starting surface.

Floating floor
A thin layer of flooring laid on top of the existing surface, designed to "float" by the use of a cushioning subfloor between the two.

Flogger
Specialist long haired, wide, flat brush, used dry to drag through a finish.

Flush fit
An exact and even fit of two joining surfaces.

Glazing
Fitting glass cut to size into a recess in a cupboard door, room door, or window.

Grain
Wood fibers running through a lumber length, indicating the direction of growth. Often used as a decorative feature.

Half-wall finish
Where the lower part of a wall has a different decorative scheme than the top half.

Halving joint
A simple wood joint, made by joining two halves, or where two rebates meet, each one half the thickness of the lumber.

Hardboard
Thin, manufactured compressed fiber board, often used as floor covering support.

Housing
Or mortise, a rectangular piece cut out of timber, across the grain, into which a tenon or tongue is slotted.

Insulation
The use of thermal materials to slow down or eliminate heat loss or the entry of cold air.

Invisible pinning
Where a matchboard or similar is nailed in such a position that the subsequent board will cover up the fixing.

Jamb
(Door jamb) the sides and top of a fixed frame.

Joist
Heavy-duty horizontal support for floors and ceilings.

Kerf
The cutting slot made when a saw blade passes through lumber.

Kettle
Small container with a handle into which small amounts of paint or varnish are decanted on site.

Key
Abrading a smooth surface, so that the roughened face will provide a grip for a paint finish.

Knot
Circular wood defect in lumber lengths where branches joined the tree.

Laminate
(Flooring) ultra-thin layer of artificial veneer with a photographic wood effect, on a base of manufactured board. Used as cheap "floating floor."

Laths
Thin wood strips pinned to studs (walls) or joists (ceiling) to act as plaster supports.

Laying off
Final long surface strokes through a paint layer, evening out the finish and preventing runs.

Locking rail
The center, horizontal support ("locking") lumber in a panelled door.

Making good
Restoring a surface to its previous standard of finish, after a repair, insertion, or alteration has taken place.

Mat
A surface finish description for dull, nonreflective paints and varnishes.

Miter
To cut wood at a 45-degree angle, so that the two equal halves form a right-angled corner.

Monochromatic
Designer's color scheme employing shades and tints of only one color.

Molding
Small wood strips cut to a decorative surface shape by a router bit.

Mortar
Bonding mix for brick and stone, consisting of cement, soft sand, water, and any additives such as plasticizer.

Muntin
Glazing bar or divider between panes of glass in a window, vertical rail in the center of a paneled door.

Glossary

Nail set
(Nail punch) small carpenter's tool used to sink a nail or pin head below the wood surface, prior to filling.

Nippers
Pincers with powerful cutting jaws, used to break off tile pieces.

Noggin
Short horizontal wood piece (stud) used to reinforce upright members in a stud or partition wall.

Nominal size
The sawn size at which lumber lengths are specified, not the finished size.

Open plan
A single large area in a property with no permanent room divisions.

Out of plumb, out of true
Not vertical, not sraight or level.

Pier
Rectangular, vertical column of bonded brickwork, used to support a beam or structure on top.

Pilot hole
Small drill hole used as a guide for a larger one, or for a screw thread.

Plinth
A rectangular wood or panel construction, acting as a base for a unit.

Plugging chisel
Special tool with a slanted leading edge, for fast waste removal when chasing along brick joints.

Plumb bob and line
A weight on a string, ensuring it hangs straight and vertical.

Pointing
Decorative and weatherproofing finish for mortared brick joints.

Primary colors
Red, yellow, and blue. Mixing these primaries in a variety of proportions creates all other colors.

Primer
The first coat applied to a face, acting as a sealer.

Proud
One surface sitting raised above another, not level.

Quarter-round molding
A narrow decorative molding, traditionally machined from hardwood.

Rafters
Support lumber forming the roof shape, meeting at the ridge and supporting the roof covering.

Ratchet
Mechanism used in screwdrivers allowing driving movement only in one direction.

Rendering
The first application of a mix (e. g., plaster) onto a brick wall.

Rip
Using a rip saw to cut wood following the direction of the grain structure.

RSJ
(Rolled steel joist) heavy steel support beam set onto slate, holding up a floor or replacing a lower support wall.

Sample board
Mix of material, texture, paint, flooring, and color-finish samples together on a board to help selection of matching decorative items.

Sanding
Generic term for using abrasives, either by hand or by machine.

Sash frame
Vertically sliding frame housed in a box and operated on runners or with cords.

Satin finish
A surface finish with a semimat sheen, offering slight luster and minimal reflection.

Screed
To lay down a mix to level a floor area.

Seasoned wood
Cut wood that has been horizontally racked and left to dry naturally over a long period of time, the ultimate in dimensional stability.

Shakes
Splits along woodgrain, caused by uneven shrinkage.

Silicon carbide
An abrasive that can be used with a lubricant (water, sugar soap) on paint finishes, or dry on bare wood.

Skew nailing
Driving nails in at different angles, for a more secure fixing.

Soft jaw
Fiber or softwood pieces used in jaws or clamps to protect the workpiece.

Stipple
Raising or texturing a surface finish with tiny dots, using the bristle tips of a brush.

Straightedge
A wooden batten, steel rule, or similar, having a true edge.

Sweating
Condensation of moisture droplets on a wall surface.

Template
Accurate shape or pattern cut from cardboard or similar thin material, used as a guide for cutting or drilling.

Tenon
Projection or tongue cut into timber, intended to slot accurately into a cut housing (mortise) or groove.

Thread
Continuous spiral groove cut into a screw, letting it grab the wood or plug securely.

Transom
A window directly above a door, letting light into a small room or corridor.

Two-way switching
Electrical wiring that lets artificial light be controlled from two different floor levels.

Undercoat
The middle application in a paint job, a mat coat covering (minor) discrepancies in the surface and providing the key for the finish.

Underlay
Hard-wearing cushioning under a floor covering, carpet, or floating floor.

Veneer
Thin sheets of decorative wood, often less stable woods, with a support core board of blocks or sheets glued at right angles to each other.

Visible spectrum
Colors recognizable to the human eye, between ultraviolet and infrared.

Wallboard
A thin, manufactured sheet of solid plaster with paper facing both sides, or one side with a damp-resistant shield.

Warped timber
Lengths twisted out of true by uneven shrinkage, or extreme changes in temperature.

Wet rot
Decay in lumber as a result of water saturation and inadequate ventilation.

Whitewash
Traditional white mat paint containing slaked lime, breathable and nonwashable.

Yacht varnish
Expensive, superior quality clear varnish intended for outside use, ideal for floors.

Zonal planning
Dividing areas up according to specific requirements.

Index

A

abrasives 44–5
accessories 224–35
adhesives 110–11, 180
adjustable room-height shelving 118–19
aerosols 47
aluminum oxide 45
arches 89
aspect 26–7

B

backsplashes 136
balusters 173
banisters 173
baseboard 115, 168–71
basic skills
- boards 158–9
- brick 122–5, 127
- floors 178–81
- painting 38–9
- preparation 134–5
- staircases 172–3
- tiles 136–7, 178–81
- wallcoverings 70–1
- wood 98–101, 104–5, 188–9

basin backsplash 136
bathrooms 15, 17, 58
bits 241
bond types 124
borders 90
boxes 152–3, 222–3, 241
brads 111
brickwork 92, 122–7
briefing 12
brushes 40–1, 46, 241
budget 13

C

cabinets 144–5, 206–7
calculators 18
canvas floor coverings 234–5
casement windows 191
catches 109
cavity walls 108–9
ceilings 86–7, 120–1
ceramic tiles 180
chair revamping 210–11
charts 246–7
chimney breast linings 80
choosing
- color schemes 28–31
- glazes 51
- paints 35
- tiles 130, 150
- wallcoverings 70–1, 130
- wood 99

cleaning 124, 161
cleating 116–17
collages 63
color
- cards 28
- checking 82
- finishes 96–7
- schemes 20–31
- washed boards 162
- wheel 24–5
- wood floors 167

colorwashing 52
complementary colors 25
containers 214–15, 222–3
conversion tables 245
cork tiles 131, 182–3
corners 90–1
crackleglazing 192–3
customizing 146–7, 153, 198–9
cut floor nails 111
cutting
- paper 82
- tiles 138–9
- tools 241
- valances 198–9
- wood 99, 104–5

D

damaged walls 42, 78–9
designer's notes
- brick finishes 94–5
- color 22–3
- floors 156–7
- painting 34–5
- paper finishes 68–9
- tile finishes 94–5
- wood finishes 94–5
- woodwork 186–7

diamond patterns 65
distressing frames 232–3
dividers 31, 91
doors 144–5, 187, 190–1
double-hung windows 191
dowels 105
dragging 54–5
drilling 102, 105, 241
dry papers 44, 45

E

eastern aspect 27
electric planers 103
electrical fittings 84
embossed paper 71
engineering bricks 122
engineer's square 240
equipment
- basic 240–1
- brick 126–7
- painting 40–1
- paper 72–3
- safety 238–9
- tiling 132–3
- wood 100–3

estimating 135, 247
exposed floor preparation 160–3

F

fabric screens 218–19
facing 122
filling 189
finishes
- crackle 192–3
- floors 165, 181
- marble 58–9

paint 35
paper 66–91
plywood paneling 116–17
previously papered 74
shelving 143
staircases 173
tiles 139, 150–1, 181
two-color 53
types 92–153
walls 119
valances 198–9
wood 151, 165, 173

fires 146–9
fittings 17, 84, 168–71
fixings 108–9, 117, 199
floating floors 174, 176–7
flock paper 71
floor-to-ceiling shelving 143
floors 154–83
canvas coverings 234–5
exposed 160–3
fitting 168–71
location 176
lofts 121
nails 111
wood 174–7

flour paper 44
flush doors 190
folding 83
frames 232–3
french polishing 194–5
furniture 75, 202–11

G

geometric art 64–5
glass tiles 131
glazes 50–1
glue 111, 173
graph paper 18, 19
grids 140–1
grouting 181

H

hammers 241
hand-printed paper 71
hanging 83, 214–15
hardboard subfloors 182
hardware 108–9
hardwood moldings 112
hawks 125, 129
hinges 109
hoops 65
horizontal paneling 115

I

infestation 158
interconnecting spaces 15

J

joinery 244

K

kitchens 15, 17, 150–1, 204
knives 241
knots 189

L

laminate flooring 175
lamps 228–31
landing areas 88–9
laying out tiles 182–3
leveling solid floors 179
lighting 26–7, 242–3
lining 70, 80
living areas 14
locating floors 176
loft areas 121
lower wall paneling 200–1

M

machine sanding 162–3
machine-printed paper 70
maintenance 41
major changes 17
marble finishes 58–9
marking 104, 135, 240
materials 244–5
measurements
conversion tables 245
rooms 18
shutters 196–7
tools 73, 240
valances 198–9
wood 98, 104

minor changes 17
mirrors 140–1
mitered corners 90–1
mixing 124–5, 129
moldings 112–13
monochromatic color schemes 30–1
montages 63
mood 26–7, 242–3
mortar 124–5
mosaics 140–1, 174–5, 208–9
murals 62–3

N

nails 110–11
needs 16–17
newels 173
northern aspect 26
nosing 173

O

oil-based stains 165–6
one-wall effects 62–3
overpainting 43

P

pads 40–1
paint
charts 246–7
doors 190–1
floors 166
guide 38–9
pads 47
pots 38–9
qualities 42
surfaces 32–65, 189
types 34–7
wood 166, 189

paneling 116–17, 190, 200–1
paper
ceilings 86–7
charts 246–7
dividers 91
finishes 66–91
hanging 83
prepasted 85
problem areas 88–9
walls 82–5

paste tables 81

pasting 83–5
patterned borders 90
pins 111
planers 103
planning 10, 18–19
plaster removal 123
plastering 128–9
plastic rules 18
pliers 241
plywood panels 116–17
pointing 124
polishing surfaces 195
power tools 102–3
practicalities 12–13, 36–7
preparation
bricks 124
exposed floors 160–3
glazes 50–1
ground 44
painting 42–3
plastering 128
surfaces 74–81
wood 188
previously papered finishes 74
primers 35
problem areas 88–9
protective clothing 239

R

racks 214–15
rag-rolling 53
reclamation yards 244–5
repairing
boards 158–9
damaged walls 42
solid floors 179
staircases 172–3
walls 76–7
revamping 210–11, 228–31
risers 173
rollers 40–1, 46–7, 64–5, 241
room measurements 18
room-height shelving 118–19
routers 103
rubbing blocks 45
rubbing down 44

S

safety 238–9
sample pots 28
sanders 103
sanding 160–1, 162–3
sandpaper 40, 45
saws 102–3, 241
scissors 18
scrapers 241
screens 218–21
screwdrivers 241
screws 105, 110
sealing 78, 163, 183
self-supporting box systems 152–3
setting out tiles 135, 182–3
shelving
adjustable 118–19
alternative finishes 143
kitchen 204
systems 216–17
wood/tile 142–5
shower areas 58
shutters 196–7
silicon carbide 45
skills
brick 122–5
identifying boards 158–9
levels 13
painting 38–9
preparation 134–5
tiled floors 178–81
wallcoverings 70–1
wood 98–9, 188–9
skimming 129
sleeping areas 14–15, 17
softwood moldings 112
solid walls 108
southern aspect 27
space savers 212–23
spattering 56–7
special effects
glazes 50–1
one-wall 62–3
other 55
papering 90–1
textured paint 48–9
wood floors 164–7
spirit levels 240
splashing 56–7
sponging 52
sprayguns 47
stabilizing 78
stains 165–6
stairs 88–9, 172–3
stamping 60–1
starter tiling kits 132–3
steamers 75
steel tapes 240
steel wool 45
stenciling 60–1
stippling 53
storage
box sections 152–3
combination 144
fabric screens 218–19
solutions 95
space savers 212–23
wood screens 220–1
stretcher bond 124
strings 173
stripes 65
stripping 74, 188–9
sugar soap 40
suppliers 244
supports 118–19
surfaces
polishing 195
preparation 74–81, 188
preparing 134
resists 192–3
walls 114
surrounds 146–9
swatches 31

T

table mosaic decoration 208–9
tacks 111
techniques see also skills 104–7
technology 16
textured paint 48–9
TGV matchboarding 200–1
tiles 136–7, 178–9
ceramic 180
cutting 138–9
equipment 132–3
finishes 92, 138–9, 150–1
floors 178–81
mirror 141
rollers 65

- shelving 142–5
- walls 97, 130–1

timber moldings 112–13
time factors 13
tips
- brickwork 126
- brushes 41, 47
- glazes 51
- mosaics 141
- tiling 139
- tools 100, 102
- wood 100, 102, 107

tools
- basic 101, 240–1
- brick 126–7
- kit 240–1
- painting 40–1
- paper 72–3
- safety 238–9
- tiling 132–3
- wood 100–3

top coats 35
tread 173
two-color finishes 53
two-tint distressing 232–3

U

undercoats 35

V

valances 198–9
varnishing 59, 163, 166
vases 226–7
vertical paneling 115
vinyl paper 71
vinyl tiles 182–3
visual tricks 28, 69

W

wallboard 108–9
walls
- cavity 108–9
- coverings 70–1
- defects 78–9
- finishing 119
- fixings 108–9, 117
- furniture 75
- hardware 108–9
- lining 80
- lower paneling 200–1
- obstacles 84
- painting 42
- paneling 114–15
- papering 82–5
- pasting 84–5
- plastering 129
- pointing 124
- repairing 76–7
- solid 108
- surfaces 114
- tiles 97, 130–1, 136–7

washable paper 71
washed boards 162
water-based stains 165–6
wax resist 193
waxing 194–5
wedges 173
weight support 152
western aspect 27
wet papers 44, 45
windows 190–1
wood 98–9, 102–7, 188–9
- cabinets 206–7
- ceilings 120–1
- chairs 210–11
- cracked finish 192–3
- equipment 100–3
- finishing 92, 151
- fire surrounds 148–9
- floors 164–7, 174–177
- graining 54–5
- materials 244–5
- panels 201
- screens 220–1
- shelving 142–5
- shutters 196–7
- staircases 173
- wax resist 193
- working 184–201

woodchip paper 71
working areas 14, 150–1
workshops 238
worktops 151
wrenches 241

Acknowledgments

The author would like to express his grateful thanks to the many working professionals whose advice and time has been willingly given during the preparation of these pages. Special thanks are due to Martin Gowar, whose depth of knowledge in finishing was frequently an inspiration; to Cheryl Owen, a fellow author in this series, for help and advice; to Russell Sadur, Theo Dorou, and Steve Tanner, whose photographic studios were virtually taken over at times during shooting; to Diana Cibil, who styled the projects; and to photographer Steve Gorton. Cheerful in all weathers, Steve's commitment to the job and unfailing logistical support made a sometimes difficult task that much easier.

The publishers would like to thank the following for the use of properties:

Oak-engineered laminate flooring on pages 178/179 supplied by EC Forest Product Sales Ltd. Units 5 & 6 The Woodland Centre, Whitesmiths, near Lewes, East Sussex BN8 6JB, England.

Moran & Co. Builders, ICI Paints, Farrell & Ball, B&Q, Wickes, Brewers & Sons Ltd, Master tiles, Covers, Travis Perkins, Paint Magic.

Picture credits

Anaglypta Wallpaper: p.6, 216L.

Crown Paints: pp. 24B, 30T, 33, 34T, 50, 117, 161.

Elizabeth Whiting & Associates:
pp. 14, 15, 16, 17, 21, 23R, 26, 27B, 34B, 35, 36, 37, 48, 54, 56, 57, 59, 60, 61, 63, 64, 67, 68R, 89, 91, 93, 94, 95, 96L, 97TL & BR, 115, 116, 120T, 130, 131L, 134, 137, 144, 146R, 147, 148, 151, 155, 156, 157, 160, 164, 173, 174, 175, 178, 179, 183, 185, 186, 187, 193, 195, 199, 200, 201, 213, 214R, 216R, 217, 218L, 219R, 237, 242, 243T.

Houses & Interiors: pp. 13, 22BR, 27T, 31, 58, 62, 96R, 97TR, 146L, 189.

Image Bank: p.11.

Jaafar Designs/Florida squares & spirals: p.131BC.

Laura Ashley: pp. 38T, 39B, 191, 219L, 223TL.

Morris & Co.Collection: pp. 68L, 70L, 168.

Next Directory: pp. 22L, 113B, 141R, 152, 162/3, 197B, 214L, 215, 218R, 220, 221, 222, 223TR & B, 243B.

Osborne & Little/V&A The Historic Collection: p. 69T.

Painted Tile Company/Wellington Tile Co/Crazy Chicken & Tulips: p.131B.

Sanderson: pp. 23T.

Stock Market: p. 2.

Front cover:
Ian Parsons, T; Elizabeth Whiting & Associates, CL & BL; Crown Paints, BR.
Front flap: Sanderson.

Back flap: Crown Paints.